The Road to Appomattox

The Road to Appomattox

Robert Hendrickson

John Wiley & Sons, Inc.

New York • Chichester • Weinheim • Brisbane • Singapore • Toronto

For my granddaughter, Kristin

Published by John Wiley & Sons, Inc.
Published simultaneously in Canada.

This publication is designed to provide accurate and authoritative information in regard to the subject matter covered. It is sold with the understanding that the publisher is not engaged in rendering professional services. If professional advice or other expert assistance is required, the services of a competent professional person should be sought.

Library of Congress Cataloging-in-Publication Data

Hendrickson, Robert.
    The road to Appomattox / Robert Hendrickson.
      p. cm.
    Includes bibliographical references (p. 227) and index.
    ISBN 0-471-14884-9 (cloth : alk. paper)
    1. Appomattox Campaign, 1865. 2. United States—History—Civil War, 1861–1865—Campaigns. I. Title.
    E477.67.H46   1998
    973.7′3—dc21   97-43474

Printed in the United States of America.

10 9 8 7 6 5 4 3 2 1

For a vast living host the word Appomattox had magic and beauty. They sang the syllables "Ap-po-mattox" as a happy little carol of harvest and fields of peace and the sun going down with no shots in the night to follow.

—Carl Sandburg, *Abraham Lincoln: The War Years*

Contents

Preface

I HAVE TRIED to tell this story of the last days of the Civil War in the words of its participants whenever possible, weaving together the voices of soldiers and civilians, accents Northern and Southern, as recorded in diaries and newspapers of the day and memoirs and biographies written after the war. Rather than burden the reader with footnotes, I've included these sources in the text and bibliography. In any case, nothing in quotes in these pages has been invented and by carefully using such voices one can better capture the spirit and flavor of the times.

It should also be noted here, as the epilogue shows at some length, that the Civil War actually lasted well beyond the surrender at Appomattox—the last shot recorded was fired as late as June 28, 1865, and some people on both sides kept on fighting in one way or another for more than a century—but the war was over for all intents and purposes when General Lee surrendered what was left of the once imposing Army of Northern Virginia to General Grant. In the South, in fact, this has traditionally been called "The Surrender."

Many people assisted me in writing *The Road to Appomattox* over the years, and my sincere thanks go out to all these friends, librarians, archivists, and scholars. I would especially like to thank Lauren and Robert Walsh in Canada, and my publisher, Gerry Helferich, and editor, Hana Lane, at John Wiley & Sons. To my wife Marilyn, as always, I can only say, "My history is your history and your history mine."

The Road to Appomattox

1

The Yankees
Are Coming

Grant, lolling in his general store in Galena . . . ready to be called
to an intricate destiny.

—F. Scott Fitzgerald

"THE YANKEES ARE COMING!"

Voices rang from the shadows of Richmond City, voices deep
in doorways, around corners, barely ahead of the advancing troops
and flames.

"Damn bluebellies everywhere!"

"If only this day could be erased from the calendar."

"If only the last *four years*."

"They'll never put it out!"

"Flames like the whip of God!"

"Here they come!"

"It's Sherman and his Bummers."

"Grant the Butcher's blue devils from out the cellar door of Hell!"

Mrs. John P. McGuire, a Confederate Commissary clerk, heard
such wild rumors outside her window, but down the street the
bluecoats . . . the bluebellies . . . the blue devils clearly were advancing through the inferno of flames and smoke that was once
proud Richmond. She hastily wrote in her diary:

The Yankees have come! Oh, who shall tell the horror of the past night! Union men begin to show themselves in Richmond. About two o'clock in the morning we were startled by a loud sound like thunder; the house shook and the windows rattled; it sounded like an earthquake in our midst. It was soon understood to be the blowing up of a magazine below the city. In a few hours another exploded on the outskirts . . . much louder than the first and shivering innumerable plate-glass windows all over Shockhoe Hill.

It was then daylight, and we were standing out upon the pavement. The lower part of the city was burning. . . . About seven o'clock I set off to go to the central depot to see if the [railroad evacuation] cars would go out. As I went from Franklin to Broad Street . . . the pavements were covered with broken glass; women, both white and colored, were walking in multitudes from the Commissary offices and burning stores with bags of flour, meal, coffee, sugar, rolls of cotton cloth, etc., colored men were rolling wheelbarrows filled in the same way. I went on and on toward the depot and as I proceeded shouts and screams became louder. The rabble rushed by me in one stream. "Who are those shouting? What is the matter?" I seemed to be answered by a hundred voices: "The Yankees have come!"

I turned to come home, but what was my horror, when I reached Ninth Street, to see a regiment of Yankee cavalry come dashing up, yelling, shouting, hallooing, screaming! All bedlam let loose could not have vied with them in diabolical roarings. I stood riveted to the spot; I could not move or speak. Then I saw the iron gate of our time-honored and beautiful Capitol Square, on the walks and greensward of which no hoof has ever been allowed to tread, thrown open and the Yankee cavalry dash in. . . .

The Federal soldiers were roaming the streets; either whiskey or the excess of joy gave them the appearance of being beside themselves. We had hoped that very little whiskey would be found in the city, as, by the order of the Mayor, casks were emptied yesterday evening in the streets, and whiskey flowed like water through the gutters; but the rabble had managed to find more secreted in the burning shops and bore it away in pitchers and buckets. . . .

The ruins of Richmond, April 1865. From *Harper's Pictorial History of the Civil War,* 1866.

The fire was progressing rapidly, and the crashing sound of falling timbers was distinctly heard. Dr. Read's church was blazing. The War Department was falling down; burning papers were being wafted about the streets. The Commissary Department, with our desks and papers, was consumed already. Warwick & Barksdale's Mall was sending its flames to the sky. Cary and Main Streets seemed doomed throughout; Bank Street was beginning to burn. . . . Almost every house is guarded. . . . The moon is shining brightly on our captivity. God guide and watch over us!

RICHMOND WAS STILL BURNING when Mrs. McGuire closed her diary on April 3, 1865. Was Grant coming? Was it Sherman? Sheridan? Had damn Yankees set the fires? Many Richmondites heard rumors that they had. There were also wild tales about a Negro unit of Yankee troops, sabers drawn, marching through the city, out to get their former masters; there were even rumors that Chimborazo Hospital, the world's largest, had been set afire by Yankee incendiaries. No one knew. What seemed certain was that the remainder of the city would burn to the ground.

Not that much was left of the once supremely proud capital of the Confederacy; even pride was in short supply there, as it often is when food is scarce. For ten months Richmond and her sister city, Petersburg, had been held under the siege that gave birth to this chaos; during the preceding summer alone some eight hundred homes in the area had been damaged by stray shells from the Union lines. "The wolf is at the door here," Richmondite Jack Middleton had recently written to his friend, the constant diarist Mary Chesnut, in Charleston, South Carolina. "We dread starvation far more than we do Grant, or Sherman. *Famine*, that is the word now."

The wolf had been at Richmond's door since about a year before in early 1864, when General Ulysses S. Grant took charge of all Union forces. Today General Robert E. Lee had begun his hasty retreat along the Appomattox River, leaving the city defenseless, and Grant was already hot on his heels, far from the streets of Richmond. *Appomattox.* A word the nation was just beginning to define. The river gave its name to the obscure town it meandered through in south-central Virginia, a sleepy hamlet more properly called Appomattox Court House, where all Confederate dreams would die. *Appomattox* itself would become a synonym for surrender or for victory or for reconciliation, depending on who pronounced it. In any case, both North and South had been on the road that would end at Appomattox ever since President Abraham Lincoln had conferred the supreme command of all Union armies on General Ulysses S. Grant, the Union's western commander at the time and known as "the man of the hour" for winning a series of brilliant though blood-drenched victories over the past two years.

General Grant would have seemed an unlikely choice for man of the hour at the beginning of the war. Up until then his life had been mostly a series of disgraces and failures, hardly the storybook background of a great military hero. Grant, who came from out of what was then the West, like most of the Union's best generals— Sherman, Sheridan, Thomas—had shown little promise outside of his expert horsemanship back when he attended the U.S. Military

Academy at West Point. He graduated in the lower half of his 1843 class and drew an infantry assignment rather than a coveted engineer post. West Point—his father's idea—was a disappointment to this lonely Ohio farm boy, a great unhappiness like most of his life save his wife, children, and his service in the Civil War. The Point had even taken his name from him. A clerical mistake there listed him as Ulysses Simpson Grant (his real name was Hiram Ulysses Grant); he accepted the error, using it from his first day at the Point until the end of his life, even in the title of his *Memoirs*. He was called Sam at the Point, however, the old story being that an upperclassman spied his name given as U.S. Grant on a bulletin board listing of new cadets and joked that this stood for United States Grant, or better yet, Uncle Sam Grant. "That's what he is," another joker supposedly chimed in. "Uncle Sam Grant—the grandson of our good old Uncle Sam."

The awkward little soldier was glad to be called Sam, too, throughout his career. He liked it better than the strange Ulysses and far better, of course, than the "Useless" of his childhood playmates. It was clearly preferable to his only other nickname, "Little Beauty," given to the good-looking soldier by the officers of his regiment before the Mexican War. At the time, according to an early biographer, Grant "had a girl's primness of manner and modesty of conduct. . . . He was almost half-woman, but this strain was buried in the depths of his soul. . . . His face was like that of a young girl's in its freshness of complexion and delicacy of outline. He was small and slender. . . . His voice was always soft, clear and musical . . . and his hands had the long, tapering fingers of a woman." Quite a contrast to the "brutal" general of later years, always pictured with unkempt beard and tobacco-stained, rumpled clothes, an ever-present stump of a cigar rooted in his mouth. A man who detested war, wouldn't kill animals, had an aversion to guns, who hated blood so much that his meat always had to be cooked charred, who was so modest that he took his baths during the Civil War with his tent flaps securely pinned closed—yet a man who would later be called a bloody butcher and much worse for the way he conducted war.

Young Sam Grant as a brevet second lieutenant, 1843. From *Personal Memoirs of U. S. Grant*, 1886.

According to his own sparse account and the often embellished stories of early biographers, Grant's years at West Point were miserable from the start. He is said to have prayed, in the way boys faced with problems do, for a train wreck as he made his way up the Hudson. Over the next four years he showed no native talent for the military, unlike his Rebel adversaries Robert E. Lee or

Stonewall Jackson, and excelled only in riding, as he had since a
child, surpassing his military instructors at the handling of horses
and once jumping his horse over a six-foot-six hurdle to set an
academy record. For a time he was indeed assigned to the class
awkward squad; he did poorly in all his subjects except mathe-
matics, and was frequently reprimanded for laziness, tardiness, and
sloppiness. Whereas Lee's rifle always glistened in his days at the
Point, Grant was marked down for not keeping his weapon clean.
Homesick and with few friends, the unmilitary cadet doubted that
he would ever graduate, but he gutted it out. Looking back in his
Memoirs twenty years after the war, he wrote: "I hear army men say
their happiest days were at West Point. I never had that experience. The most trying days of my life were those I spent there,
and I never recall them with pleasure." Strong words for a man
who rarely showed his emotions.

During the Mexican War, which he personally thought "wicked,"
a landgrab at best, Grant served in the Quartermaster Corps and
met Captain Robert E. Lee at least one time, though years later
Lee could not remember him or their brief chat. Grant distinguished himself in combat near Mexico City by breaking down a
howitzer and carrying it piece by piece up narrow stone stairs to a
church steeple, where he assembled the weapon and turned it on
Mexican forces below, inflicting great damage. Another time he
rode Comanche-style on the side of his horse through enemy lines
for reinforcements. Pointing him out on the street one day, his
commander remarked, "There goes a man of force!" Despite his
feelings about the war and war in general, he served valiantly and
was promoted to brevet captain.

Grant had been introduced to Julia Dent, a St. Louis belle from
a family of slaveholders, by her brother, West Point cadet Frederick T. Dent, soon after the young lieutenant began active military
service. They were quickly engaged. Four years had passed since
their engagement—they met only once in all that time—when the
couple decided to marry on Grant's return from the Mexican War
in 1848. One of the attendants at the gala wedding was Sam
Grant's good friend Lieutenant James Longstreet, who was to become one of the South's best fighting generals. After four years of

a happy married life, however, Grant's regiment was ordered to the Pacific Coast, and the couple decided it would be best for Julia to stay in St. Louis until her "Ulyss" came home.

Over the next two years Grant's loneliness seems to have led to a drinking problem that got out of hand, but this is by no means certain and may never be proved, like most of the rumors and gossip he attracted during his military career. In his *Memoirs* he claims that he had no chance of supporting his family out of his pay as an army officer on the Pacific Coast: "I concluded therefore to resign, and in March applied for a leave of absence until the end of the July following, tendering my resignation to take effect at the end of that time." The story persists, however, that drunkenness led to his resignation. Historian Bruce Catton believed Grant was "as abstemious as any man needs to be," but the general had many detractors in his day, ranging from those who claimed he drank "four fingers" several times daily and went on drunken sprees periodically, to those who claimed that he merely couldn't hold even small portions of liquor, had "no brain for drinking." His friend Rufus Ingalls, who roomed with him at the Point and served with him on the West Coast, believed that Grant was drinking at Fort Humboldt in northern California; others, including his respected biographer Hamlin Garland, supported this belief. It seems fairly certain that Grant never drank while involved in any fighting during the Civil War, but it appears likely that his tendency toward depression and the lonely life he led while a captain at Humboldt did lead to excessive drinking. According to one often-told story, Grant was warned by his superior, Lieutenant Colonel Robert Buchanan, that his drinking was setting a bad example for the troops at the remote fort. He was forced to sign a blank resignation, which would be sent to the War Department if he couldn't control himself. Grant couldn't, and his martinet of a commanding officer—the two men despised each other—sent in his resignation.

One of F. Scott Fitzgerald's stories describes "Grant lolling . . . in Galena" waiting "to be called to an intricate destiny" after he left the army. Sam Grant never talked about "destiny," but if depression was his curse, patience and endurance beyond most men were surely virtues of this rather plodding, shy family man whose strongest words even among hardened army veterans were "dog-gone" and "by lightning," and whose lodestone word was always "duty" rather than "glory." Patience enough to wait out all the failures he would face in civilian life and all the long, bloody defeats and victories he would suffer when war came. Out of the army, Grant failed at raising potatoes on Hardscrabble Farm back east, even with the help of two slaves given to Julia by her father, slaves Grant returned to the Dents before the Civil War. He failed at wood hauling; at bill collecting; at a job as customhouse clerk; at a St. Louis real estate business he established with his wife's cousin. In one early letter he wrote of the *"poverty, poverty, poverty"* that always stared him in the face. He was "poor Sam Grant" to most who knew him, few but Julia ever calling him Mr. Grant. Once he had to pawn his watch to buy his wife and children Christmas presents. Ague and rheumatism plagued him; he was turned down for the post of county engineer; he borrowed money and couldn't repay his loans. Finally he moved from St. Louis back to Galena, where he was still remembered as a shy child who loved the company of horses better than people and had few if any close friends. The West Point graduate and Mexican War hero became a mere clerk in Grant and Sons, his father's harness shop, making about $800 a year. He was not much good at his job and stoically put up with the abuse of his brothers and fellow employees, possibly drinking to forget his failures.

Only with the coming of the Civil War did Sam Grant's life begin to take on shape and meaning again. He immediately began training local youth for the militia, and soon sat down to write the adjutant general of the army:

> Galena, Illinois
> May 24, 1861
>
> Col. L. Thomas
> Adjt. Gen. U.S.A.
> Washington, D.C.
>
> Sir:—Having served for fifteen years in the regular army, including four years at West Point, and feeling it the duty of every one who has been educated at the Government expense to offer their

services for the support of that Government, I have the honor, very respectfully, to tender my services, until the close of the war, in such capacity as may be offered. I would say, in view of my present age (39) and length of service, I feel myself competent to command a regiment, if the President, in his judgement, should see fit to intrust one to me.

Since the first call of the President I have been serving on the staff of the Governor of this State, rendering such aid as I could in the organization of our State militia, and am still engaged in that capacity. A letter addressed to me at Springfield, Illinois, will reach me.

I am very respectfully,

Your obt. svt.
U.S. Grant

Grant's offer wasn't formally accepted or rejected—no one ever answered him. The letter was found after the war, seven years later, unfiled, with no comments, in some dusty corner of the adjutant general's office. Whether Grant was deemed unfit to command because of his previous tarnished record will probably never be known to history. Certainly, he himself had doubts at the time about his abilities. When a neighbor in Galena asked him if he'd like to be a colonel, he reportedly replied, despite his confident letter, "I would rather like a regiment, yet there are few men really competent to command a thousand soldiers, and I doubt whether I am one of them." Nevertheless, he was determined enough to pursue the matter after his letter brought no answer. He rode to the state capital at Springfield, Illinois, where he was promptly made a colonel and given a regiment. A month or so later he received a promotion to brigadier general, a rank he hadn't asked for and always suspected—with good reason—was the work of Illinois congressman Elihu B. Washburne, a close friend of President Lincoln's.

Almost a year would pass before Lincoln gave much thought to his new general. On February 16, 1862, Grant's forces captured Fort Donelson from the Confederates, losing five hundred men compared with Confederate casualties of fifteen hundred soldiers and thirteen hundred taken prisoner. Kentucky and Tennessee were in the control of the North now. Donelson was the first glimmer of light, a bloody dawn after a long Union night in the netherworld. U. S. Grant here won the nickname "Unconditional Surrender" Grant when he issued his famous laconism to the enemy for the capitulation of the fort: "No terms except unconditional and immediate surrender can be accepted." Here he also acquired the famous cigar chain-smoking habit (sometimes twenty-four a day) that contributed to his untimely death twenty years after the war. Grant was pictured in one newspaper drawing puffing away on a cigar in the thick of battle. "I had been a light smoker previous to the attack on Donelson," he later told his aide-de-camp General Horace Porter. "In the accounts published in the papers I was represented as smoking a cigar in the midst of the conflict; and many persons, thinking, no doubt, that tobacco was my chief solace, sent me boxes of the choicest brands. . . . As many as *ten thousand* were soon received. I gave away all I could get rid of, but having such a quantity on hand I naturally smoked more than I would have done under ordinary circumstances, and I have continued the habit ever since."

Major Union victories were rare at the time of Donelson, and Grant was promoted to major general of volunteers for his leadership. Nevertheless, when he went to consult with the commander of Union forces in Nashville, he was falsely charged with leaving his command for nonmilitary reasons.

This false accusation most likely finds its explanation in jealousy on the part of Generals George McClellan and Henry Halleck, the latter of whom even repeated a rumor to higher-ups that Grant had resumed his excessive drinking habits. "Old Brains," as the owlish-faced, pop-eyed Halleck was called (Grant somewhat sarcastically called him the perfect staff officer), had good reason to be concerned about drinking among Union officers and men. Drinking was an enormous problem in both the Northern and Southern armies and probably caused more deaths than anyone will ever know—deaths attributable to foolish decisions made under the influence and deaths caused by bad booze itself. According to one Southern newspaper editor, the rotgut available to

Bluebellies and Butternuts alike "would conglomerate the vesicles of the aorta, phlogistify the phylacter maximus, hem-stitch up the depatic ducts, insulate the asperifollis gland, deflagate the dudonian process, and wilt the buttons on the waistcoat."

But Grant wasn't guilty this time. It seems very likely, though, that he did go on a bender after his famous Vicksburg victory, one of the most brilliant strategic campaigns of the war. The original source for this story, rarely quoted at any length, is Sylvanus Cadwallader, an excellent, respected war correspondent covering Grant's headquarters for the *Chicago Times* and *New York Tribune* from 1862 to 1865. Cadwallader first noticed "symptoms of intoxication" in General Grant after the siege of Vicksburg, when they were traveling on the steamboat *Diligence* up the Yazoo River to Satartia. The two men thought highly of each other at this point—Cadwallader was convinced that Grant had no equal as a general—and they remained on good terms after the *Diligence* affair, possibly even more so because Cadwallader almost single-handedly pulled Grant through this embarrassing scrape.

Cadwallader told the story in his *Three Years with Grant*, the manuscript of which wasn't finished until 1896, and wasn't published for another fifty-nine years. Finding Grant "stupid in speech and staggering in gait," the reporter first persuaded the ship's captain to close the barroom and "lose the key" to it. As he wrote:

> I then took the General in hand myself. I enticed him into his stateroom, locked myself in the room with him (having the key in my pocket), and commenced throwing bottles of whiskey, which stood on the table, out the windows . . . into the river. . . . On finding himself locked in he became quite angry and ordered me peremptorily to open the door and get out instantly. This order I firmly, but good-naturedly declined to obey. I said to him that I was the best friend he had in the Army of the Tennessee; that I was doing for him what I hoped someone would do for me, should I ever be in his condition; and that he must for the present, act upon my better judgement, and be governed by my advice. As it was a very hot day and the State-room almost suffocating, I insisted on his taking off his coat, vest and boots, and

lying down on one of the berths. After much resistance I succeeded, and soon fanned him to sleep.

The comedy continued. When Grant awoke that night, still in a stupor, he insisted on going ashore at Satartia, a nest of desperadoes and Rebel sympathizers, but Cadwallader and the troopers guarding the general talked him out of it. "His first intention was to mount and return overland to his headquarters in front of Vicksburg, through a section of country as hostile as any in the Confederacy," Cadwallader wrote. "I have never doubted but he would have ridden off into the enemy's lines that night had he been allowed to do so."

Grant captured by the Rebels? A strong possibility if he hadn't been stopped, Cadwallader clearly implied. At any rate, Grant woke up the next morning as if nothing had happened, "came out to breakfast fresh as a rose, clean shirt and all, quite himself," remembered Charles A. Dana, the War Department investigator and former *New York Tribune* editor who also accompanied him. Which made Cadwallader all the more astounded to find the general drunk again soon after breakfast: "I . . . was almost thunderstruck at finding an hour afterward that Grant had procured another supply of whiskey from on shore (at Haynes's Bluff) and was quite as much intoxicated as the day before. The same tactics were resorted to [he locked Grant in his cabin again] but I encountered less fierce opposition. . . . To be seen in his present condition would [have been] to his utter disgrace and ruin."

But Grant's spree was far from over. Having ordered the steamboat on to Chickasaw Bayou, he could be restrained no more when it reached its destination. On landing at sundown, he went on board a headquarters sutler boat that generously dispensed free liquor and cigars to all Union officers. Cadwallader, finally realizing what had happened, found the general in front of a table filled with bottles of liquor and wine, in the act of downing a glass of whiskey that obviously wasn't his first.

The perfect Keystone Kop serial continued in the midst of one of the most horrible wars the world had ever known. For the ride back to headquarters Grant chose a horse called Kangaroo, so named because he always reared up and plunged forth whenever mounted. Grant, in the bellicose state of his drunkenness, spurred the horse as soon as he got in the saddle and Kangaroo leaped off at full speed before anyone could follow. "Grant paid no attention to roads or sentries," Cadwallader remembered. "He went at full speed through Union camps and corrals . . . literally tore through and over everything in his way. The air was full of dust, ashes, and embers from campfires and shouts and curses from those he rode down in his race. Fortunately horse and rider escaped impalement from bayonets . . . and were not fired upon by guards."

Cadwallader only caught up with the general when Grant, growing comatose, slowed his horse down to a walk. The correspondent tied the general's bridle rein to his own saddle and again took charge in no uncertain terms. "His intoxication increased so in a few minutes that he became unsteady in the saddle," Cadwallader noted. "The [military] escort was not in sight. . . . Fearing discovery of his rank and situation [by the Rebels], I took refuge in a thicket near the foot of the bluff. Here I induced the General to lay down on the grass with the saddle for a pillow. He was soon asleep."

Grant slept peacefully under the stars while, unknown even to Cadwallader, his escort searched the woods for him, fully expecting to find their commander dead. It took only an hour of sleep and the ride back to headquarters in an ambulance before Grant was sober again, before he "shook himself together, as one just rising from a nap, bid all goodnight in a natural tone and manner, and started to his tent as steadily as he ever walked in his life."

So ended what must be one of the most spectacular sprees in American military history, the wildest evening ride since Longfellow's galloping account of Paul Revere, purposeless though it was. General John A. Rawlins, Grant's devoted friend and aide-decamp, who controlled Grant's drinking during the war as well as any man could, thanked Cadwallader warmly for what he had done. (Cadwallader never published his account during the war, "unwilling to jeopardize Grant's reputation by adding anything to the rumors and stories in circulation concerning his inebrity.") The reporter was thereafter treated as a trusted member of Grant's staff, and on several occasions was "introduced to others as a member of his personal staff" by the general. He would even be an invited witness to the historic surrender meeting at Appomattox, according to his testimony. As for his opinion of Grant's reputation for drunkenness, Cadwallader wrote:

> The truth was General Grant had an inordinate love for liquors. He was not an habitual drinker. He could not drink moderately. When at long intervals his appetite for strong drink caused him to accept the invitation to take "just one glass before parting," he invariably drank to excess unless someone was with him whose control he would acknowledge to lead him away from temptation [someone like Rawlins, Mrs. Grant, or Cadwallader]. Both extremes of public rumor (that Grant did or did not drink) rested on some foundation in fact. Though absolutely refusing to drink on one day or occasion, there was no certainty that he would not be inebriated on the next.

Some scholars question the Cadwallader story, written thirty years after the event, claiming that he was not there, or that he had embellished the tale, or that it just hadn't happened. But Dana's reference to Grant's condition as due to an illness could well be a diplomatic way of saying that he was drunk, and Rawlins did write a scalding letter to Grant just a day before the alleged incident on the Yazoo:

> Tonight I find you where the wine bottle has just been emptied, in company with those who drink and urge you to do likewise. . . . You have the full control of your appetite and can let drinking alone. Had you not pledged me the sincerity of your honor early last March that you would drink no more during the war and kept that pledge during your recent campaign, you would not today have stood first in the world's history as a successful military leader. Your only salvation depends on your strict adherence to that pledge.

Much later, some twenty-two years after the war, Dana wrote a *New York Sun* editorial entitled "General Grant's Occasional Intoxication."

Grant would be charged with drunkenness many times during the war; delegations often called on Lincoln to demand that he be removed from command for his intemperance. There is no evidence that he was ever drunk on the field of battle, however; and never so drunk, as the old story goes, that he could not sit on his horse while commanding, or even so soused—as the famous James Thurber satire has it—that he surrendered his sword to Lee at Appomattox. The strongest testimony of this came from General John M. Thayer, who told the president: "It has been charged in northern newspapers that Grant was under the influence of liquor on the fields of Donelson and Shiloh. The charge is atrocious, wickedly false. I saw him repeatedly during the battles of Donelson and Shiloh on the field, and if there were any sober men on the field, Grant was one of them."

Another blot on Grant's reputation was the infamous General Order Number 11 that he issued in December 1862. It read in part: "The Jews, as a class violating every regulation of trade established by the Treasury Department and also department orders, are hereby expelled from the department within twenty-four hours from the receipt of this order." This nasty bit of anti-Semitism was rescinded as soon as President Lincoln heard about it a week later, but the damage was done. It appears that Grant's unscrupulous father went into partnership with a firm of traders, Mack and Brothers, who happened to be Jewish, after offering them Grant's special protection. Grant may have struck out at Mack and Brothers to avoid confronting and offending his father, but this seems a lame excuse for such blatant bigotry.

In any case, Lincoln retained his far-from-perfect, hard-drinking general; he liked this plain man's fighting style, rare among Union commanders at the time, of running his military operation from the field instead of behind a desk in the capital, far removed from the troops and any danger. Lincoln had defended him even before Vicksburg—after the terrible battle at Shiloh, in Tennessee, on April 6, 1862, when Grant was surprised by Confederate forces and only won the day by sheer force of numbers, losing over thirteen thousand men in the process. "I can't spare this man," Lincoln said. "He fights." A year later he was supposed to have wisecracked (actually it was a hoary story fabricated by humorist Charles G. Halpine, a former Union general, in a report of an imaginary banquet) that he wished someone would tell him what brand of whiskey Grant drank so he could "send a barrel to the other generals."

Lincoln's faith in Grant was rewarded with the brilliant victory at Vicksburg on July 4, 1863, which again resulted in massive Federal casualties but effectively split the Confederacy in two, giving Union forces use of the Mississippi River. Few cared if Lincoln's general went on the famous steamboat bender at the close of the Vicksburg campaign. Later that year fewer still cared about his tippling when Grant became a national hero with his victories at Missionary Ridge and Lookout Mountain outside Chattanooga, Tennessee. Congress awarded him a gold medal in March 1864 and revived the three-star rank of lieutenant general for Lincoln to bestow upon him, a rank only the legendary George Washington and the brilliant, vainglorious Winfield Scott had held before Grant.

Soon the North's new hero responded to an invitation of Secretary of War Edwin Stanton and took the train to Washington to meet Lincoln for the first time. He traveled with no aides or secretaries, just his eldest son, thirteen-year-old Fred, who had witnessed every battle of the Vicksburg campaign at his father's side and now would watch him formally receive his new commission. On the eve of the president's weekly reception, so many people turned out to see the idol of the hour that one reporter called it "the only real mob I ever saw in the White House." Grant was asked to stand on a sofa so all the crowd could see him and did so for almost an hour. The shy general, wearing a badly fitted, somewhat wrinkled, lackluster uniform, and "blushing like a schoolgirl," struck sophisticates in the Blue Room as a "stumbling seedy hick," an "awkward hayseed." He piqued some politicians for his lack of interest in them or his newfound fame. Distinguished author Richard Henry Dana Jr. even brought up the drinking rumor again: "He had a cigar in his mouth, and rather the look of a man who did, or once did, take a little too much to drink. . . . He does not march, nor quite walk, but pitches along as if the next step would bring him on his nose." He seemed to be always alone, one perceptive woman noted; he "walked through a crowd as if solitary." Lincoln, for his part, hit it off well with the flushed, rather embarrassed little general. They talked about the next day's ceremonies, when the president would formally promote Grant to his new rank as supreme Federal commander, general in chief of the armies of the United States. He would head what was called "the greatest army in the world," at least in numbers—over 800,000 men enrolled, 533,000 present and ready to fight. The Confederacy, on the other hand, had about 400,000 men on its muster rolls, half of them under arms.

In his diary, Lincoln's secretary John G. Nicolay wrote that Grant's speech accepting the president's promotion on March 9, 1864, was a bit of a disappointment:

> The General had hurriedly and almost illegibly written his speech on a half sheet of note paper, in lead pencil, and being quite embarrassed by the occasion, and finding his own writing so very difficult to read, made rather sorry and disjointed work of enunciating his reply. I noticed too that in what he said, while it was brief and to the point, he had either forgotten or disregarded entirely the President's hints to him [about what to say] of the night previous.

Grant's speech was a humble one of only three sentences, trusting in "the favor of that Providence which leads both nations and men." At their first private meeting shortly afterward, Nicolay wrote, Lincoln advised Grant that he especially wanted him "to take Richmond . . . and asked if the Lieutenant-General could do it. Grant, without hesitation, answered that he could if he had the troops. These the President assured him he could have."

Nothing was decided or even suggested about *how* the capital of the Confederacy was to be taken, for Lincoln agreed to leave the fighting of the war up to Grant, something he hadn't been able to do with the six commanding generals preceding him, each of whom had seemed more inept or indecisive than the last. As Grant put it in his *Memoirs*:

In my first interview with Mr. Lincoln alone he stated to me that he had never professed to be a military man or to know how campaigns should be conducted, and never wanted to interfere in them; but that procrastination on the part of the commanders, and the pressure from the people at the North and Congress, *which was always with him,* forced him into issuing his series of "Military Orders" one, two, three, etc. He did not know but that they were all wrong, and did know some of them were. All he wanted or had ever wanted was someone who would take responsibility and act, and call on him for all the assistance needed. . . . Assuring him that I would do the best I could with the means at hand and avoid as far as possible annoying him or the War Department, our first interview ended.

Grant was quickly on his way with his son, glad to be rid of what he called the "show business" atmosphere of the capital. Lincoln's promise not to meddle in military affairs was taken literally by the new supreme commander and he did not confide his specific plans to the president—possibly because the loquacious Lincoln was widely believed to be loose-lipped about secret military operations. Grant's basic strategy was simple: the hero of Donelson, Vicksburg, and Chattanooga was to go after General Lee, for whom he had the greatest respect but hardly idolized, as some early writers claimed. He did not believe in the myth of Lee's invincibility. "I had known Lee personally," Grant said after his appointment as supreme commander, "and I knew that he was mortal." Once he called Lee a "headquarter's general"; still another time he snapped, "I'm tired of hearing about Bobby Lee!" In any case, it was Grant's plan to go for Lee relentlessly, never letting him take the initiative again, while the commander of all the western armies, General William Tecumseh Sherman, would capitalize on Lee's constant involvement by attacking General Joseph Johnston's forces in Georgia and eventually capturing Atlanta. As Sherman succinctly put it, "[Grant] was to go for Lee and I was to go for Joe Johnston." With the North's far greater numerical superiority—and Lincoln had promised Grant all the men he needed to replace casualties—what the press was calling "the greatest army in history" would wear the enemy down. The

General U. S. Grant, 1864. From *Men and Things I Saw in Civil War Days*, 1899.

over-half-a-million-man force would hammer the Rebels into sub-mission, neither Lee nor Johnston being able to help each other.

Grant summed up the plan in his official report as chief of staff at war's end:

> From an early period in the rebellion I had been impressed with the idea that active and continuous operations of all the troops that could be brought into the field, regardless of season and weather, were necessary to a speedy termination of the war. The resources of the enemy, and his numerical strength, were far in-

ferior to ours; but . . . we had a vast territory, with a population hostile to the government, to garrison, and long lines of river and railroad communications to protect. . . .

The [Union] armies in the East and West had acted independently . . . like a balky team, no two ever pulling together, enabling the enemy to use to great advantage his interior lines of communication for transporting troops from east and west, reinforcing the [Confederate] army most vigorously pressed, and to furlough large numbers [of men], during seasons of military inactivity . . . to go to their homes and do the work of producing [food] for the support of their armies. . . .

From the first I was firm in the conviction that no peace could be had that would be stable . . . until the military power of the rebellion was entirely broken. I therefore determined, *first*, to use the greatest number of troops practicable against the armed force of the enemy; preventing him from using the same force at different seasons against one and then another of our armies. . . . *Second*, to hammer continuously against the armed force of the enemy and his resources, until by mere attrition, if in no other way, there should be nothing left to him but [surrender] . . .

Lincoln liked this strategy when he learned of it, if only because he had long ago proposed it to generals moribund almost to the point of rigor mortis, generals with the "slows," as the president put it. But the major trouble with Grant's plan was that it took over a year to accomplish and, of far more importance, would be paid for with the lives and limbs of tens of thousands of soldiers on both sides.

Grant was fully aware of this. He later wrote in his *Memoirs*:

Soon after midnight, May 3rd–4th, the Army of the Potomac moved out from its position north of the Rapidan, to start upon that memorable campaign, destined to result in the capture of the Confederate capital and the army defending it. This was not to be accomplished, however, without as desperate fighting as the world had ever witnessed, not to be consummated in a day, a week, a month, or a single season. The losses inflicted, and endured, were destined to be severe; but the armies now

Union troops crossing the Rapidan at the start of Grant's Virginia campaign. From *Harper's Pictorial History of the Civil War,* 1866.

confronting each other had already been in deadly conflict for a period of three years, with immense losses . . . and neither had made any real progress toward accomplishing the final end. . . . The campaign now begun was destined to result in heavier losses to both armies, in a given time, than any previously suffered; but the carnage was to be limited to a single year.

And so the rich, verdant southern spring of 1864 saw three vast Union armies on the march, Grant ultimately responsible for them all: General George Meade at the head of the Army of the Potomac, with Grant and a staff of his own traveling with and overseeing him; the inept and notorious General Benjamin Butler leading the Army of the James in Virginia against Lee's support; and General William Tecumseh Sherman aiming the Army of the Tennessee against Atlanta, from which Sherman would make his famous—or infamous—march to the sea and then into South Caro-

lina, where Fort Sumter, the place where it all started, would ultimately fall again into Union hands.

Clearly, Grant shared General Sherman's "war is all hell" philosophy and believed that almost any method was justified to end
the Great Rebellion. If he never said this exactly, it is evident in
his words and actions. There would be many bloody battles east
and west to suffer through, but the first, on the gentlest of spring
mornings, was what might be called an "accidental battle"—the
Wilderness campaign.

The Wilderness is an area across the Rapidan in northern Virginia, so named for its thick, tangled woods and dense brush. The
region was dark and forbidding even to those veteran soldiers who
knew its pitted terrain of swampy black muck, sand, and red clay.
Grant had no intention of fighting a major battle in this maze
where the Rebels had trapped General Joe Hooker a year earlier;
what he wanted to do was attack quickly *across* the Wilderness,
cutting Lee off from Richmond and capturing his entire army.
This proved a vain hope. Grant was a few hours too late, and the
Gray Fox guessed his strategy. He quickly moved his troops *into*
the Wilderness to fight the Yankees there, a vast wooded area
where his men, outnumbered two to one, would be safer from the
superior Federal artillery. Lee had fought and won before in this
eerie place where, uncovered by the winter rains, the bleached
skeletons and grinning skulls of men and horses lost in the first
battle all but cried "Turn back!" to the skittish Federals advancing across the same ground. Herman Melville wrote of it in *Battle-
Pieces*:

> In glades they meet skull after skull
>   Where pine-cones lay—the rusted gun,
> Green shoes full of bones, the mouldering coat
>   And huddled-up skeleton

No longer were Grant's men the confident troops crossing the
Rapidan with virtually no resistance, marching in quick swinging
gait to the music of Grand Army bands. They stepped carefully.
No enemy could be seen all around them save sardonic bones
laughing, a troop of bones out of step mocking them. Skulls bobbed

in ditches of muddy water; Federal private Warren Goss found a bird's nest in the cavity of one skull, a wasp's nest in another: "Life in embryo in the skull of death." One angry, frightened Union soldier kicked a skull staring up at him. "This is what you are all coming to," he told the infantrymen flanking him, "and some of you will start toward it tomorrow!" Still the woods were ironically beautiful, filled with bright wildflowers, flowering white dogwoods, and flickering shades of green. "It is a glorious spring day on which all the bloody work is being done," wrote a soldier in Lee's badly depleted Army of Northern Virginia. Grant and his 122,000 men were caught in this treacherous, unfamiliar near-jungle, twelve miles wide and six miles deep, of which the Confederates at least had sufficient knowledge to set up effective positions, offsetting the North's superior numbers and big guns. Visibility was at best fifty feet in any direction. Men on both sides fell into pits, stumbled in gullies, were stopped in their tracks by tangles of vines, briers, and brush. "It was a blind and bloody hunt to the death," Private Goss wrote, describing disoriented men wandering around in circles. "They were two wild animals hunting each other," according to another contemporary account. "When they heard each other's steps they sprang and grappled. Here in blind wrestle as at midnight did men in blue and gray clutch at each other. Bloodiest and weirdest of encounters. War had seen nothing like it."

The battle could have been a symbol of the blind stupidity of war itself, ignorant armies clashing by perpetual night in the dense battle smoke; it brings to mind the German general Helmuth von Moltke's quip that the U.S. Civil War was fought between two armed mobs. But it was far worse, the men slowly burning to death, screaming, choking to death on their own blood, the stomachs ripped open like doors to hell. Grant's aide Horace Parker wrote: "[Men were] piled upon each other in some places four layers deep, exhibiting every ghastly phase of mutilation. Below the mass of fast-decaying corpses, the convulsive twitching of limbs and the writhing of bodies showed that there were wounded men still alive and struggling to extricate themselves from their horri-

Fighting in the Wilderness, 1864. From *Harper's Pictorial History of the Civil War,* 1866.

ble entombment." General Grant could hardly have been blamed if he took to his Old Crow again, though there is no evidence that he did. At one point in the slaughter Grant did "throw himself face down on his cot and give way to the greatest emotion . . . stirred to the very depths of his soul."

The Wilderness has been called the battle no one saw, but close up it looked, sounded, and felt like a battle in hell itself when the woods caught fire, trapping soldiers on both sides. Over two hundred wounded Union infantrymen burned to death in the leaves and wildflowers, unable to crawl away fast enough. "I stumbled, fell and my outflung hands pushed up a shoulder of leaves," Maine major Abner Small wrote. "The fire sprang into flame, caught in the hair and beard of a dead sergeant, and lighted a ghastly face and wide open eyes. I rushed away in horror."

In horror, in terror, they ran from the fires and burning bodies. "With a crackling roar, like an army of fire, it came down upon the

Union line," Private Goss recalled. "The winds drove the blinding smoke and suffocating heat into our faces . . . then, reaching out its tongue of flame, ignited the breastworks of resinous logs, which soon roared and crackled along their entire length. The men fought the enemy and flames at the same time. Their hair and beards were singed and their faces blistered. . . . Their rifles . . . became so hot . . . that they were unable to hold them."

Other Federals and Confederates actually worked together, moving their wounded, screaming comrades out of the flaming woods. So confused was the battle over the two days that Union troops were fired on by their own artillery. Confederate general Micah Jenkins was killed by troops of a Virginia brigade; soon after, General Longstreet was shot in the throat by these same Virginians, and General Lee had to personally assume command of the Old Warhorse's troops. Earlier, Lee had insisted on advancing with the Texas Brigade, until the unit to a man shouted, "Lee to the rear! General Lee go back! We won't go on unless you go back!" Only then did he turn toward safer ground.

But General Lee's bravery in front of his troops, General Grant's faith and stolidity—they were as nothing in sight of the human suffering in this mysterious, maddening no-man's-land. When the battle in the "devil's garden" was over on May 6, 1864, the North had lost 17,666 (possibly more) men, 2,246 of them killed in the action over two days, while the South sacrificed more than 7,500 of its 60,000 troops, about the same percentage of casualties considering the Union's almost two-to-one superiority in numbers. Both sides withdrew from battle, neither having won as much ground as the dirt under the fastidious General Lee's fingernails. Surgeons estimated they had worked one hundred hours just sawing off arms and legs. Hundreds of wooden legs would be tapping out a code of loss for the next half century on the boardwalks and sidewalks of America, marching for a while, some of them, with maimed veterans of the War to End All Wars and even World War II.

"What awful, what sickening sights," Union chaplain A. M. Stewart wrote. Then he caught himself: "No, we have ceased to get sick at such sights!" Yet even in the midst of all this carnage an angel of mercy appeared every morning in the form of a young Southern girl unable to speak or hear since birth. She came through the woods to the wounded Union soldiers stranded beneath the trees, ladling them milk from a pail she carried, a silent flower of the Virginia spring keeping many alive by her presence. Nineteen-year-old Joseph H. Johnson, of a New Paltz, New York, unit, drank the rich milk mornings while lying under a blanket of leaves red with blood from his shattered thigh. He at least lived long enough to be evacuated, to see all of his family one last time and tell of the beautiful, unknown child who could have been his little sister.

Finally, on May 7, 1864, after two days someone said were "far too terrible for any forgetting," Grant, smoking one of the two dozen cigars he stashed in his pockets each morning and whittling down a stick as was his custom, is said to have decided on the spur of the moment that Lee would be moving south from the Wilderness. More carnage. Instead of retreating as Hooker, cutting his losses, had done after the first battle here, Grant would advance. "If you see President Lincoln," he told a departing battlefield correspondent, "tell him, from me, that whatever happens, there will be no turning back." He would surprise Lee, boldly flank him, and march to the crossroads of Spotsylvania and around the Army of Northern Virginia toward Richmond. It was a good plan; but, again, it didn't work. Lee hadn't retreated south. His hunches, if not his grand strategy, were almost always better than Grant's or any Union general's. "Grant is not going to retreat," he assured an aide. "He will move his army to Spotsylvania. . . . I am so sure of his next move that I've already made arrangements to march by the shortest practicable route, so that we may meet him there."

Grant's men—initially glad that the Army of the Potomac was moving forward for the first time after a defeat, proud that their new leader "didn't scare," sure they wouldn't "skedaddle" this time, that they were on their way to Richmond and final victory and home—were the ones to be surprised. At the end of their long, forced march they found a wall of Confederate troops blocking their path. In front of them was a curved salient of Confederate breastworks, the "Mule Shoe," which was to become known to history as the "Bloody Angle" for the 6,800 Federal dead and wounded and the 5,000 Southern casualties suffered there. This protruding Mule Shoe salient of the Rebel line, protected by huge tree branches sharpened into hundreds of spikes, pointed ominously at the Union troops, but they charged into battle as ordered that May 9 morning. They failed in a series of furious attacks, Lee's troops dug in too deep, and continued to fail through the brutal ten-day battle, never breaking the Confederate lines. Horace Porter recalled:

> It was chiefly a savage hand-to-hand fight across the breastworks. Rank after rank was riddled by shot and shell and bayonet thrusts, and finally sank, a mass of torn and mutilated corpses; then fresh troops rushed madly forward to replace the dead; and so the murderous work went on. . . . Muskets were fired with muzzle against muzzle. Skulls were crushed with clubbed muskets and men stabbed with swords and bayonets thrust between the logs in the parapet which separated the combatants. Wild cheers, savage yells, and frantic shrieks rose above the sighing of the wind and the pattering of rain and formed a demonical accompaniment to the booming of the guns. . . .

Both sides suffered tremendous casualties. "How immense the butcher's bill has been," Lieutenant Oliver Wendell Holmes Jr. wrote in a letter to his parents. "I steadily believe that Grant is going to succeed, and that we shall have Richmond," Walt Whitman wrote his mother from Washington, "but oh what a price to pay for it." Among the Confederate dead was the dashing young cavalry general Jeb Stuart, cloak lined with scarlet, ever-present red flower in his lapel, his personal banjo-player Sweeney always at his side. The "Cavalier of Dixie," "Beauty," the "Eyes of the Army," was mortally wounded on May 11 at Yellow Tavern while defending the road to Richmond, six miles away. He had been shot by a Union cavalryman thrown from his horse in battle and trying to escape on foot. General Lee said he could "hardly think of him without weeping." Stuart was only thirty-one. His troops remembered his standing order to them: "We gallop toward the enemy, and trot away, always."

But most of the horror at Spotsylvania, worse even than the Wilderness, was as usual up close among the ranks. In a gruesome charge through the fog and smoke on May 12 a blue wave of twenty thousand troops hit the Bloody Angle and took it against all odds, only to have the Rebels fall back behind supporting breastworks and mow them down. Never before in the history of warfare had the exchange of fire been so fierce and relentless. Bodies were found completely laced with bullet holes, not three inches of space between each shot. Thick trees two feet in diameter were chopped down and bodies literally ripped to red shreds by *rifle bullets*, the bodies coming apart in midair. Wrote Confederate artillery major Robert Stiles: "The musketry fire is said to have been heavier than it ever was at any other place in all the world, or for any other hour in all the tide of time." Infantrymen arranged the hands of nearby corpses to hold cartridges for them so that they could fire faster. When men ran out of bullets in this furious encounter, they chucked their bayoneted rifles like spears at each other.

One Confederate counterattack was led by an enraged "old Captain Hunter," whose only weapon was a frying pan; it seems he had been cooking a nice piece of meat that a Yankee shell destroyed. But there was little time for humor or rest. The sharpshooters on both sides were busy at work. Among the first Union dead, killed before the initial engagement on May 9, was kindly General John Sedgwick ("Uncle John" to his troops), picked off by a Reb sharpshooter just as he quipped to a soldier at his side, "Posh, they couldn't hit an elephant at this distance." The hated snipers were barely tolerated by their own comrades. A Confederate officer wrote:

> Sharpshooting at best is a fearful thing. The regular sharpshooter seemed to me little better than a human tiger lying in wait for blood. His rifle is frequently trained . . . upon a particular spot—for example, where the head of a gunner must appear when sighting his piece—and the instant that target appears and

"darkens the hole," *crash* goes a bullet through his brain. . . . One can understand now the supreme . . . suffering of the lines. Thousands of men cramped up in a narrow trench, unable to get out, or get up, or to stretch or to stand without danger to life and limb; unable to lie down, or to sleep, for lack of room . . . ; night alarms, day attacks, hunger, thirst, supreme weariness; squalor, vermin, filth, disgusting odors everywhere . . . ; the first glance over the way at day down bringing the sharpshooter's bullet singing past your ear or smashing through your skull, a man's life often exacted as the price of a cup of water from the spring.

These angry words from Confederate major Willy Dame's *Reminiscences* could have just as well described the Union lines any place throughout the war. At Spotsylvania men were killed in the line after waking up and yawning, arms outstretched, after kneeling in prayer at night, while out in the open trying to find a lost pocketknife, or wedding ring, or crucifix. The best that can be said for this insidious form of murder is that it killed relatively few of the war's 620,000 dead. When the Spotsylvania campaign ended after twelve days on May 19, the Union had lost 17,500 men of the 110,000 force; the Confederates put 50,000 men in the field, but their drastic losses of well over 6,000 casualties and 4,000 captured would never be accurately recorded.

"This has been the most terrible day I have ever lived," a Union soldier said after one bloody Spotsylvania engagement. When it rained, wounded soldiers drowned in the muddy water flooding the trenches; others were shot during charges and fell face forward into mud holes, choking to death. Over 150 dead Union bodies were counted in a twelve-by-fifteen-foot area no larger than a parlor or living room. Union chaplain Stewart told of Rebel dead mixed with Yankees in a rifle pit that became a mass of putrefaction within one week, "the hair and skin fallen from heads, and the flesh from the bones—all alive with disgusting maggots." Passing soldiers had to stuff their nostrils with green leaves, he recalled, apologizing that "such a scene seems too revolting to record . . . yet how else convey any just conceptions of what is done and suffered here?" Later he said, "Much of this may never, *can* never be written, and were it, could not be understood."

A Southern officer wrote of Grant, "We have met a man this time who either does not know when he is whipped, or who cares not if he loses his whole Army." With Grant's coming the Union strategy seemed to have changed from lethargy to butchery. Grant himself, on May 11, told Chief of Staff Halleck, "I propose to fight it out on this line if it takes all summer." More than one soldier would have cursed his words and hoped that he wouldn't fight it out here another hour, but nevertheless most of the troops soldiered stoically and bravely through the terrible days on the road to Richmond, as shown by this extract from the diary of an anonymous Union veteran published at the time in *Harper's Weekly*:

> *May 8.*—Marched all night down through Spottsylvania—Went into the fight at 10 o'clock, made two charges on the Rebs, got drove back—loss very heavy.—Rested.—Ordered out in front: only 200 men left.—Stand picket all night.
>
> *May 9.*—Pleasant morning.—Started early, marched out, formed a line of battle.—Laid down. Laid all day in the hot sun, with our straps on.—Attacked the Rebs a little before night, drove them back, then laid down and slept.
>
> *May 10.*—Pleasant morning.—The battle commenced anew at noon, lasted till 9 o'clock, when we passed to the front to support the skirmishers.—Staid there until dark; drew back, lay down for the night.
>
> *May 19.*—Cloudy.—All quiet on the line.—Our boys changed papers with the Rebs this morning. Wrote a letter home.—Relieved from picket at 9 o'clock: laid behind breast-works all night.
>
> *May 23.*—Cloudy and cool.—All quiet this morning.—We are in Bowling Green, beginning to move forward.—Marched nine miles, forded the North Anna River at 2 o'clock.—The Rebs attacked us at 6 o'clock.—Fought an hour and a half; whipped them.

So went the alternately dreary and fearful life of the common soldier, the "mudcrusher," the Billy Yank and the Johnny Reb (though the Rebels themselves called the typical Secesh soldier "Bolivar Ward"). As a Confederate infantryman put it later on: "Cavalry are the eyes of the army, they bring the news; the artillery are the boys to make a noise; but the infantry do the fighting, and a general or so gets all the glory."

General Grant wasn't getting much glory in the press or anywhere else at the time, but the dogged Grant, who possessed a one-track mind if ever there was one, moved forward again. His troops raced toward Richmond. Lee, in yet another small masterpiece of second-guessing strategy, eventually divided the Union army into three parts at the Battle of the North Anna River; but suffering from a severe case of diarrhea and burning with fever, he was unable to press his advantage. Grant finally moved around the Confederate right flank and occupied Hanovertown, but Lee got in front of the Army of the Potomac again at the important crossroads town of Cold Harbor. Although Grant was only ten miles or so from Richmond, Lee's troops had dug in deep again for the "King of Spades"; the spade had become the South's best weapon, but it was easy to dig with just one's hands in this dry, sandy soil.

Grant decided to try breaking through anyway, strongly influenced by his staff officer Lieutenant Colonel Cyrus B. Comstock, who advocated a "smash 'em up" frontal assault strategy against the Confederates. Grant also wanted the big definitive victory the newspapers and public were clamoring for and which seemed necessary to raise morale throughout the North. Union troops, however, seemed to know better than their commander what would happen when he ordered the general assault on Lee's intricate, heavily fortified Cold Harbor lines, often only a few yards away from their own. Another red battle to come. Horace Porter told of walking among the troops the night before the opening action on June 1 and watching them fashion the first crude dogtags used in any war: "I noticed that many of the soldiers had taken off their coats and . . . were calmly writing their names and addresses on slips of paper and pinning them on the backs of their coats, so that their dead bodies might be recognized and their fate made known to the families at home."

The first Cold Harbor battle resulted in a fearful slaughter of the Federal troops, but it was just a sample of what was to come. The main engagement at Cold Harbor began two days later, at 4:30 A.M. on June 3, 1864, and within a mere half hour—some say *seven or eight minutes*—more than seven thousand Union troops were killed and wounded—possibly a thousand men a minute. "In that little period more men fell bleeding as they advanced than in any other like period of time throughout the war," recalled Union adjutant Martin McMahon. "This is an order to slaughter my best troops," Union general William Smith said angrily. Waves of thousands of men had been sent from the trenches straight on against the enemy breastworks with no protection at all. Relentlessly they moved forward in this terrible charge. They were mowed down with little more chance than executed men facing a firing squad, their bodies soon a thick blue-and-gold, red-threaded quilt covering the ground. One man running forward saw his entire company fall dead in front of him. "That dreadful storm of lead and iron seemed more like a volcanic blast than a battle," a Union captain remembered. "Heads, arms, legs, guns, were seen flying high in the air," said a Rebel artilleryman. "It seemed like murder to fire upon you," a Confederate officer told a Union soldier during a short truce. "It was not war, it was murder," Confederate general Evander Law recalled later. Not a millimeter of ground was gained by the three hopeless assaults Grant ordered that day. According to a letter written by Colonel Theodore Lyman, an officer on General Meade's staff, "We lost four or five to one. We gained nothing save . . . proof of the unflinching bravery of our soldiers." Adding the casualties of the first two days of the battle to those of the main engagement brought the total Union dead and wounded to over twelve thousand, making Cold Harbor one of the bloodiest battles of the Civil War and all human history. It was widely joked at the time that Cold Harbor was wrongly named—it was sweltering hot, almost one hundred degrees, and it wasn't a harbor. But it was a cold harbor for the human heart.

Some sources actually put the number of Cold Harbor dead and wounded at about seventeen thousand, not including the fifteen hundred Confederate dead. Certainly it was seen from the beginning as organized mass murder, a bloody slaughter that justified Northern newspapers calling Grant a butcher. There is also no doubt that Grant's order for the third advance on June 3 was virtually ignored by the troops, who almost to a man refused to move when the bugles sounded. Private Frank Wilkeson, an artilleryman, wrote in his *Recollections of a Private Soldier in the Army of the Potomac*:

> About four o'clock in the afternoon I heard the charging commands given. With many an oath at the military stupidity which would again send good troops to useless slaughter, I sprang to my feet and watched the doomed infantry. Men, whom I knew well, stood rifle in hand no more than thirty feet from me, and I am happy to state that they continued to so stand. Not a man stirred from his place. The army to a man refused to obey the order, presumably from General Grant, to renew the assault. I heard the order given, and I saw it disobeyed. Many of the enlisted men had been up to and over the Confederate works. They had seen their strength, and they knew that they could not be taken by direct assault.

Respected New Hampshire captain Thomas Barker agreed with the private. "I will not take my men in another such charge if Jesus Christ himself should order it!" he vowed. On the eve after the battle Grant himself told his officers, "I regret this assault more than any one I have ever ordered." Years later, in his *Memoirs*, he admitted the same:

> At Cold Harbor no advantage whatever was gained to compensate for the heavy loss we sustained. Indeed, the advantages, other than those of relative losses, were on the Confederate side. Before [Cold Harbor] Lee's Army of Northern Virginia seemed to have acquired a wholesome regard for the courage, endurance and soldierly qualities of the Army of the Potomac. They no longer wanted to fight them "one Confederate to five Yanks." . . . They seemed to have given up any idea of gaining any advantage of their antagonist in the open field. . . . [Cold Harbor]

seemed to revive their hopes temporarily; but it was of short duration. The effect upon the Army of the Potomac was the reverse. When we reached the James River, however, all the effects of Cold Harbor seemed to have disappeared.

But such butchery would not be forgotten in the lifetimes of these soldiers. Many blueshirts charged that the Confederates in the main battle at Cold Harbor could not miss when they fired. Some Confederate riflemen wept while firing, but hit their targets even though their aim was blurred by tears. Yet the brave, brutalized troops on both sides could be hard, cruel—they almost had to be. Frank Wilkeson wrote:

A wounded man suffered intensely from a wound through the foot. My sympathy was excited for the young fellow. . . . We lifted him on the rude [operating] table. A surgeon held chloroform to his nostrils, and under its influence he lay as if in death. The boot was removed, then the stocking, and I saw a great ragged hole on the sole of the foot where the ball came out. Then I heard the coatless surgeon who was making the examination cry out, "The cowardly whelp!" So I edged around and looked over the shoulders of the assistant surgeon, and saw that the small wound on the top of the foot, where the ball entered, was blackened with powder! I, too, muttered "The coward!" and was really pleased to see the knife and saw put to work and the craven's leg taken off below the knee. He was carried into the shade of a tree, and left there to wake up. I watched the skillful surgeon probe and carve other patients. The little pile of legs and arms grew steadily, while I waited for the object of my misplaced sympathy to recover his senses. With a long breath he opened his eyes. . . . I will never forget the look of horror that fastened on his face when he found his leg was cut off. Utter hopelessness and fear that look expressed. I entered into conversation with him; and he, weakened and unnerved by the loss of the leg and the chloroform, for once told the truth. Lying on his back, he [had] aimed at his great toe, meaning to shoot it off; but being rudely joggled by a comrade at the critical instant, his rifle covered his foot just below the ankle and an ounce ball went crashing through the bones and sinews. The wound, instead of being a furlough, was a discharge from the Army, probably into eternity.

"Cowardly whelp" or not, there were many soldiers who tried to escape the bloody war via self-inflicted wounds. Desertion was a great problem, too. To this point in time the North had suffered over two hundred thousand desertions; accurate figures for the South are unavailable, but desertions were rife among the Southern rank and file, who often believed it was "a rich man's war and a poor man's fight." Thoughts of desertion were especially common after horrible battles like Cold Harbor, where the men began to think they were treated as so many sacrificial cattle. It had already been proved to the Union at Fredericksburg and to Lee at Gettysburg that the old tactics of mass frontal assaults against good, entrenched troops were sorrowfully outmoded due to the new, more efficient rifles used by Civil War soldiers. The soldiers knew this and knew that their generals did.

To make matters worse at Cold Harbor, in addition to the failure of generalship, the Union wounded trapped under fire were abandoned, crying for help between the lines, for a full *three days* because Grant delayed in sending out stretchers for them. Their heartrending cries went unanswered, one story goes, because Grant would not request a truce to retrieve his wounded. Why? Because military tradition held that the side that requests such a truce is the losing side, and Grant would not admit a defeat that would psychologically slow the Army of the Potomac's momentum. Others say the fault lay with Lee for demanding a customary flag of truce rather than a cease-fire and refusing to call off his sharpshooters. In any event, the two generals stupidly argued the quibble for three days before Grant gave in. Only *two* men would survive of the thousands lying wounded and dying out in the blistering sun. Rebel soldiers, venturing bravely into the field, probably saved more Union lives than the Yankees themselves did. The stench of bodies rotting in the sun masked the smell of spring flowers. "The wounded and slain have a peculiarly horrible look," an observer wrote, "by reason of biting the ends off their paper cartridges, blackening lips and faces. Mix blood and the sweat of agony with the black." These boys in black face, wounded in the advance, often wounded again by Confederate sharpshooters, could crawl nowhere. They could only scream or sob for water or mother or God or death. Before the truce General Lee ordered one young soldier saved, then turned away. While comrades of war on both sides watched helplessly an abandoned soldier slashed his throat with a bayonet. Another boy nearby futilely tried to bash in his own skull with a rifle butt. "So much for the glory of war," someone muttered.

Another letter of Colonel Lyman's describes the Cold Harbor field when it was all over:

> And there the two armies slept, almost within an easy stone-throw of each other; and the separating space ploughed by cannon-shot and clotted with the dead bodies that neither side dared to bury! I think nothing can give a greater idea of deathless tenacity of purpose than the picture of these two hosts thus lying down to sleep with their heads almost on each other's throats! Possibly it has no parallel in history.

By the time the Confederates reached Cold Harbor the well-founded fear of starvation had also struck their ranks. "I have been so hungry that I have cut the blood off from crackers [found on dead Yankees] and eaten them," wrote Rebel private John Casler. Confederate sergeant George Eggleston recalled:

> But what is the use of writing about the pangs of hunger? The words are utterly meaningless to persons who have never known actual starvation. . . . Hunger to starving men is totally unrelated to the desire for food as that is commonly understood and felt. It is a great agony of the whole body and of the soul as well. It is unimagineable, all-pervading pain inflicted when the strength to endure pain is utterly gone.

Some observers count Cold Harbor as Lee's last major victory in the war, while others say it was just a temporary and short-lived stemming of the Union blue tide until lack of food and manpower finished his army. The only undisputed victors were buzzards, heads red with blood. Certainly many held this opinion. Southern and Northern newspapers resumed their cries of "Butcher Grant"; was he miraculous or simply murderous? others wondered. "Grant doesn't care a damn if men fall like the leaves of fall," Mary Chesnut wrote from South Carolina. "Grant is a butcher," declared Mary Lincoln, who had taken a dislike to the general when she first met him in the White House three months earlier and he refused an invitation to one of her soirees.

Colonel Walter H. Taylor, Lee's able aide-de-camp, had little good to say of General Grant. "[Grant's] losses have already been fearfully large," he wrote in his notebook on May 23, 1864. "Our list of casualties is a sad one to contemplate, but does not compare with his terrible record of killed and wounded; he does not pretend to bury his dead, leaves his wounded without proper attendance, and seems entirely reckless as regards the lives of his men. This and his remarkable pertinacity, constitute his sole claim to superiority over his predecessors. He certainly holds on longer than any of them." *Them* in this case specifically referred to Union generals McDowell, McClellan, Pope, Burnside, Hooker, and Meade—all of whom had unsuccessfully fought the Army of Northern Virginia before Grant took command.

Others North and South disagreed with such assessments. Lee found little fault with Grant's strategy, aware that the war had a new psychological dimension now that Grant was moving forward at any cost. "That man Grant will fight us every day and hour till the end of the war," General Longstreet remarked. Grant's own officers found him clearheaded and cool in battle at all times, "a man who could be quiet in several languages." Said Union colonel Lyman, "[He has] three expressions: deep thought; extreme determination; and great simplicity and calmness. . . . He habitually wears an expression as if he had determined to drive his head through a brick wall and was about to do it." Mrs. Grant told a *New York Herald* reporter: "I have no doubt Mr. Grant will succeed, for he is a very obstinate man."

Already the great debate had begun as to who was the greatest general, Grant or Lee, a question that will probably never be answered to everyone's satisfaction and whose answers are almost much more emotional than coolly reasoned. One Confederate colonel at least tried to be fair. In a June 7 letter he wrote:

> From first to last, Grant has shown great skill and prudence, combined with remorseless persistency and brutality. He is a scientific Goth . . . destroying the country as he goes and delivering the people over to starvation . . . [whereas] Lee is almost unapproachable, and yet no man is more simple or less ostentatious, hating all pretension. It would be impossible for an officer to be more reverenced, admired and respected. He eats the rations of the soldier and quarters alone in his tent. Without parade, haughtiness or assumption . . . he is worthy of the cause he represents and the army he commands . . . [yet] Lee has at least met with a foeman who matches his steel. . . . Each guards himself perfectly and gives his blow with a precise eye and cool and sanguinary nerve.

General Sherman, on the other hand, spoke of Grant's great "simple faith" in a letter to his new boss:

> I believe you are as brave, patriotic, and just as the great prototype Washington—as unselfish, kind-hearted, and honest as a man should be—but the chief characteristic is the simple faith in success you have always manifested. . . . This faith gave you victory at Shiloh and Vicksburg. Also, when you have completed your best preparations, you go into battle without hesitation . . . no doubts, no reserves; and I tell you, it was this that made us act with confidence.

Charleston diarist Mrs. Chesnut hardly agreed. She compared Grant with the cruel Russian field marshal Aleksandr Vasilyevich Suvorov (1729–1800), who is celebrated in several cantos of Byron's *Don Juan*. "He [Grant] is their right man, a bull-headed Suvorov," she wrote, echoing many Southerners and some Northerners of the day. "He fights to win that chap does. He is not distracted by a thousand side issues; he does not see them. He is narrow and sure—sees only in a straight line . . . from a battle in the gutter, he goes straight up. . . . If General Lee had Grant's resources he would have [already] bagged the last Yankee, or have had them all safe back in Massachusetts."

There were similarities between Suvorov and Grant. Both were great strategists; Suvorov, the son of a Swede who emigrated to Russia, enlisted in the army as a boy and worked his way up the ranks. Like Grant, the greatest of Russian field marshals was known for his courage in battle, and he too came out of retirement to aid his country, during the French Revolutionary Wars. Both Suvorov and Grant were plain men of great simplicity, with few airs, Suvorov living and fighting as a private soldier during his campaigns. Grant, of course, became head of all the Union armies, and later president, while Suvorov was made a count and then a prince. Both men had many enemies, too, and were intimate with failure and disgrace. But here the comparison ends. For although the two generals often won battles by the sheer overwhelming numbers of their armies, at a terrible sacrifice of life, Grant never displayed the cold streak of contemptuous cruelty that ran through Suvorov's military and personal life. Suvorov showed no mercy to the enemy or his own troops; he had only contempt for those who disagreed with him. His name will always be linked with the capture of Ismail in Bessarabia, which became one of the worst sacks and massacres in history, among other horrors. Grant would never be accused of such intentional evil. He did fail his wounded in the no-man's-land at Cold Harbor, but he was no Suvorov or Philip of Macedon, who told the Athenians after they requested a truce to bury their dead: "Let them lie and rot in the field till they stink to heaven."

Yet Grant's losses were grotesque in his relentless march toward Richmond: fifty-five thousand dead and wounded in one month of fighting to make an advance of just seventy miles, almost as many men as were in Lee's army, more than 41 percent of the army he had started with. "[The Union army] has literally marched in blood and agony from the Rapidan to the James," wrote Charles Francis Adams Jr., a great *supporter* of the Union general. But Grant, who always carried the big picture in his capacious mind, looked at other statistics. The Confederates had suffered thirty-two thousand casualties, some 46 percent of their original forces, including twenty-two of their fifty-eight generals; and Lee, unlike his opponent, had no great reservoir of manpower to replace his fallen soldiers. The way the numbers stood, to balance the casualty rate the Confederates had to kill and wound not two but three times as many Yankees. The end could already be foreseen. As Confederate artilleryman Stiles mused: "If one army outnumbers another two to one, and the larger can be indefinitely reinforced and the smaller not at all, then if the stronger side will but make up its mind to do all the killing the weaker can do, and will keep it so made up, there can be but one result."

Though the mood among many in the Union ranks was now close to mutiny—corps commander General Gouverneur Warren quipped, "For thirty-six days now it has been one funeral procession past me"—Grant still firmly believed that Lee's dwindling numbers meant the Federal master plan was working. Even he, however, gave up on Cold Harbor, leaving the black and bloated bodies to the buzzards with bloody beaks. While he waited there, secretly preparing to outsmart Lee and cross the James River toward Petersburg, the gateway to Richmond, he sent General Philip Sheridan and his cavalry out on a diversionary move to link up with General David Hunter at Charlottesville and destroy all-important Confederate railroads. Sheridan never managed to join Hunter, but inflicted much damage before being repulsed in his attack on Trevilian Station and retracing his steps back to Grant. There were 20 percent losses on both sides at Trevilian, arguably the bloodiest cavalry action of the war.

Grant finally did outsmart Lee this time. Lee erred twice. In less than half a day, Grant's engineers constructed a remarkable 2,100-foot-long pontoon bridge over the James, then built others nearby. By June 14, in one of history's great army movements, an unusually wily Grant had marched his entire army to the south bank of the river, concealing his massive movement by leaving a corps of men on the left flank. As Major Stiles put it, he had "folded his tents like the Arabs and silently slipped away." General Lee didn't realize Grant was moving until it was too late to

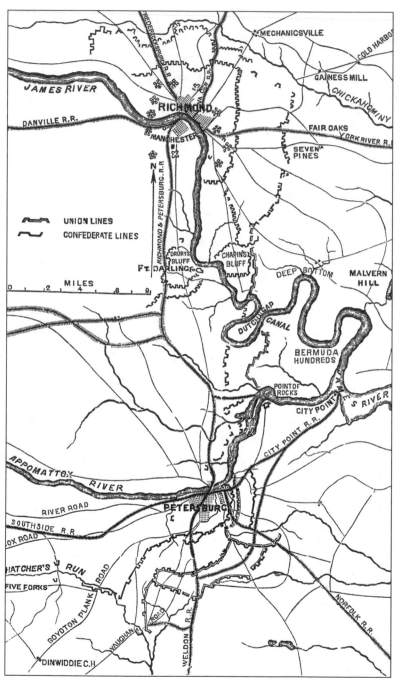

The Union and Confederate lines at Petersburg and Richmond, June 1864. From *Harper's Pictorial History of the Civil War,* 1866.

stop him. In fact, Lee refused to reinforce Petersburg on June 15, when General Pierre Beauregard requested aid to fight the large force of Yankees he reported in the area. "They aren't there," Lee told Beauregard's messenger, at almost the exact time that Union forces began attacking the city, "they are heading toward the capital!" It was June 17, at least five days since Grant made his move, before the Gray Fox realized what had happened.

Fortunately for the Confederates, the Union forces also erred badly. Petersburg might have fallen on June 15, and Richmond not long after, if the force of sixteen thousand Northern troops led by General W. F. "Baldy" Smith had joined with Union general Winfield Hancock's men and attacked Beauregard's force of fifty-four hundred men. But Smith was slow in getting started, and Hancock was delayed in joining him due to an unholy series of mishaps. Hancock, finally arriving on the field, proposed that he and Smith lead a moonlight attack against the Rebels, an attack that most military strategists believe would have succeeded. Smith refused, preferring his own rather vague plans, thus enabling General Beauregard to reinforce Petersburg with troops from his position facing the bottled-up General Butler at Bermuda Hundred. Beauregard had fourteen thousand men now and soon received many more from an abruptly awakened General Lee. He pulled back to a better position, still blocking the Yankees from Richmond. The Union had lost a great chance to end the war at least several months sooner. The long siege of Petersburg—ten months of gruesome trench warfare—had begun.

2

The Siege
of Petersburg

The siege became a continuous battle by day. By night spurts of
flame along the works showed that Death was vigilant.

—Major Giles B. Cooke,
aide to General Lee

GENERAL ROBERT E. LEE, already physically and psychically worn
by the war, sat like some powerless god, ramrod straight if not
strong, aboard his gray charger Traveler. Surveying Petersburg in
the distance, he knew his lines were bound to grow thinner every
day now that the Yankees were at the gate. Imposing Confederate
defenses and poor Union leadership would prolong the siege, but
Lee must have already sensed the outcome; a frisson of terror may
have swept through him.

But who can pretend to know General Lee's mind? His great
biographer Douglas Southall Freeman wrote: "I can account for
every hour of Lee's life from the day he went to West Point until
his death . . . but I never presumed to know what General Lee was
thinking."

Robert E. Lee, an enigma like Grant—will anyone ever really
know either of them? They remain enigmas fighting a mystery
despite the billions of words written about them. Robert E. Lee,
next to Lincoln the most legendary figure of the Civil War (Grant

Lee's famous warhorse Traveler carried him from his first campaign through his last. From a portrait made in 1853; Library of Congress.

ranking a distant third or fourth), in his own time a living monument, the "man in marble." He is widely known as Robert E. Lee, but actually he was most often called R. E. Lee during the war, sometimes Marse Robert, Uncle Robert, the King of Spades (for always urging his men to dig in deeper, deeper), even Granny Lee (he was fifty-seven and constantly fretted about his troops), but rarely Robert E. Lee or Robert Edward Lee, and never Bobby Lee to his face, if one didn't want to provoke that famous temper of his. Yet the more stately Robert E. Lee is the name found today in all the histories of the "Brothers' War" and on a myriad of statues throughout the South.

The aspiring warts-and-all biographer has little trouble portraying Ulysses S. Grant, full of wens and warts, but is baffled by Robert E. Lee, who often seems to have been all but wartless. The almost six-foot-tall, erect, impeccably dressed Lee was the exact opposite of the stubby, bearlike General Grant in most every outward way excepting a love of horses. Lee's father was the legendary cavalryman Light-Horse Harry Lee, George Washington's favorite, who served brilliantly in the Revolutionary War—a war that also featured a lightweight fighting a heavyweight, an army far superior in numbers. Light-Horse Harry, the same man who eulogized Washington as "first in war, first in peace, and first in the hearts of his countrymen," later became governor of Virginia. Lee could trace his family back to an ancestor who fought with William the Conqueror. Two Lees signed the Declaration of Independence; another had been president of Virginia. R. E. Lee was to the military and to the manner born; he was shaped by tradition even before he was born. One of the Southern chivalry, he, "the most perfect gentleman of a State above all States celebrated for its chivalry," would have ignored the plebeian Grant anywhere but on the battlefield; he couldn't even remember, or wouldn't admit, that he had met the younger man during the Mexican War. But though he was to the manner born—the Lees of Virginia were in the vanguard of American life from the very beginning of colonization—Robert E. Lee did not live the life of a Virginia squire, as the story so often goes. His father spent some time in debtor's prison. Financial problems and poor health eventually forced Light-Horse Harry to live in the West Indies for five years, almost until his death in 1818, and young Robert never saw his father after his sixth year. The family moved from their Stratford, Virginia, mansion with its "several hundred acres of lawn" to a much humbler home in Alexandria, where they lived in what has been called "genteel poverty," and where Robert, according to one relative, learned "to practice self-denial and self-control, as well as the strictest economy in financial concerns," all traits that would serve him well on the battlefield.

As the youngest male in the family—his two brothers were off to school—it was Robert's duty to run the house and care for his ailing mother, which may account partly for the gentleness and quietness of his nature. "He is both son and daughter to me," Anne Lee once said, which recalls the obvious male-female nature of his rival Grant. One of his great pleasures, however, was to spend hours each evening studying the books in Light-Horse Harry's extensive military library. He seemed to know from the start that he would make the army a career, and when he turned eighteen it did not take much convincing by relatives to get General Andrew Jackson to give the son of Light-Horse Harry, always an outstanding student, an appointment to West Point.

In his four years at West Point the responsible and reserved Robert E. Lee made only one close friend, Joseph E. Johnston, one of the few close friends he was to have all his life and an especially great consolation to him during the dark days of the Civil War. There was not much fun, no drinking buddies—nor would there ever be—but the standoffish Lee was an exemplary student and soldier. "Robert was a model cadet," his nephew Fitzhugh Lee, later a general under his command, wrote of him; "his clothes looked nice and new, his crossbelts, collar, and summer trousers were as white as the driven snow. . . . It was a pleasure for the inspecting officer to look down the barrel of his gun; it was bright and clean, and its stock was rubbed so as to almost resemble polished mahogany." The facts seem to bear the nephew out. Robert E. Lee became adjutant of the Cadet Corps and graduated second in his forty-six-man West Point class of 1829, receiving not one demerit in his time there. His academic success and Grant's comparative failure were contrary to the usual scholastic standings at the Point, where statistics show future Union officers typically did better than their Southern counterparts.

Unlike Grant, Lee was posted to the coveted Corps of Engineers upon his graduation, several days after which his invalid mother died. Two years later he married Mary Custis, the great granddaughter of Martha Washington. They were to have seven children, Lee and this woman he had known since he was three years old, and she was always to be "the beat of his heart"; but they were separated many times in the next fifteen years, while Lee served ably if routinely as a highly regarded army engineer and surveyor throughout the country, including Fort Hamilton in New York Harbor. The loneliness that was to be so great a part of his destiny showed itself in an 1841 letter he wrote to Mary telling

Second Lieutenant Robert E. Lee on his graduation from West Point, 1829. From a portrait painted at the time; Library of Congress.

of his "sympathy with the trees and birds, in whose company I take delight" while walking in the woods, but his total lack of interest in any "crowd of strangers." He always wanted to be home, like most soldiers on both sides in the wars he would fight.

Lee was already thirty-nine when he saw his first action in the Mexican War of 1846–1848. Captain Lee, chief engineer under the imperious, vainglorious, three-hundred-pound General Winfield Scott—"a parade in himself," and a man who often spoke of himself as the royal "we"—helped plan the siege of Veracruz and was breveted to major by Scott, who commended him in a dispatch to Washington for both his planning and for "conducting columns from stations under the heavy fire of the enemy." Seven times Mexican bullets nicked Lee's chestnut mare, Grace Darling. In another report Scott called him "the gallant and indefatigable Captain Lee" and made him a brevet lieutenant colonel. Finally, after Lee was slightly wounded charging up Chapultepec to the "Halls of the Montezumas," his commander promoted him to brevet colonel. Of all the bright young officers in Mexico who were to become Civil War legends—Grant, Jackson, Jefferson Davis, Beauregard, McClellan, Meade, Pickett, Early, and a dozen more—Lee's star shone the brightest. The bemedaled General Scott, in fact, predicted that he would become the "world's greatest soldier" and vowed that he was responsible for the American victory. He called Lee "the very best soldier I ever saw in the field."

Lee didn't have much contact with Grant at the time; according to one story, Lee, in fact, had to admonish Grant at headquarters for his sloppy, stoop-shouldered, hands-in-pocket appearance: "Lieutenant, you had best go back to your tent and clean up a bit." But both men had their strong reservations about the Mexican War. "We hold and can continue to hold their country," Lee wrote to his wife, "and have a right to exact compensation for the expenses of a war continued, if not provoked, by ignorance and vanity on the part of Mexico. It is true we bullied her. For that I am ashamed."

Lee resumed his work with the Board of Engineers in Baltimore after the war, supervising the construction of Fort Carroll in Baltimore Harbor. In 1852 he was appointed superintendent of West Point, where he served for three years (almost expelling his nephew Fitzhugh one time) before he was transferred to the Second Cavalry Division and promoted to the regular rank of lieutenant colonel.

Lee's correspondence during these years with the Second Cavalry, which took him as far west as Texas, was devoted far more to his various cats than it was to matters political. He did write in a letter to Mary that "slavery as an institution is a moral and political evil in any country," though he held that "the blacks are immeasurably better off here than in Africa . . . the painful discipline they are undergoing is necessary for their instruction as a race." He believed that the length of black subjection was "ordered by a wise and merciful Providence. . . . emancipation will sooner result from a mild and melting influence than the storms and contests of fiery controversy." While "the final abolition of slavery is onward . . . we must leave the progress as well as the result in His hands." The progress, he implied, would be slow.

Lee's last prediction was dead wrong, of course, but he had been a soldier now for over thirty years and no one in the army was less a political theorist or politician. His spare time was spent studying the campaigns of Napoléon, who was unequaled as a strategist, he believed; or simply longing to be home, writing letters to his wife. As with Grant, there is no indication that he had any idea of his destiny.

The death of his father-in-law brought Lee back to Virginia for an extended stay, during which strange old John Brown—"Saint John" to some, an insane zealot to others—made his storied raid on Harper's Ferry, Virginia. Since Lee was the nearest qualified officer, the War Department ordered him to lead a battalion of Marines to put down Brown's "slave rebellion."

John Brown and his band of sixteen whites and five blacks had seized sixty hostages and the government arsenal at Harper's Ferry on October 16, 1859, barricading his followers in the engine house with their hostages. Colonel Lee's forces encircled the engine house while he sent in Lieutenant J. E. B. "Jeb" Stuart, another future romantic legend of the South, to negotiate with Brown, who threatened to kill all his prisoners if attacked. The dauntless Stuart, heeding the words of a hostage—"Never mind us, fire!"—signaled for Lee to attack. As Lee put it matter-of-factly in a memorandum: "Tuesday, about sunrise, with twelve Marines under Lieutenant Green, broke in the door of the engine-house, secured the insurgents, and released the prisoners unhurt. All the insurgents killed or mortally wounded but four—John Brown, Stevens, Coppie, and Shields."

Old Brown of Osawatomie was to swing from the gallows six weeks later for multiple murders and treason at Harper's Ferry. "Weird John Brown hung there," Herman Melville would later write, "his streaming beard the meteor of war." But Lee soon journeyed back to his post in Texas, well aware of the storm clouds to the east yet unable to decide where his loyalty lay. On the one hand he believed the South had "been aggrieved by the acts of the North" and would defend his home state. On the other, as he wrote to his son Custis after South Carolina seceded on December 20, 1860: ". . . I can anticipate no greater calamity for the country than a dissolution of the Union. . . . Secession is nothing but revolution. . . . If the Union is dissolved . . . I shall return to my native State and share the miseries of my people, and, save in defense, will draw my sword on none." After this, on January 23, 1861, a few months before Fort Sumter fell to the Rebels, he would state:

> As an American citizen, I take great pride in my country, her prosperity and institutions, and would defend any State if her rights were invaded. But I can anticipate no greater calamity for the country than a dissolution of the Union. It would be an accumulation of all the evils we complain of, and I am willing to sacrifice everything but honor for its preservation.

He later told a clergyman that if "he owned every slave in the South he would willingly give them all up if by so doing he could preserve the Union"; and at the end of the war, according to Charles A. Dana in *Recollections of the Civil War* (1898), he assured Grant "he had always been for the Union in his heart, and could find no justification for the politicians who had brought on the war, the origin of which he believed to have been the folly of extremists on both sides."

Shortly before spring in 1861 Colonel Lee was posted to Washington to strengthen the city's defenses. At this time he was offered the position of field commander of all *Union* troops. Winfield Scott, general in chief now, Secretary of War Simon Cameron, and President Lincoln all wanted him, considering Lee a great soldier, and he spent agonizing days and nights walking the floor and "weeping tears of blood," as his wife put it, while making up his mind. But he finally refused, submitting his letter of resignation to the secretary of war. His first loyalty, he decided, was to the state of Virginia. Writing to General Scott, who believed he was "worth 50,000 soldiers to the Union," he repeated his words to his son: "Save in defense of my native State, I never desire again to draw my sword."

But he did draw his sword two days after Virginia seceded from the Union on April 17, 1861. And because it was the greatest sword in the South or the country, an almost magic Excalibur, some would say it became the bloodiest sword, prolonging the war and thus causing more death and suffering than any other. Clearly this great, gallant, and moral soldier was not one to be fooled by or caught up in the patriotic rhetoric and fantasies that had replaced reason in Richmond. He was aware of the Union's vast superiority in numbers and matériel—had even predicted that a war between North and South would last four years, dismissing as nonsense the rantings of Southern fire-eaters that it would all be over in a few months or by Christmas at most. In his heart he had always been for the Union, yet this most reasonable of men against all reason chose loyalty to his state first. It has been argued that his decision was the worst he made in his life and that intentionally or not, he was to be responsible, ironically, for more bloodshed than Grant the Butcher.

For his first year in service to the Confederacy Lee, appointed a general, acted as a troubleshooter—officially, the personal military adviser to Confederate president Jefferson Davis. It wasn't until late spring of 1862 that he received his first field command— the Army of Northern Virginia—a position he held until the last months of the war, when he was too late appointed general in chief of all Confederate armies. Only a few weeks before he received his first army to command he was still full of doubts. In a letter to Mary he wrote that their son Custis "must consult his own judgement, reason and conscience as to the course he may take" in choosing whether or not to resign his Union commission (which he did) and join the Confederates: "I do not wish him to be guided by my wishes and example." Admirable words to one's son: "If I have done wrong, let him do better." Like Grant, he was a good father, a family man, lonely outside the family. He would much rather be home caring for his children and invalid wife than a Napoléon on "fields of glory." An aide found him head on desk, sobbing after word reached him that his second daughter Annie had died of a lingering illness in 1862 while Lee was deep into the blood and horrors of battle. The despairing, bitter letter he wrote to Mary is a classic of its kind and between its lines reveals many of his innermost feelings about the war:

> I cannot express the anguish I feel at the death of our sweet Annie. To know that I shall never see her again on earth, that her place in our circle, which I always hoped one day to enjoy, is forever vacant, is agonizing to the extreme. But God in this, as in all things, has mingled mercy with the blow in selecting that one best prepared to leave us. . . . When I reflect on all she will escape in life, brief and painful at the best . . . I cannot wish her back.

Once Lee took command of the Army of Northern Virginia, the war did seem to turn around for the South. Lee's chief strength as a general proved to be his ability to rapidly size up a situation, guess what his opponents' next move would be, and quickly exploit their weaknesses. Unrivaled for his audacity, his willingness to take risks, he was also far ahead of his time in his skill in maneuvering and using field defenses to aid maneuvers. But most important was the unprecedented loyalty his noble character and courage inspired in his men, a quality surpassed only by George Washington among military leaders. His worst faults were his tendency to trust his subordinates too much, not to insist strongly enough that they carry out his orders to the letter, and, ironically enough, his strong sense of devotion to duty.

Lee's devotion to duty, the importance of the concept to him, is clearly seen in a letter he wrote to Custis in 1860:

> In regard to duty, let me, in conclusion of this hasty letter inform you that, nearly a hundred years ago, there was a day of remarkable gloom and darkness—still known as "the dark day"—a day

when the light of the sun was slowly extinguished, as if by an eclipse. The Legislature of Connecticut was in session, and as its members saw the unexpected and unaccountable darkness coming on, they shared in the general awe and terror. It was supposed by many that the last day—the day of judgement—had come. Someone, in the consternation of the hour, moved an adjournment. Then there arose an old Puritan legislator, who said that, if the last day had come, he desired to be found at his place doing his duty, and therefore, moved that the candles be brought in, so that the House could proceed with its duty. There was quietness in that man's mind, the questions of heavenly wisdom and inflexible willingness to obey present duty. Duty, then, is the sublimest word in our language. Do your duty in all things, like the old Puritan. You cannot do more, you should never wish to do less. Never let me or your mother wear one gray hair for any lack of duty on your part.

But it was a double-edged sword, Lee's religious devotion to duty. A British observer of the Civil War, General Viscount Wolseley, wrote:

His nature shrank with such horror from the dread of wounding the feelings of others that upon occasions he left men in positions of responsibility to which their abilities were not equal. This softness of heart, amiable as that quality may be, amounts to a crime in the man intrusted with the direction of public affairs at critical moments. Lee's devotion to duty and great respect for obedience seem at times to have made him too subservient to those charged with the civil government of his country. He carried out too literally the orders of those whom the Confederate constitution made his superiors, although he must have known them to be entirely ignorant of the service of war. He appears to have forgotten that he was the great revolutionary chief engaged in a great revolutionary war, that he was no mere leader in a political struggle of parties carried on within the lines of an old well-established form of government. It was very clear to many at the time . . . that the South could only hope to win under the rule of a military dictator. If General Washington had had a Mr. Davis over him, could he have accomplished what he did? . . . General Lee was given command over all the

Confederate armies [only] a month or so before the final col-
lapse; the military policy of the South was all throughout the war
dictated by President Davis. . . . Lee, for example, was opposed
to the final defense of Richmond that was urged upon him for
political, not military reasons. It was a great strategic error.

Not Grant's but General McClellan's Union troops were attacking Richmond for the first time when Lee took command. His
campaign forced the Federals to withdraw. Soon the Confederate
victory at Second Bull Run raised morale throughout the South.
But the military situation did not improve. At Sharpsburg, or Antie-
tam, on September 17, 1862, Lee had to draw back from Maryland
into Virginia after what is called "the bloodiest single day of the
Civil War," with the South losing 2,700 men and the North about
2,100, not counting almost 10,000 wounded on each side. Three
months later at Fredericksburg—"a great slaughter pen," as one
soldier called it—Lee turned back General Burnside's troops even
though outnumbered, but not without suffering 5,300 dead and
wounded, compared with Federal losses of 12,700 killed and
wounded. "I wish these people would go away and leave us alone,"
Lee said in frustration after the battle, but he knew of course that
this was not to be.

General Lee was still calling the Union forces "these people"
or "those people"—he rarely used the term "the enemy" for them—
the next spring, when he confronted the Yankees at Chancellors-
ville in May 1863. Here Lee defeated General Hooker's superior
numbers, though with losses almost as heavy as the North's, thanks
in great part to Stonewall Jackson's brilliant execution of Lee's
strategy. But Jackson was accidentally shot on the field by one of
his own men; his arm had to be amputated (oddly, it was buried
alone where it still remains in the Lacy family graveyard in Chan-
cellorsville) and he died ten days later of pneumonia contracted in
his weakened condition. This great loss to Lee marked another
turn for the worse, especially when he made one of his rare mis-
takes in reorganizing the Army of Northern Virginia. "I do not know
how to replace him," he said when Jackson died, and he truly
didn't. Trying to compensate for the loss of Jackson as he pushed

Thomas J. "Stonewall" Jackson, 1862. From *Marse Robert*, 1929.

northward, he chose too many green officers to command units they had no experience with, put too much faith and trust in others.

Soon after Lee made his decision to invade the North, his army suffered over twenty-eight thousand casualties at the battle of Gettysburg, lasting from July 1 to July 3, 1863. When the smoke cleared, he told his aide Colonel Charles Venable, while running his forefinger over a map: "If I had Stonewall Jackson with me, I should have won the battle . . . so far as man can see." Though his generals were clearly more responsible for the loss in this major turning point of the war—especially Longstreet, for failing to attack on time—he characteristically took full blame for the defeat and offered to resign. He wrote to President Davis:

> The general remedy for want of success in a military commander is his removal. . . . I, therefore, in all sincerity, request your

Excellency to take measures to supply my place. I do this with the most earnestness, because no one is more aware than myself of my inability to discharge the duties of my position. . . . I sensibly feel the growing failure of my bodily strength. I have not yet recovered from the attack [of dysentery] I experienced this past spring. I am becoming more and more incapable of exertion, and am thus prevented from making the personal supervision to the operations in the field which I feel to be necessary. I am so ill, that in undertaking to use the eyes of others I am frequently misled. . . . Everything therefore, points to the advantage to be derived from a new commander. . . . I have no complaints to make of anyone but myself. I have received nothing but kindness from those above me, and the most considerate attention from my comrades and companions in arms.

Davis, to his credit, quickly rejected his gracious offer and a seriously ailing, broken Lee (there was a rumor he suffered a heart attack at Gettysburg) retreated south from Pennsylvania with his torn, tired troops. Yet, after a long, hard winter, his army, many shoeless and close to starving, rose up like a phoenix to inflict terrible losses on Grant in the Wilderness campaign that led up to Petersburg.

In all these battles and many more Lee had demonstrated great defensive and offensive skills as a general. More important to the Confederate cause, he had won the complete devotion of his men and people throughout the South. He was said to be the glue holding the Confederacy together. Lee appeared cold and fastidious, never allowing a wrinkle in his gray uniform, but he was basically a kind person who always had time to hear his men's problems and was lenient regarding their shortcomings, never court-martialing even those who were clearly insubordinate. As for his famous temper, it quickly flared and disappeared; his self-control was far stronger. At Gettysburg, one story has him raising his hand as if to strike Jeb Stuart when, for the first time, the general arrived late to the field with his cavalry, but he soon regained his usual calm manner. He once apologized to his secretary after an outburst, saying, "Colonel when I lose my temper, don't let it make you angry."

This was a man who dismounted under fire to place a fallen fledgling back in its nest, who upbraided a messenger for mistreating his horse and fed the horse a buttered biscuit before reading the battle dispatch. Brave and imperturbable, he once fell asleep in his chair, according to the poet Sidney Lanier, while Yankee shells were repeatedly exploding a few yards from him; more than one time his men had to urge him to move farther back from enemy fire. No commander of troops was ever more beloved than Lee. Stonewall Jackson said, "Lee is a phenomenon—the only man I would follow blindfolded." A Rebel infantryman vowed, "I'd follow that man through Hell." The North certainly did not have any commander so admired by all his men—not Grant, surely not Sherman or Sheridan.

But if General Grant couldn't hope to inspire the same devotion among his troops as General Lee, he certainly commanded more respect than any Union military chief before him. Despite all the blood and gore of the Wilderness campaign, he was moving forward, "getting things done"; his men felt closer to the most important cause of all—going home. Grant's "strategy of exhaustion," as it has been called, was meant primarily to destroy not the Confederacy's armed forces, a task he thought impossible, but their logistical support: the weapons, food, and clothing they needed to wage war. In May 1864, a month before the siege of Petersburg began, he had ordered General Sherman to move his one-hundred-thousand-man army into Georgia as part of the overall plan, "to move against [General Joseph E.] Johnston's army, to break it up, and to get into the interior of the enemy's country as far as you can, inflicting all the damage you can against their war resources." This Sherman would succeed in doing beyond anyone's wildest reckoning; by September he would take Atlanta, a vital communications and supply center, before beginning his fabled march to the sea, an operation that ranks with the greatest in military history.

Who was this cold-eyed "damn Sherman," the most hated general of the Civil War, whose name even today remains a curse in parts of the South? William Tecumseh Sherman was named

General Sherman in 1864.
From *Men and Things I Saw
in Civil War Days*, 1889.

Tecumseh by his parents after the great Shawnee Indian warrior
chief, and received his Christian name from the priest who bap-
tized him on St. William's Day. Foster son of the noted Ohio lawyer Thomas Ewing, one of eleven siblings his widowed mother
raised, he had a difficult childhood, due in part to his flaming red
hair, which made him the butt of schoolyard jokes and which he
made even more conspicuous for a short while by dyeing it a sickly
shade of green. But by the time the tall, skinny boy entered West
Point he seemed to have surmounted his early frustrations and was
a bright, popular cadet known as an accomplished storyteller, con-
versationalist, and bold, daring comrade never averse to having a
drink or a good time. He graduated sixth in his class but had so
many demerits he was almost expelled.

    Sherman married his foster sister Ellen Ewing after graduation
and decided, like Grant, to leave the army after seeing action in
the Mexican War rather than be separated from his wife on the

frontier. Here his life parallels Grant's. He worked as a lawyer and banker, losing all his savings and property in the Panic of 1857. As he wrote his wife: "I look upon myself as a dead cock in the pit, not worthy of further notice." But he soldiered on and took a position first as the superintendent of a military academy that later became Louisiana State University and then as president of a St. Louis transit company, for forty dollars a month. He loved the South, he said, but thought secession was absurd, telling a friend in Louisiana: "This country will be drenched in blood. . . . You people [Southerners] speak so lightly of war. You don't know what you are talking about. War is a terrible thing. You mistake, too, the people of the North. They are peaceable but earnest and will fight too. . . . you are rushing into war with one of the most powerful, ingeniously mechanical and determined people on earth—right at your doors. You are bound to fail."

Sherman's years of service in the south led to the offer of a commission in the Confederate Army when the war commenced, but he refused the offer and accepted a commission as a Union infantry colonel, turning down a political generalship proffered by Lincoln because he wanted to be beholden to no one. After the Union defeat at First Bull Run in July 1861, he was promoted to brigadier general and soon made commander of the Department of Cumberland, but his quarrels with superiors—who considered him erratic and all but removed him from command—and his strained relations with the press (one time he jailed a reporter who ignored his orders) led to a breakdown, bouts of depression, and thoughts of committing suicide. Again he recovered, thanks in part to General Grant's support of his bold strategy during the battle of Shiloh, in which he was wounded and had three horses shot from under him, but whose loss his enemies in the press tried to blame on him. This time his recovery was not without a price. Physically he seemed a broken man, thinner than ever, nervous, a chain-smoker of cigars puffing even more furiously than Grant. In 1863, when he was just forty-three, his wife wrote that "he looks more wrinkled than a man of sixty"; to another observer he suggested "Lazarus risen from the grave." He was completely devoted to General Grant, at one point saying, "Grant stood by me when I was crazy, and I stood by him when he was drunk, and now we stand by each other."

Sherman believed that "war is hell," but he was a war lover, too; he once wrote his wife of "the grand and beautiful game of war." His philosophy might be summed up in his reply to a woman who charged his troops with stealing in 1863. "Madam, . . ." he replied, "war is cruelty. . . . the crueler it is, the sooner it will be over." Grant shared this philosophy, and so Sherman, Grant's military superior in the Mexican War, was glad to be considered Grant's chief general by now, divining a greater genius for strategy and leadership in the younger man.

By the time of the Petersburg siege, however, Grant's strategy was stalled; while Sherman the destroyer moved forward in Georgia, devastating everything military or civilian, animal or vegetable in his path, Grant was standing still in Petersburg. Grant quickly abandoned the idea of direct assaults on the now reinforced Confederate lines when, on June 18, such a regimental attack resulted, within a mere half-hour period, in the death of 632 of the 900 men sent into battle. About all he could do for the moment was support another aspect of the grand strategy—to hold Lee's troops in Petersburg so that they could not join Johnston in Georgia to fight Sherman, just as Sherman was keeping Johnston's troops so busy that they couldn't join Lee in Virginia.

Grant's immediate strategy was to try and steadily extend the Petersburg siege westward, forcing Lee to stretch his lines even thinner. Soon, he hoped, his forces would form a thirty-three-mile semicircle around the city. It is true that Grant wasn't fighting Lee's army of old now—a contemporary joke claimed "both the cradle and the grave had been robbed" for the present Army of Northern Virginia—but Grant always thought that his numerical superiority was grossly exaggerated, as he indicated when writing his *Memoirs* years later.

> In the Confederate army, often only bayonets are taken into account [in estimating numbers], never, I believe, do they estimate more [men] than are handling the guns of the artillery [or are] armed with muskets or carbines. Generally, the latter are far

enough away to be excluded from the count. . . . In the Northern armies the estimate is most liberal, taking in all connected with the army and drawing pay. Estimated in the same manner as ours, Lee had not less than 80,000 men at the start [of the Wilderness campaign]. . . . He was on the defensive, and in a country in which every stream, every road and every natural defense was familiar to him and his army. The citizens were all friendly to him and his cause, and could and did furnish him with accurate reports of our every move. Rear guards were not necessary for him, and always having a railroad at his back, large wagon trains were not required. All circumstances considered, we did not have any advantage in numbers.

He went on to throw a few more jabs at Bobby Lee, certainly thinking of his own place in history:

General Lee . . . was a very highly estimated man in the Confederate army and States. . . . His praise was sounded throughout the entire North after every action he was engaged in: the number of his forces was always lowered and that of the National forces exaggerated. . . . To be extolled by the entire press of the South after every engagement, and by a portion of the press North with equal vehemence, was calculated to give him the entire confidence of his troops and to make him feared by his antagonists. It was not an uncommon thing for my staff officers to say (at about the time of Vicksburg), "Well, Grant has never met Bobby Lee yet." There were good and true officers who believe now that the Army of Northern Virginia was superior to the Army of the Potomac man to man. I do not believe so. Before the end I believe the difference was the other way.

In evaluating the two commanders, it should be remembered that Grant had already successfully besieged the Confederates at Fort Donelson and Vicksburg, capturing entire armies at each place, while Lee never conducted a successful siege. Lee would certainly make a brilliant and gallant *defense* at Petersburg, but it does not rank at the head of such great military defenses as Napoléon's in 1814, when the master of war, outnumbered six to one, held back six hundred thousand troops of the Grand Alliance for one hundred days. Lee, the great student of Bonaparte, must have known, in fact, that Napoléon believed that forty thousand men should be able to hold against three hundred thousand of the enemy. This would especially be true if the enemy, like Grant, did not have enough troops (he had less than half Napoléon's estimate) to invest the defense completely, and the defender, like Lee, had cities like Richmond and Danville at his back to provide reinforcements and supplies. These reasons, along with poor leadership by Grant's generals in many cases, were important factors in enabling Lee to hold out for over three hundred days.

Yet as Alfred H. Guernsey pointed out as early as 1866 in *Harper's Pictorial History of the Civil War,* great credit must be given to Lee:

> When Lee fell back within the lines of Richmond, his fortifications bore little resemblance to the formidable works constituting the defenses of the fortified cities of Europe, which Napoleon probably had in mind [in his formulations]. They consisted of redoubts of low profile, with ditches, parapets [protective walls], and abatis [obstacles or barricades], and forts at all salient points from which the lines could be swept by artillery. . . . Lee was to demonstrate at Petersburg that the defensive power of such works, resolutely held by an adequate force, is fully equal to the elaborate masonry of Vauban and Vohorn.

In any event, as Grant's tenacious infantry moved left to the west and his artillery incessantly pounded the Rebels, it seemed only a matter of time before the Confederate lines would become too thin to hold. By the time President Lincoln visited Grant on June 21, 1864, the general in chief's headquarters were already well established at City Point on the James River outside Petersburg, where they would remain until the end of the siege almost ten months later. Beside the usual tents crowding the plains, the headquarters site was filled with shanties, restaurants, and sutler's wagons, not to mention the sightseers and reporters who were present day and night gawking at Grant and his staff. The west end of the camp lay fifty feet above the bluff bank of the Appomattox River, which flowed west to the town of Appomattox Court House, a place-name that would later become as legendary as any in American history. Neither Grant, nor Lee, nor anyone else could have guessed the future significance of this place-name so uniquely American—it was a common American practice, adding "Court House" to the name of a county town, the practice more prevalent in Virginia than anywhere else.

President Lincoln, his son Tad, and Assistant Secretary of the Navy Gustavus Fox had sailed from Washington, one hundred miles away, on the steamer *City of Baltimore* to meet Grant at City Point. Lincoln was high-spirited, full of jokes as ever; when an officer advised him to try a glass of champagne for his mal de mer, he quipped, "No, my friend, I have seen too many fellows seasick ashore from drinking that very stuff." No admonition to Grant was intended, so far as is known. In his tall black hat, black frock coat, and black trousers Lincoln put several onlookers in mind of a "boss Undertaker"; he was "a long, gaunt, bony looking man, with a queer admixture of the comical and the doleful in his countenance that reminded one of a professorial undertaker cracking a dry joke," correspondent Cadwallader wrote. One story has it that Old Abe tried to find Grant's tent himself, scrambled over a hedge, and was halted by an adamant sentry who wouldn't believe he was President Abraham Lincoln. But the tale is probably untrue. Apparently, Grant met Lincoln's white steamer and they conversed a while in his cabin before the general took him on a tour of the Union trenches and rifle pits. Lincoln riding to the front on Grant's thoroughbred Cincinnati, Tad aboard the pacing pony Jeff Davis, they headed toward a location where the enemy camp on the opposite side of the Appomattox could clearly be seen.

Troops along the route cheered "Uncle Abe!" and "Old Abe!" as the president and his cavalry escort passed by, Lincoln shaking the hands of several veterans. Grant directed him toward the camp of the Eighteenth Corps, black troops who had performed gallantly in Baldy Smith's assault on the Petersburg defenses a week earlier, capturing six of the sixteen enemy guns taken that day. This particularly pleased Lincoln, who had urged a "color-blind" policy in recruitment, "though opposed on nearly every side," as he remembered it. The black soldiers encircled the man they called

"Father Abraham," "the Liberator," or "Chainbreaker." "Hurrah for the Liberator!" one man cried. Another shouted, "God bless Massa Lincoln!" Another: "Lord save the Giver of Freedom, the day of Jubilee am come!" Laughter and songs were heard, tears ran down both black and white faces. Lincoln himself cried. "He rode with bared head," Horace Porter recalled, "the tears had started to his eyes and his voice was broken."

Lincoln dined with Grant that night and regaled him with stories from the past so numerous and detailed that they inspired a listening sentry to say: "That man's got a powerful memory and a mighty poor forgettery." The next morning the party visited the ultimate politician—General Benjamin Butler, an incompetent officer the president couldn't get rid of until after his reelection. Lincoln praised Grant for his fortified positions on the line: "When Grant once gets possession of a place, he holds on to it as if he had inherited it." His general in chief was completely confident, advising the president: "I am as far from Richmond now as I ever shall be. I shall take the place, but as the Rebel papers say, it may require a long summer's day." Lincoln for his part expressed the wish several times during this first of frequent visits that there be no more Spotsylvanias or Cold Harbors. "I cannot pretend to advise, but I do sincerely hope that all may be accomplished with as little bloodshed as possible," he told Grant.

Despite these subtly cautionary words, Grant knew that Lincoln still trusted him completely. No one else, after all, seemed able to get things done; he was succeeding where all others had failed. As Lincoln had said of him, "Grant is the only one of our generals who has fought twenty-eight great battles and won twenty-eight great victories." Another time, a year before, the president had told Grant how he defended him when a party of "cross-roads wiseacres" visiting the White House criticized Grant for paroling or releasing General John Pemberton's Confederate troops when Pemberton surrendered after the siege of Vicksburg. Old Abe had leaned back in his chair and launched into a long, humorous tale that concluded with the remark, "I guess Pemberton's forces will never be much account again—as an army."

It seemed at this point that Grant would have little trouble with the president, even with Lincoln's implicit reservations about the mounting Union casualties. His chosen lieutenants stood squarely behind him, too, and (excepting his initial selections of Butler and Burnside) he was a great judge of officers, as witness his choice of Sherman, Sheridan, and James B. McPherson. Sherman flatly told General James Rusling after the war that "Grant is the greatest soldier of our time, if not of all times. . . . some others of us on both sides were pretty good generals; but not one of us could compare with Grant, nor begin to compare with him."

Grant still hated war, thinking it unnecessary, foolish, and brutal, but he had hardened toward all the violence around him. Something of this was reflected in his April refusal to exchange prisoners with the South because exchanges up until then had not been on a man-for-man basis. A good move strategically, considering the South's dwindling manpower, but a deathblow to many Union prisoners suffering horribly in Andersonville and other Confederate prison camps. Then there was the case of the convicted black rapist hanged facing the Confederate lines on June 20, the day before President Lincoln arrived at City Point. He was hanged there as a propaganda ploy, presumably approved by General Grant, to show the Rebels that all violent criminals would be dealt with harshly where the Yankees ruled. Several weeks later two white soldiers from New York were hanged for raping a woman who years later confessed on her deathbed that she had "swore the lives of these men away in order to contribute her mite toward the extermination of the Yankee army."

On the other hand, Grant showed great mercy in the case of a Union deserter who had been captured armed, in a Confederate uniform, and sentenced to death by a firing squad. His wife, somehow learning of his fate, came to the front to plead with General Grant for his life. For hours the woman begged the general to spare the man's life, on the sole grounds that he had been a good husband to her, and Grant finally had the deserter brought to him. He would gladly watch his execution without an iota of pity, for he might have caused the death of thousands, Grant told the soldier, but out of pity for his wife he would give him one more chance. He ordered the man back to the company he deserted from, where he would be kept under close surveillance and shot within the day upon the slightest dereliction of duty. The soldier apparently served out his enlistment honorably. Grant would later proudly say that he had never signed a death warrant while in command, but there was more to it than that. "No, he didn't," General Sherman once said in reply. "No he didn't; but he left the prisons full of miserable devils, deserving death, whom *I* had to execute or turn loose!"

Important as they were, Grant's problems at Petersburg might have seemed the least of his troubles when Lee dispatched General Jubal A. Early to the Shenandoah with a dual mission—to evict the marauding Yankees from the fertile valley and possibly drive toward Washington, D.C. Forcing General David Hunter's forces to retreat into West Virginia, Early and his eighteen thousand troops met relatively little resistance, crossing the Potomac on July 5. By the next day, marching hard, he had captured Hagerstown, Maryland, and demanded $20,000 in Union greenbacks, which he claimed were reparations for Union raids in the Shenandoah. After several skirmishes around Middletown the "invading army" of hungry and often shoeless men reached the Monocacy River near Frederick City. There Baltimore department commander Lew Wallace—later to be much better known as the best-selling author of *Ben Hur*—met him with an army of six thousand Federals. Outnumbered over three to one, General Wallace's inexperienced men were routed, suffering casualties of more than one-third their forces, but at least succeeded in delaying Early.

Early pushed on after exacting $200,000 in "reparations" from the officials of Frederick by threatening to burn the city to the ground. His troops ripped up twenty-five miles of railroad track and set afire factories and government buildings before reaching the outskirts of Baltimore.

By now all Washington was expecting the worst. "Long guns with bayonets are going about in company with short clerks," one wag wrote. "Everybody is tugging some sort of death-dealing tool." Rumors were rife. *One hundred thousand men* were advancing on the capital, someone telegraphed Lincoln from Baltimore. "Baltimore is in great peril," the city's mayoral commissioner cabled, pleading for reinforcements. "I have not a single soldier but whom is being disposed by the military for the best protection of all," President Lincoln wired back. "By latest accounts the enemy is moving on Washington. Let us be vigilant, but keep cool. I hope neither Baltimore nor Washington will be sacked."

Rumors continued to fly throughout the country; in New York, the price of gold shot up to its highest price in years. Burning down the house of Maryland's Governor Bradford, Early marched on to Silver Spring, the Capitol dome clearly seen in the distance. Early could have freed and armed seventeen thousand Confederate prisoners of war in the vicinity but didn't think he had the time.

At this point, on July 11, the Confederate flag might soon have been flying from the Capitol. Unknown to Lincoln, a steamer was waiting on the Potomac to speed him away if the city fell. The president, staying at the Soldiers' Home, just a few miles from Early's advance forces, was hurried back to the White House. Early had cut all communications lines. All that seemed to stand between the capture of Washington with its war offices, arsenals, and hoard of gold was a force of twenty thousand men composed mostly of raw recruits, clerks, and wounded, convalescing veterans. But the next morning fifteen thousand crack troops dispatched from City Point by General Grant landed in Washington, met at the wharf by a grateful Lincoln, waving his hat. Astride his horse on Seventh Street Road leading directly into the capital, Early quickly noticed these same soldiers beginning to march from the transports down the streets and he decided to give up his direct assault on the city.

Fort Stevens, Early had observed, was "fully manned" and he had ordered an attack on the fort blocking his path before he knew of the Union reinforcements. Lincoln and his wife foolishly watched the action from the parapets and came under the fire of rebel sharpshooters to whom Old Abe presented a tall target. "Amid the whizzing bullets," his secretary wrote, "the President [stood] with grave and passive countenance." He was pulled down once but later stood again to watch, although one officer was wounded and another was killed barely three feet from him. "Get down, you fool!" young Union officer Oliver Wendell Holmes Jr. shouted at him. According to official accounts of the action, several men were "picked off by rebel sharpshooters" that afternoon from windows in a house some 1,100 yards distant. A six-foot-four-inch man must have been an inviting target indeed, and Lincoln was lucky he didn't become the one and only U.S. commander in chief killed in action. But this was the first time during the war that he had seen men close-by killed in action—the real horrors of bone breaking, blood spurting, and men screaming in pain—and he must have been dazed by it all, by the realization that this was not a ten-thousandth of what others were seeing and suffering. Mrs. Lincoln, for her part, seemed unfazed by battle. Later War Secretary Stanton teased her about her sightseeing. "Mrs. Lincoln," he said, "I intend to have a full-length portrait of you painted, standing on the ramparts at Fort Stevens overlooking the fight!" Replied the first lady, without missing a beat: "That is very well, and I can assure you of one thing, Mr. Secretary—if I had had a few *ladies* with me the Rebels would not have been permitted to get away as they did!"

But get away is just what General Early did. Early, discouraged by the regiments he saw tramping through Washington, abandoned his attack on the reinforced fort. By July 13 he was retreating toward the Potomac, leaving 600 Union casualties and the home of Postmaster General Montgomery Blair burning behind him, quipping to one of his officers: "Major, we haven't taken Washington, but we've scared Abe Lincoln like hell!" An army of fifteen thousand led by Grant's choice General Horatio Wright pursued him, but Wright for some reason stopped when he reached the Potomac, letting Early's men escape across the river. Perhaps he thought Early's army consisted of forty thousand men—over twice the real number—as General Halleck, little more

than Grant's glorified clerk now, had wired General Grant. Some blamed all on Wright. "He feared he might come across the rebels and catch some of them," Lincoln himself said. Others opted for Halleck. "Put Halleck in command of 20,000 men," Ben Wade said, "and he could not scare three sitting geese from their nests." But no matter who was to blame, Early got away, his wagons filled with loot, $220,000 in his pocket, and his men all well-clothed and shod, ready for more raiding in the Shenandoah.

Early himself, however, got his share of criticism. Many believed General Wallace had saved Washington from invasion at the battle of Monocacy by delaying Early's advance by one day. Grant himself claims in his *Memoirs* that "if Early had been but one day earlier he might have entered the capital before the arrival of the reinforcements I sent," and went on to say "General Wallace contributed . . . by the defeat of the troops under him a greater benefit to the cause than often falls to the lot of a commander . . . by means of a victory."

Correspondent Cadwallader, however, was in a better position to judge Early's advances on Washington than Grant, and he held that Wallace's delaying action should have made no difference. Cadwallader had left Grant's camp at City Point for Washington twenty-four hours before Grant sent troops, guessing that Early would raid the city. He found Washington's defenses "in a deplorable condition" and believed Early could easily have entered it "without any loss of men worth a moment's consideration, when playing for such a stake."

The coarse, cynical Early—a man "ashamed to be detected doing an act of kindness"—always claimed that his object was never to capture Washington, but to raid the city, seizing horses and provisions; capture Lincoln, if possible; and draw Grant's forces from Petersburg. But he only succeeded in his looting—Lincoln, of course, was not captured, Washington wasn't burned down, and although Grant had to send two regiments to the capital, this did not relieve Federal pressure in the siege of Petersburg. Cadwallader contended that Early could have done much more than he did and definitely had the time to do it, writing:

I have always wondered at Early's inaction throughout the day, and never had any sufficient explanation of his reasons. Our lines in his front could have been carried at any point, with the loss of a few hundred men. Washington was never more helpless. Several wide turnpikes led directly to it. Any such cavalry commander as Sheridan, Wilson, Hampton or Stuart could have ridden through all its broad avenues, sabred everyone found in the streets, and before nightfall could have burned down the White House, the Capitol and all public buildings. It has been stated that Early supposed Washington was fairly protected by Federal troops. But this is a very poor excuse. As an army commander, it was his business to inform himself in such cases. His spies and Provost Marshalls could have given him all these facts. Yet he spent the day supinely; and when he was about ready (in his own mind) to swoop down upon it, he found it strongly and sufficiently reinforced. Wright's corps arrived during the night of the 11th. . . . Thus ended the most imminent danger Washington was subjected to during the war.

Two weeks after the first and last Confederate raid into Washington, General Grant took to the bottle again. This may have been precipitated by the raid itself, or by Lincoln's decision to appoint General Halleck commander in charge of the defense of Washington, as Secretary of War Stanton urged him to do after Early's raid. Grant wanted a proven field commander put in charge, and Lincoln for the first time broke his promise not to interfere in military affairs by going against his general in chief. Grant, however, showed no resentment in his *Memoirs*, making no mention at all of the political infighting at the time. He might just as well have been so deeply saddened by the death of Major General James B. McPherson on July 22 that he turned to drink.

The brilliant, dashing McPherson, first in his class at West Point, had been killed during the battle of Atlanta when he rode off to investigate heavy firing on the left of General Sherman's lines. Intercepted by Rebel skirmishers who beckoned him to surrender, he is said to have tipped his hat in reply and bolted off, only to be shot from his mount. The wounded horse galloped back to Sherman, whose men later found the gallant officer with a bullet through his heart. Only thirty-five, "young in years but full of honors," as General James F. Rusling put it in his memoirs, McPherson—who was engaged to be married as soon as Atlanta was taken—had already been chosen by Grant to replace Sherman if anything happened to his chief general, and certainly had a great future in front of him. Wrote Sherman: "General McPherson fell in battle, booted and spurred, as the gallant knight and gentleman should wish." At Petersburg, Grant cried when informed of his death, saying "the country has lost one of its best soldiers, and I have lost my best friend." Late in life he wrote, "In his death the army lost one of its ablest, purest and best generals."

The Petersburg siege itself must also have been getting to Grant at the time—his forces were trying to tighten their hold on the city by attacking the railroads supplying it and the incompetent General Burnside was making final preparations for his disastrous mine under the Confederate lines. All these factors could have contributed to Grant's depressed state of mind, and he again did not have his trusted aide-de-camp General John A. Rawlins at his side to help him. Rawlins, a lawyer without any military experience who had befriended Grant in Galena, was one of five or six generals from that little town who had benefited from knowing Grant. In Grant's words, he became "the most nearly indispensable" of all his officers after the general in chief recruited him for his staff in 1861, a key adviser as well as a close friend and a strong personality who could control him when he went astray, as Cadwallader did after Vicksburg. But Rawlins was away in Washington on July 27, arriving back the next day to find Grant still drunk. He wrote to his wife that morning:

> I found the General in my absence digressed from his true path. The God of Heavens only knows how long I am to serve my country as the guardian of the habits of him whom it has honored. It shall not be always thus. Owing to this faltering of his, I shall not be able to leave here. . . . Active operations have commenced, which with the fact of the General's forgetting himself . . . renders my being here of an importance that you can appreciate as fully as any person living.

Grant's friend and trusted aide, John A. Rawlins. From
Meet General Grant, 1929.

How and how much Rawlins guarded Grant's bad habit on this
occasion remains unknown. Rawlins seems to have prevailed, however, and Grant got sober and stayed sober for a long while, though
he never came close to the old promise he made to Rawlins that
he wouldn't "touch a drop."

Which is remarkable, considering Burnside's Mine—or Burnside's Blunder, as it might better be called—an attempt to tunnel
under the Confederate lines at Petersburg. Burnside did not con-
ceive the plan, nor should he alone be charged with its failure (the
buck shouldn't stop until Grant), but the luckless soldier's name
has always been attached to it.

Luckless Burnside almost always was. On Ambrose Burnside's
first wedding day, for example, his wife-to-be studied him one last
time and responded with a resounding "No!" when the minister
asked her if she took this man to be her lawful wedded husband.

Whether this had anything to do with the doubtlessly abrasive whiskers, or sideburns, Burnside wore remains unknown to history, but the story does show how unusual situations simply happened to the unfortunate soldier. Not only did the wrong things happen, but General Ambrose Everett Burnside, who later married another bride successfully, had a flair for doing the daring, innovative thing in war as well as fashion, a quality that kept his photographs in the papers and his countenance in the public's mind. Burnside started off on the wrong foot from the moment he entered the military. After serving as a tailor's apprentice in his native Liberty, Indiana, he had been appointed a cadet at West Point, graduating low in his class and excelling more in extracurricular singing and cooking than in military tactics. Following a tour with the cavalry in the West, he resigned from the army in 1853 to set up the Bristol Rifle Works in Rhode Island, where he manufactured the breech-loading Burnside carbine of his invention. Things went badly for him, as usual, his business failing despite his new rifle's success, but not so badly as they would after he reentered the army at the outbreak of the Civil War. Burnside's expedition to the North Carolina coast in 1862, resulting in the capture of Roanoke Island, New Bern, Beaufort, and Fort Macon, won him the rank of major general and much acclaim. Yet when he took command of the Army of the Potomac later that year, he proved to be a distinct failure both as a leader and a strategist. His plan to capture Fredericksburg by crossing the river resulted in a slaughter so bloody that a special truce had to be called to bury the Union dead, making Fredericksburg long known as Burnside's Slaughter Pen.

Victories would come later for the ill-starred general, but they somehow never rivaled his spectacular setbacks, including the much-publicized Mud March, when Burnside marched his men out of camp near Fredericksburg and had to march them directly back again due to a heavy rainstorm that made maneuvers impossible. Relieved of his command early in 1863, the unlucky general was next officially reprimanded by President Lincoln when, while heading the Department of the Ohio, he "court-martialed" ex-congressman Clement Vallandigham for an antiwar political speech and closed the *Chicago Tribune* when the paper protested. Finally, Burnside was transferred back to the Ninth Corps he had originally commanded when he enlisted (it was called Burnside's Peripatetic Geography Class because it traveled so widely on foot), only to face a final spectacular defeat at Petersburg in 1864.

Burnside's Mine at Petersburg was really the brainchild of a lowly private, who mentioned it to his commanding officer, mining engineer Lieutenant Colonel Henry Pleasants of the Forty-eighth Pennsylvania Volunteers, a regiment from Schuylkill composed mostly of former coal miners. The mining tactic had been tried a year before at Vicksburg, when twenty-two hundred pounds of gunpowder had been detonated in a tunnel to open up a route into the city. "The effect was to blow the top of the hill off and make a crater where it had stood," General Grant wrote. "The breach, however, was not sufficient to enable us to pass a column through. In fact, the enemy had thrown up a line further back."

This time both Pleasants and Burnside, as head of the Ninth Corps, strongly backed the plan, which would be directed against the southern earthworks of the Confederate lines, where guns and bayonets had failed to penetrate. "That God-damned fort is the only thing between us and Petersburg, and I have an idea we can blow it up!" Pleasants had said. Burnside submitted the plan to General Meade, commander of the Army of the Potomac, and to Grant himself. Both men rather reluctantly approved or consented to it, leading correspondent Cadwallader to observe that Grant "should have known better than to have trusted any necessary preparations to such an incompetent officer as Burnside had proved himself to be long before that. For this he deserves great blame."

Actually, Pleasants himself gave Burnside more credit than the rest of his superiors, who only made the many difficulties facing him worse. He later reported to the Congressional Committee on the Conduct of the War:

> My regiment was about four hundred strong. At first I employed but a few men at a time, but the number was increased as the work progressed, until at last I had to use the whole regiment—noncommissioned officers and all. . . . I found it impossible to

get assistance from anybody. . . . Whenever I made application [for equipment] I could not get anything, although General Burnside was very favorable to it. The most important thing was to ascertain how far I had to mine, because if I fell short or went beyond the proper place, the explosion would have no practical effect. Therefore I wanted an accurate instrument with which to make the necessary triangulations. I had to make them on the farthest line, where the enemy's sharp-shooters could reach me. I could not get the instrument I wanted, although there was one at army headquarters, and General Burnside had to send to Washington and get an old-fashioned theodolite [a kind of transit]. . . . General Burnside told me that General Meade and Major Duane, chief engineer of the Army of the Potomac, said the thing could not be done—that it was all clap-trap and nonsense; that such a length of mine had never been evacuated in military operations, and could not be; that I would either get the men smothered, for want of air, or crushed by the falling of earth; or the enemy would find it out and it would amount to nothing.

Ignoring such advice, working in three shifts around the clock for almost a month in the sweltering Virginia heat, hearing Southern voices above their heads, Colonel Pleasants and his miners dug a tunnel 20 feet deep and 510.8 feet long that would reach directly under the Confederate redoubt, excavating about eighteen thousand cubic feet of dirt. The job would have been done in at least a third of the time if Pleasants had been supplied with the proper equipment. Because no suitable mining equipment was supplied, pickaxes had to be remodeled by Ninth Corps blacksmiths to do the job, small wheelbarrows were fashioned from hardtack cracker boxes, and timbers needed to reinforce the tunnel were torn from a nearby railroad bridge ripped down for the purpose. When they reached their goal, the miners began digging a 75-foot cross gallery or crossbar that formed a T with the main shaft of the tunnel and ran beneath the enemy works. This was divided into eight strategically placed chambers, each filled with a thousand pounds of powder connected by spliced fuses (about two tons less powder than Burnside had requested from the headquarters' engineers).

The miners tried to work secretly and quietly, even hiding the excavated dirt under freshly cut bushes in the ravine separating the lines. But the Rebels, only about a football field away, could see what was going on; in fact, wild rumors spread in Petersburg itself that the Yankees had undermined the entire city, that they were sitting on a volcano that might erupt at any moment. Lee's aide Giles B. Cooke recalled late in life:

> General Lee always read the Northern newspapers. From mysterious references to great events, he decided that something unusual was in the wind. Deserters and prisoners (always a major source of information for both sides) divulged information, until we knew where the tunnel was being driven, how many men were at work and when it should be completed. Then we started a counter tunnel. The men in each could hear the others at work. But in the end we gave up on our tunnel, lacking suitable tools to carry it on. Besides, General Lee had conceived a better plan, mounting a line of cannon directly behind the salient, ready for the day it might be destroyed.

The Federal mine was completed on July 23, the miners packing the last thirty-five feet with dirt so that the explosion wouldn't blast out through the entrance. But Grant made another move before ordering it exploded. He wrote:

> I wanted to take the occasion to carry Petersburg if I could. It was the object therefore, to get as many of Lee's troops away from the south side of the James River as possible. Accordingly, on the 26th, we commenced a movement with Hancock's corps and Sheridan's cavalry to the north side by the way of Deep Bottom, where Butler had a pontoon bridge laid. The plan, in the main, was to let the cavalry cut loose and, joining with Kautz's cavalry of the Army of the James, get by Lee's lines and destroy as much as they could of the Virginia Central Railroad, while, in the meantime, the infantry was to move out so as to protect their rear and cover the retreat back when they . . . got through with their work. We were successful in drawing the enemy's troops to the north side of the James as I expected. The mine was ordered to be charged and the morning of the 30th of July was the time fixed for its explosion.

Grant had also given general orders about how the assault was to be conducted after the explosion:

> All officers should be fully impressed with the absolute necessity of pushing entirely beyond the enemy's present line if they should succeed in penetrating it, and of getting back to their [own] present line promptly if they should not succeed in breaking through. To the right and left of the point of assault all the artillery possible should be brought to play upon the enemy in front during the assault. . . . One thing, however, should be impressed on corps commanders. If they see the enemy giving away on their front or moving from it to reinforce a heavily assaulted portion of the line, they should take advantage of such knowledge and act promptly without awaiting orders from army commanders.

General Meade, despite reservations about the mine, issued excellent specific instructions to Burnside and his other generals regarding the operation, which would be one of the few frontal assaults of the Petersburg siege—in part because Lincoln had resigned himself to a long siege and would later even urge Grant not to risk actions "desperate in the sense of great loss of life," but instead to "hold on with a bull-dog grip, and chew and choke as much as possible."

Burnside had all along been training special troops to lead the first charge after the mine explosion. These were his Ninth Corps division of comparatively fresh black soldiers commanded by General Edward Ferrero. Basically, Burnside's original plan was to mass the black troops in two close columns. As soon as these columns passed through the breech made by the explosion, two regiments of each column would seize the enemy lines to the right and left and the rest of the black division was to rush up Cemetery Hill and take it before proceeding into Petersburg itself.

It was a good plan, depending in large part upon the special black troops. But General Meade decided that these crack infantrymen should not be used because if the attack failed the army would be charged with recklessly and callously using its black soldiers in an experimental operation. Grant says in his *Memoirs* that "Meade interfered," but he clearly approved his action. Up to this point Burnside could be blamed for little, was in fact helpful. Then he got mad. Cursing his superiors under his breath, the Ninth Corps commander peevishly decided that if his superiors could be indifferent about his choices, so could he. Burnside actually drew straws among his three remaining division commanders to see who would get the job. As his perennial bad luck would have it, the two commanders equal to the task—Generals Potter and Wilcox—lost the draw. General James H. Ledlie of the First Division got the short straw, and this proved as bad a choice as could have been made.

Though Burnside was a little slow with his final preparations (and even then not nearly careful enough), the explosion was set for 3:30 on the morning of July 30. The 320 kegs of powder, 25 pounds in each, 40 kegs in each of the eight chambers—a total of four tons of explosive—were all in place. The miners lit their match, fired the fuse. The massed columns ready to charge through the breech heard the fuse sputtering, waited silently. A minute passed, *two . . . ten . . . twenty . . . thirty minutes . . . an hour.* The troops, more fearful with every moment of waiting, saw the sun rising over the imposing Confederate works, the glinting guns that would be the end of many of them.

No explosion came. It was finally determined by the mine boss, Sergeant Harry Reese, that the fuse had been improperly spliced about halfway down its length, among several other complications. Another intrepid volunteer, Lieutenant Jacob Douty, crawled to the end of the tunnel with the materials Reese needed to resplice and relight the faulty fuse to the huge store of powder.

At 4:44 Reese lit the fuse again and in what seemed instants troops North and South witnessed an explosion no man among them had ever seen the likes of in this war or in any other. "There she blows!" someone shouted. "A fort and several hundred yards of earth work with men and cannon was literally hurled a hundred feet in the air," wrote a Southern soldier after viewing what he called "probably the most terrific explosion ever known in this country." The Confederate fort literally disappeared in the explo-

The explosion of the Crater, or Burnside's Mine, 1864. From *Harper's Pictorial History of the Civil War,* 1866.

sion. Men awoke from sleep to find themselves "wriggling up in the air" or descending. "Petersburg swayed and trembled as men, guns and earth were thrown skyward," wrote Confederate Major Cooke in recalling the blast.

Correspondent Cadwallader depicted it best from the Union side:

> The scenic affects surpass all powers of description. . . . I happened to be looking directly at it when the enormous mass of powder was at last ignited. Contrary to the usual expectation, the noise and roar of the concussion . . . comes a few seconds later.

My first perception was that of seeing the earth commencing to rise on a line a hundred yards in length, then to split open by fissures, from which emerged a dense volume of smoke, dirt and dust followed by sulfurous flames, as if the whole center of the globe was belching forth some monstrous volcanic masses. The smoke and flames rose perpendicularly at first, then spread out into a great sheet and commenced slowly to fall in the form of a great water spout. This was soon followed by the detonation of the combustibles. The sound of the explosion . . . came so late that those whose eyes were not turned that way missed much of its sublimity.

The huge mushroom cloud—great-grandfather to those of a distant war no one could have foreseen—broke apart and rained in slow motion chunks of earth big as hills and houses, giant wrecked weapons of war, hundreds of bloody, mangled human bodies and blackened body parts dancing and diving through the air. At least 278 Confederate soldiers were dead, some of them buried alive. The fearsome explosion had ripped a crater in the earth 170 feet long, up to 80 feet wide, and 30 or more feet deep that extended into Confederate territory. "Then commenced a furious cannonading from the Union line for a mile to the right and left, under cover of which the assault was to be made," Cadwallader observed. "It is believed that no such thunder of cannon was ever heard on the American continent, and probably not in the world." In all, 110 cannon and 50 mortars opened fire.

In the midst of this pandemonium, even before the smoke had cleared, the Union bugles blew the charge. General Ledlie's troops were first, but Ledlie was nowhere among them; pointing his boys in the right direction, this known drunkard and coward had found "some safe retreat," in Grant's words, was cowering in a bomb-proof shelter well behind the lines, drinking rum for courage while his men were being killed. Grant would say he was inefficient and "proved also to possess disqualifications less common among soldiers." Cadwallader was blunter about the politically connected boozer. "He did not even accompany his men, but remained behind in a safe place, and was written down coward by all from that time forth."

Ledlie's men had more than enough time to seize the summit of the hill—and open the way to Petersburg—for the Confederates had fled in every direction; but the untrained, leaderless troops faltered, unsure where to go or what to do in the maze created by the explosion and bombardment. To make matters worse Burnside had incredibly failed to obey orders and level the eight-foot trench in the *Union* line so that his divisions could charge in a wide formation. Men ran forward only two or three abreast, forced to climb out of their own trench, slowing down the assault. All plans were soon forgotten. Man after man plunged wildly into the huge bomb crater, which seemed to offer some protection.

Recovering from the explosion after over half an hour, the Confederates concentrated at the back of the crater and counterattacked under General William Mahone, recapturing what ground the Federals had gained. By now fifteen thousand men had been herded into the area of the bomb pit, not one division commander up front leading them. Confederate artillery was trained down point-blank upon the thousands densely packed in the crater, blasting them to pieces. Other attackers leaped into enemy trenches trying to hide from the murderous fire of mortars and muskets all around them. In a last desperate move the black troops originally chosen to lead the attack were ordered to charge by *their* commander, General Ferrero, who showed them the way from a safe distance and then doubled up with General Ledlie and his bottle of rum in his bombproof shelter. Still the forsaken black soldiers made a valiant suicidal charge. They took 250 prisoners, but without support they were overwhelmed by a countercharge and tumbled into the crater, where there was barely standing room. They literally fell over into the crater on their hands and knees, a Union officer recalled: "Troops were so thick in there that a man could not walk." Bodies were piled up three and four deep in the crater as the black soldiers, trying to get out, ran into a counterattacking brigade of Confederates enraged by both the terrible new tunnel bomb ("a mean trick") and the fact that former slaves were fighting them on their home ground. It was like shooting fish in a barrel. The Confederates potshot them until they ran out of ammunition, then hurled down their bayonet-fixed rifles like spears, and resumed firing with new loaded rifles passed from the rear. Prisoners were killed; many a Rebel gunstock bore blood-clotted hair. Those who could not get out of the crater had to run devil-take-the-hindmost like everyone else back to their lines. Most, black and white alike, remained, figuring it was even more perilous to retreat. For over eight hours Burnside's troops were crowded in the narrow slaughter hole, without water, under a blazing sun. In the words of Major William H. Powell: "The midsummer sun caused waves of moisture produced by the exhalation from the mass of men to rise above the crater. Wounded men died there begging piteously for water, and soldiers extended their tongues to dampen their parched lips until their tongues seemed to hang from their mouths."

By morning's end thousands of Union soldiers had run and crawled in every direction out of the crater, often leaving their weapons and even limbs behind them in the mad escape. None of the other corps, some 35,000 men, were put into action to help them. In the pit, literally at the feet of Robert E. Lee at one point, were 3,748 Union casualties (of the 20,708 Union troops engaged), some 1,500 Confederate casualties mixed in with them. From a distance the bodies looked like rag dolls, until you came closer and saw they were often screaming, squirming men, still trying to escape if they had legs. As for the Confederates buried alive, you could see an arm or leg sticking up here and there, hear soft Southern accents calling from the grave for help. Later, bodies were raised from the pit on taut line, like weird puppets dancing on strings.

General Lee, coming up close and staring down at the carnage, was heard to say, "I wish that we could do something for those men, but I suppose it is impossible now." We have no record of what General Grant said at the moment, but in a letter to General Halleck he called the crater rout "the saddest affair in the war" and claimed that he could have taken Petersburg had the plan been properly executed. In his *Memoirs* he termed the effort a "stupendous failure." He blamed it mainly on General Ledlie's "incompetency," but did "blame Ledlie's seniors, also, for not seeing that he did his duty, all the way up to myself." A Court of Inquiry sharply censured Ledlie and Ferrero for absolute inefficiency, if not cowardice, in hiding in the bombproof shelter. Burnside was mildly censured, mainly because he failed to clear the way, as Meade had directed, making the charge so crowded and slow. A congressional committee pinned the failure chiefly on Meade's refusal, sanctioned by Grant, to let the trained black division lead the assault. Burnside's plan, said the congressmen, was "entirely disregarded by a general who had evinced no faith in the successful promotion of the work."

Confederate general Mahone later wrote that if the Burnside Mine had been followed up by an effective attack, Lee would have been forced to retreat: "After the explosion there was nothing on the Confederate side to prevent the orderly projection of any column through the breach which had been effected, cutting the Confederate army in twain . . . [and] opening wide the gates to the rear of the Confederate capital."

Grant would be haunted by the crater disaster for the rest of the war. It led to another drinking bout in December, when the Congressional Committee on the Conduct of the War visited Grant at City Point for several hours to investigate the fiasco. "While at dinner with us on our steamer," Congressman George W. Julian wrote, "he drank freely, and its effect became quite manifest. It was a painful surprise to the committee and was spoken of with bated breath; for here [apparently drunk] was the Lieutenant-General of all our forces. . . . The great movements then in progress, for aught we knew, might possibly be deflected from their purpose by his condition."

Correspondent Cadwallader in his usual caustic way speculated that the one good result of the affair was that "General Burnside ceased to command the Ninth Corps." But almost miraculously Burnside became popular again after Grant sent him off on a permanent furlough. Entering politics, despite his checkered army career, he went on to be elected governor of Rhode Island for three terms and United States senator for two terms, until his death in 1881, at age fifty-seven. His winning personality and patriotic spirit doubtless played an important role in his political triumphs. From the constant publicity given him, the flamboyant feathered *Burnside hat* that he wore in the field came to be named after the big, bluff, and hearty general, as were the *burnside whiskers*, or *burnsides*, he affected. Innovative as ever, he had chosen to wear the hair on his face in a new way, shaving his chin smooth below a full mustache and big muttonchops or sidebar whiskers. Thousands imitated him, and soon his *burnsides*, because they were situated on the sides of the face, were called *sideburns*—this reversal of his name evidently having nothing to do with his military reversals, though that might have been appropriate. Burnside's name became one of the most familiar eponymous words; ironically, it remains much better known than the names of most Civil War generals, including even his direct superior Meade, who wrote to his wife of his subordinate: "I feel sorry for Burnside, because I really believe the man half the time don't know what he is about, and is hardly responsible for his acts."

With the failure of the Burnside Mine "passed away the finest opportunity which could have been given to us to capture Petersburg," Regis de Trobriand wrote in *Four Years with the Army of the Potomac*. A great risk had lost much and gained nothing; major direct frontal assaults had passed out of favor at Petersburg now. For eight months more Grant would steadily extend the left of his lines westward, Lee sidestepping along with him until the fortifications spread out over fifty miles. Lee had been deprived of his vaunted mobility and his overstretched lines grew skeleton thin, but Grant had lost the chance to end the war quickly and the long delay would mean more fratricidal slaughter.

Hour after hour brought new casualties in action ranging from sniping to attacks involving brigades and even divisions. Often the Confederate wounded were brought into Petersburg, where they

General Ambrose E. Burnside, 1862. From *Men and Things I Saw in Civil War Days,* 1889.

were nursed by Southern women. General Gordon told a touching story of one such nurse and her patient:

> A beautiful Southern girl, on her daily mission of love and mercy, asked a badly wounded soldier boy what she could do for him. He replied: "I'm greatly obliged to you, but it is too late for you to do anything. . . . I can't live long." "Will you not let me pray for you? I hope that I am one of the Lord's daughters, and I would like to ask him to help you." Looking intently into her be-witching face, the boy replied: "Yes, pray at once and ask the Lord to let me be His son-in-law."

3

Marching to the Sea, Through the Shenandoah— and into Vermont!

There is many a boy here who looks on war as all glory, but, boys, it is all hell.

—General William Tecumseh Sherman,
in a Columbus, Ohio, speech, 1880

As THE SIEGE WARFARE at Petersburg dragged on, the hungry, ragged Confederates resisted so tenaciously largely because they realized what the alternative would be. At the same time they understood their comrades who were already quitting. Rebel infantryman Luther Rice Mills wrote:

> I go down the lines, I see where fell my comrades, the Crater, the grave of fifteen hundred Yankees. When I go to the rear I see little mounds of dirt, some with headboards, some with none, some with shoes protruding, some with a small pile of bones on one side near the end showing where a hand was left uncovered; in fact, everything near shows desperate fighting. And here I would rather "fight it out." If Petersburg and Richmond is evacuated . . . our cause will be hopeless. It is useless to conceal the truth any longer. Many of our people at home have become so demoralized that they write . . . that desertion now is not dis-

honorable. . . . I have just received an order . . . to carry out on picket tonight a rifle and ten rounds of cartridges to shoot men when they desert. The men seem to think desertion is no crime and hence never shoot a deserter when he goes over—they always shoot but never hit.

Day after day General Lee suffered as much as his demoralized army. He ate as little, slept as little, and worried even more. His health was close to breaking from a persistent chest cold he contracted months ago, his voice hoarse from a chronic throat infection, his hair completely silver now, and the lines in his face deeply drawn. Come to Richmond and rest a spell, his wife Mary, ailing herself, wrote early in September; here you can have the comforts of home and guard your health. "But what care can a man give himself in time of war?" he asked her in reply. "It is from no desire of exposure or hazard that I live in a tent, but from necessity. I must be where I can speedily at all times attend to the duties of my position, and be near or accessible to the officers with whom I have to act."

The siege enlivened only by the spirited flanking actions of Grant, General Lee often rode Traveler all day along the lines, leaving most of the night for military planning. His aide Major Cooke remembered:

> The needs of our men worried him more than the chances of battle. Every day regiments were on the move to keep up with Grant's changes of force. It was not unusual to see our commander sitting erect on his horse watching the ranks as a father might have done. His face bore an expression that I cannot describe. No man that I have ever seen had General Lee's soft, luminous eyes, inexpressibly kind. Every one of those ragged, shoeless soldiers was dear to him. He used to say he was always ashamed of them, except upon the field of battle.

An army of scarecrows, someone called them. Lee's thin, hungry, shabby troops lacked everything except belief in their commander, widely known as "the soul of the Confederacy." Ammunition was in short supply, soap in shorter supply; many men went barefoot. The typical daily ration was four ounces of salt pork and a handful of cornmeal—often there was less or nothing—while the Billy Yanks fared comparatively well. Lee, who ate spartan meals (his usual dinner boiled cabbage and corn bread), felt guilty whenever he had a chance to dine better than his troops, who were rumored to be roasting rats and dogs over their campfires. When a saddle of mutton sent to him by his wife went astray, he wrote to her, "If the soldiers get it, I shall be content." When three little girls brought him baskets of eggs, popcorn, and pickles from their poor homes, he insisted that they keep the food for their hungry families, adding a few apples to each basket.

At the Confederate hospitals supplies had long been exhausted. "Everywhere there was gangrene, amputations without chloroform, men dying needlessly," Major Cooke recalled. With the passing days Lee's army was worn down by disease, malnutrition, and desertion as much as by casualties in the vigorous skirmishes along the line. Though the defense lines appeared strong to the Yankees, they were thinly manned, Lee sadly outnumbered. Speaking in *The Lost Cause* (1866) of the way the Confederate ranks were recruited at the time, Richmond newspaper editor Edward A. Pollard noted:

> It was not unusual to see at the railroad stations long lines of squalid men with scraps of blankets in their hands or small pine boxes of provisions, or whatever else they might snatch in their hurried departures from their homes, whence they had been taken almost without an hour's notice and ticketed for the various camps of instruction in the Confederacy. In armies thus recruited, it is no wonder that desertions were numerous, but for every Confederate soldier who went over to the Federal lines, there were hundreds who dropped out from the rear and deserted to their homes.

Lee and his dwindling army faced a line of works at Petersburg that Grant's troops had built only one hundred to two hundred yards from their own, following the general course of the Confederate works. "A great mud wall," Major Cooke called it many years later, "including bags of earth, sections of logs and trees covered by dirt. . . . At intervals they built bastions such as you see in the pictures of ancient castles. . . . [Their] mortars threw shells over our entrenched lines, compelling us to dig sheltered places which we called bombproofs. Later, in the World War, they were named dug-outs and became celebrated as something new!"

Little action was seen in these elaborate lines while the Confederates repaired the extensive damage caused by the Burnside Mine, but on August 9 another tremendous explosion rocked City Point when two daring Confederate agents, John Maxwell and R. K. Dillard, smuggled a crude time bomb aboard a Union ammunition barge. The blast killed 43, injured 126, and destroyed about a million dollars' worth of property. "Fragments of flesh, hands, feet and other parts of human bodies were literally gathered by the basketful, one-fourth mile distant," correspondent Cadwallader wrote. "Showers of shot, shell, grape and canaster, minnie balls and other missiles rained down in every direction. The ridge pole of my tent was snapped in two by a solid shot. . . . Singularly, no one connected with headquarters was injured." General Grant, however, was showered with debris from the explosion while sitting in front of his tent at noon that sweltering day. Many speculated that the blast was in retaliation for the Burnside Mine, but there is no certain proof of this.

No Union retaliation followed for the possible Rebel retaliation, but in the heavy rain on August 18 a Federal corps under General Warren extended the line around Petersburg, occupying the Weldon Railroad, an important route for Confederate supplies. Over a mile of the Weldon was occupied in this first substantial action since the Crater. The battle for the railroad line continued sporadically throughout the month and into fall and early winter, with the Union forces destroying over thirty miles of track in all. The Federals prevailed at a cost of some 4,455 casualties to the South's 1,600, and Lee had to accept the loss of the whole northern section of this important supply railroad. By the time the Weldon battle ended, the commissary general reported that only nine days' food remained for Lee's army; hunger was causing men to desert now. Lee himself telegraphed Davis that his men were without any meat. His army was saved only by the arrival of a wagon train of food from several supply ships at Wilmington, North Carolina, the sole port remaining open to Confederate blockade runners. This was not as dramatic as the September 16 ride of General Wade Hampton and his "cowboys," who skirmished with Union soldier-herders south of the James River at Coggins' Point and rustled some twenty-four hundred head of cattle back to Lee, along with three hundred prisoners. But the meat tasted just as good—better at this point in time.

Major actions along the Petersburg line were few aside from the Weldon Railroad engagements, the siege remaining relatively quiet until the spring of the next year, though there were always harebrained schemes that came up like the proposal to build a wall around Richmond and then flood the city with water pumped in from the James River. On September 29, Grant did order an attack on Forts Harrison and Gilmer, Confederate fortifications in front of the Petersburg line. The battle for Fort Harrison was considered so important that both Lee and Grant directed operations in the field. Grant's two-pronged, eight-thousand-man attack succeeded in capturing the fort west of Petersburg when a Union division rapidly stormed Harrison. The attack north of the James against Fort Gilmer, however, proved unsuccessful. General Lee launched vigorous counterattacks against Fort Harrison, trying to retake it the next day, but the Federal troopers held and later turned the fort into a Union bastion. They had, however, failed to act quickly after first taking Harrison and lost still another golden opportunity to march on and capture Richmond, only eight miles away.

It was at about this time that diarist L. B. Jones, hearing the incessant roaring of Union and Confederate cannon from Richmond, wished all the destruction would end. He noted that every tree on Governor Wise's farm had been cut down by Grant's booming guns. "What for?" he wrote pleadingly. "What harm have the poor trees done the enemy? I love trees, anywhere."

But the carnage, of course, continued. In four days of fighting at Peebles' Farm the Federals won less than a mile a day in extending their lines westward; by October 2, there were well over 3,000 Union casualties—more than a thousand a mile. The Southern figures were uncertain. Another assault ordered by Grant on October 27 to gain control of the Boydton Road and Southside Railroad was an even bloodier failure. Lee's troops turned back the daylong assault, which cost Grant 1,758 casualties out of his 40,000-man attacking force.

Yet Lee and his men were fighting a defensive action their general never wanted to fight. Lee had already made it clear to President Davis that he did not believe Richmond should be defended, arguing that the capital of the Confederacy be moved elsewhere. During a November visit to Richmond, he urged Davis to let him retreat from Petersburg to North Carolina or westward to the mountains, "where we could fight twenty years." It is only a matter of time before Grant exhausts us, he implored; Richmond holds no strategic importance, we must leave while we can and carry on the war elsewhere, let us abandon Petersburg "at the earliest practicable moment." Davis remained adamant, rejecting the great strategist's pleas. "Richmond is the heart of the Confederacy, and must be held," the armchair strategist vowed. "If we lose our capital we lose all." Lee left Richmond without making any public comment, but he was clearly disgusted with both Davis and the Confederate Congress, about which he said to his son, "Custis, I cannot see that Congress is doing anything but eating peanuts and chewing tobacco, while my men are starving."

Just as fed up with politicians was General Grant, who had in August put an abrupt end to all talk of him as a candidate for president of the United States against Lincoln by adamantly ruling out even a draft. "They can't do it! They can't compel me to do it!" he told a visitor, clenching his fists. "I consider it as important to the cause that Lincoln be elected as that the army be successful in the field!"

Grant's grand strategy in the field was working. Throughout all the Petersburg battles mentioned and others at Hatcher's Run and Fort Holly, he worked to extend his line westward, but he had another motive in mind. "The operations in front of Petersburg and Richmond until the spring campaign of 1865 were confined to the defense and extension of our lines," he wrote, "and to offensive movements for crippling the enemy's lines of communication, *and to prevent his detaching any considerable force to send south.*" These last words indicated his intention to protect General Sherman, whom he had long since ordered to capture Atlanta.

Grant and Sherman had first planned the simultaneous assault on Atlanta and Richmond shortly after Grant's appointment as general in chief, first poring over their maps back on March 17, 1864, in Nashville, Tennessee. As a Union officer phrased it, Grant would hit at the head of the Confederacy at Richmond or Petersburg, whose helmet was Lee's Army of Northern Virginia, and Sherman would hit at its heart at Atlanta, whose shield was General Joe Johnston's Army of Tennessee. There would be a unity of operations, they decided, a continuous series of battles in both theaters of action that would result in the attrition of the already vastly outnumbered Confederate armies. They believed the results would be worth the great cost in Union lives.

By April 1 Grant began to issue orders for his grand strategy and all the operations supporting it. "Wherever Lee goes, you will go also," he told General Meade, though he himself actually directed the operations of the Army of the Potomac, which he had made his official headquarters. By May 1, the same day Grant started after Lee in the Wilderness, Sherman's troops were already skirmishing with Rebels outside Stone Church in northern Georgia, his one-hundred-thousand-man army ready to set out toward the interior of Georgia and Atlanta. Johnston's Army of Tennessee was only half as large.

The Atlanta campaign soon saw Sherman and Johnston contending for Resaca, Georgia, a strong position which the Union forces took after Johnston pulled out on May 15, fearing he would be flanked with the Oostenaula River at his back. After this battle Sherman was criticized for not taking the chance he had there and then to destroy Johnston's army. Instead, he slowly moved toward Atlanta, fighting many battles and skirmishes on the way. Early in June his cavalry under General George Stoneman finally captured Allatoona Pass, so important because through it ran the Chattanooga Railroad, which gave the Federals an indispensable supply

General Joseph Johnston, about 1863. From *Marse Robert*, 1929.

line. His progress continued, Johnston always walking backward, slipping ahead of him, until Sherman lost the battle of Kennesaw Mountain near Marietta, in "villainously bad" rainy weather, as he described it, suffering over two thousand casualties in an assault that should never have been attempted against Johnston's well-entrenched positions. Still he pushed on closer and closer to the great rail hub and arsenal of Atlanta, his campaign a masterpiece of strategy and engineering. Johnston retreated in front of him, to the hills around the Gate City of the South. One mill owner in a town along the way, seeing so many Yankee and Confederate troops, ran up a neutral French flag over his building. Sherman didn't think it was funny; he thought the man ought to be hanged.

Jefferson Davis, who had already upbraided Johnston about the withdrawal from Resaca and his seeming inability to attack, had by now heard enough of "Retreating Joe" Johnston, as his detractors called the general. "Genl. Johnston has failed," he wrote Lee on July 12, "and there are strong indications he will *abandon Atlanta*. . . . It seems necessary to *relieve him* at once. Who should succeed him? What do you think of Hood for the position?" Sending his discredited military adviser General Braxton Bragg to investigate, Davis concluded that Bragg was right in believing that "the case is helpless in present hands," and on July 17 replaced Johnston with General John Bell Hood, a combative daredevil by nature, as commander of the Army of Tennessee. Johnston's defense was that he had definitely intended to hold Atlanta in a final stand and needed all the men he could salvage to do so. He pointed out that "General Lee, in keeping on the defensive and retreating toward Grant's objective point [Petersburg-Richmond], under circumstances like mine, was adding to his great fame . . . [so] I supposed that my course would not be censored. I believe then, as I do now, that it was the only [course] which promised success."

Davis's decision has been the subject of controversy ever since. He and Johnston were in fact two incredibly thin-skinned men with a long history of insulting each other. In any case, Hood's policy of aggressive, hard fighting against the huge Yankee army, at whatever the cost, proved no more successful than Johnston's conservative tactics and yielded far more casualties—over eighteen thousand men, one-third of his army, in his first ten days of command. By July 22 Atlanta was effectively under a state of siege, like Petersburg; and by the second of September it was Hood who had to save what was left of his army by evacuating the city, failing in his major task of holding it. Unable to carry off his much-needed munitions, he blew them up in a tremendous explosion heard and felt miles away. Sherman was elated that Hood came out from Atlanta's elaborate defenses, which would have cost many Union lives to penetrate.

"So Atlanta is ours and fairly won," Sherman telegraphed Lincoln on September 2. Lincoln wrote him a letter of thanks, saying, "The marches, battles, sieges, and other military operations that have signalized this campaign must render it famous in the annals of war, and have entitled those who have participated therein to the applause and thanks of the nation." Added Grant in his official report: "General Sherman's movement from Chattanooga to Atlanta was prompt, skillful, and brilliant. The history of his flank movements and battles during that memorable campaign will ever be read with an interest unsurpassed by anything [similar] in history." On September 4, Grant ordered a salute in honor of the victory to be fired "with shotted guns from every battery bearing upon the enemy" at Petersburg. Lincoln soon after made September 5 a national day of celebration and commissioned Sherman a major general in the regular army.

Prospects for Sherman were brighter than ever before now. "Cump" or "Uncle Billy," as he was called, had proved wrong every "dirty newspaper scribbler" who doubted him, and his victory virtually assured Lincoln's reelection in November, offsetting the stall at Petersburg. Though he lost thirty thousand men in the many battles of the Atlanta campaign, reinforcements left him commanding as large an army as he set out with; while the tatterdemalion Confederate army, having lost ten thousand men, was down to forty thousand poorly equipped troops.

Sherman's next move was to evacuate the entire civilian population of Atlanta except blacks. "I am not willing to have Atlanta encumbered by the families of our enemies," he proclaimed; "I want a pure Gibraltar, and will have it so by the first of October." To a protesting General Hood and civilian authorities he wrote a long reply which, reduced to its simplest terms, said the Confederacy had sown the wind and they were now reaping the whirlwind. In the full and clear terms are found his famous pronouncements "War is cruelty and you cannot refine it" and "You might as well appeal against the thunder-storm as against these terrible hardships of war." There was to be no bargaining. A ten-day truce was declared beginning on September 12, and 446 families, composed of 784 adults and 860 children, were sent north and south from Atlanta. Adult, child, sick, crippled, blind—there were no exceptions, and most of the refugees were forced to leave almost all their possessions behind. Wailing and howling was heard on the country roads and in the press, but Sherman had coldly written: "If the people raise a hand against my barbarity and cruelty, I will answer that war is war and not popularity-seeking."

Sherman certainly often acted barbarically, as events were to show more clearly, but he was a brave man and a great strategist as well. His rival General John Bell Hood—who lost the use of an arm at Gettysburg and a leg at Chickamauga, and fought many a battle strapped to his saddle after that—ranks among the bravest of combat soldiers but was no strategist at all. In tandem with Jefferson Davis, who seemed to fancy himself the Napoléon of the Confederacy, he at times acted like Sherman's ally. Both Grant and Sherman had expected that after the truce was over and Atlanta evacuated, Hood's army would be outside the gates of the city trying to prevent Sherman from advancing farther into Georgia—the fabled March to the Sea hadn't yet been conceived and Hood's Army of Tennessee was perceived as the primary target. But Hood, urged on by Davis, moved out of the way, shifting his whole army to Sherman's rear. Their plan was to eventually cut Sherman's long supply line and communications from Chattanooga to Atlanta, trying to draw Sherman northward from Georgia. By November Hood had invaded Tennessee, but Sherman didn't follow, sending General George Thomas and sixty thousand of his troops to deal with Hood's army while he began his historic march through Georgia to the sea. General John Schofield dealt Hood a disastrous defeat at the battle of Franklin, Tennessee, in which six Confederate generals were killed among the over six thousand Southern dead and wounded. Schofield then joined General Thomas for the battle of Nashville fifteen days later, on December 15. Here, as Thomas reported, "hopelessly broken, the Confederates fled in confusion," suffering some fifteen hundred casualties and forty-five hundred men captured—losses which ended the effectiveness of the Army of Tennessee for the war and made the valiant Hood "cry like his heart was breaking," according to eyewitness Private Sam Walker. So much for the strategy of Jefferson Davis.

Sherman, of course, now well on his way in his March to the Sea, was at the gates of Savannah, hoping eventually to cut from there through the Carolinas and into Virginia again, ending the thousand-mile march by joining up with Grant. "If you can whip Lee," he told Grant, "and I can march to the Atlantic, I think Uncle Abe will give us a twenty day leave." He was going to "make Georgia howl!", the fiery Man on Horseback declared, and both Grant and Lincoln gave him their full support. Certainly nothing stood in his way after Davis and Hood had sent the only Confederate army in Georgia into Tennessee. Davis had further aided Sherman by making speeches revealing Confederate strategy that were widely reported by Southern newspapers, leading Grant to write Sherman at one point: "It is evident from the tone of the Richmond press, and all other sources, that the enemy intends making a desperate effort to draw you from where you are. I have directed all new troops from the West, and from the East too, if necessary . . . to be sent to you." Secrecy, so essential to Confederate strategy, was overlooked entirely. So, often, was good political sense. In one disjointed speech at Macon, Georgia, reported by the *Macon Telegraph* on September 23, Davis managed to call Georgia's governor Joseph E. Brown a "scoundrel" for saying the Confederacy had abandoned his state; to abusively denounce General Johnston; to charge that over half of the Confederate army was absent without leave; to advise Georgia that there could be no aid from Virginia; to advise the world that the Confederacy had few men left between eighteen and forty-five—and yet still claim that Sherman was doomed. He told the crowd:

> Sherman can not keep up his long line of communication, and retreat sooner or later he must, and when that day comes, the fate that befell the Army of the French empire in its retreat from Moscow will be re-enacted. Our cavalry and our people will harass and destroy his army as did the Cossacks that of Napoleon;

Atlanta in ruins. From *Harper's Pictorial History of the Civil War,* 1866.

and the Yankee general, like him, will escape with only a body-guard.

Davis was as bad at fortune-telling as he was at strategy. Sherman had far more than a "body-guard" with him when he began his March to the Sea the morning of November 15, and the South certainly had no Cossacks at hand. Sherman led a force of sixty-two thousand men in two columns and a supply train of wagons twenty-five miles long. "Behind us lay Atlanta in ruins," he wrote. "Atlanta became a thing of the past."

Fully a third of Atlanta, some eighteen hundred buildings, had been burned, and the city was in ruins. Major George Nichols, among the last to leave Atlanta, in his *Story of the Great March,* observed:

A grand and awful spectacle is presented to the beholder in this beautiful city, now in flames. By order, the chief engineer has destroyed by powder and fire all the store-houses, depot buildings, and machine-shops. The heaven is one expanse of lurid fire; the air is filled with flying, burning cinders; buildings covering two hundred acres are in ruins or in flames; every instant there is the sharp detonation or the smothered booming sound of exploding shells and powder concealed in the buildings, and then the sparks and flame shoot away up into the black and red roof, scattering cinders far and wide. These are the machine shops where have been forged and cast the rebel cannon, shot and shell that have carried death to many a brave defender of our nation's honor. These warehouses have been the receptacles of munitions of war, stored to be used for our destruction. The city, which, next to Richmond, has furnished more material for provoking the war than any other in the South, exists no more as a means for injury to be used by the enemies of the Union.

But not only enemy supplies were burned. Sherman's "fiends" laid waste to the entire city, and civilian looters helped to spread the blaze, setting stores and public buildings on fire. Desolate, smoldering Atlanta, its economy eradicated, became a bitter symbol throughout the South of Northern barbarism, one that would rankle over a hundred years. "My aim was to whip the Rebels . . . make them fear and dread us," Sherman recalled later. He did, and made many unreconstructed Rebels and their descendants hate all the North as well. Mrs. Chesnut called "Red" Sherman "that ghoul, that hyena." He was also known as the Hun, the Burner, the Killer. The *Richmond Examiner* called his troops "scabs, scavengers and scum of creation," "hellborn," "Godforsaken," "lecherous," "hateful," "despised," and "human fungi."

Atlanta lay in ashes, but much worse was to come. Sherman's mobile city of soldiers was marching in two wings through the heart of Georgia, taking forty days' rations in their wagons, but living off the land with a vengeance. "Sherman" and "Sherman's Bummers"—the plunderers composing his foraging parties—became the only words more anathema to Southerners than that hated word "Yankee." Bayonets glinting, carrying fifty rounds of cartridges each, the general's well-dressed and -equipped troops were more confident than ever. The men saw that the Confederacy was dying and hoped they would soon be united with Grant in Petersburg to fight the final battle. They were to march 15 miles a day until they reached Savannah, 255 miles away, passing some 15 major towns and cities on the way, the enormous army ranging over a belt of country 30 miles wide that was the most fertile land in Georgia. "A gigantic pleasure excursion," one Union soldier called the Grand March. "A picnic," said another. Foraging parties from the supply wagons brought back pigs, cattle, chickens, vegetables, grain, and honey, destroying what they left so the Confederates couldn't use it, salting the ground, some claimed, mixing kerosene with the flour left behind.

The line of march followed the Georgia Central Railroad and Macon Railroad and tracks were destroyed every inch of the way, the 265 miles of rails twisted beyond use into what came to be called "Sherman hairpins," or "Jeff Davis neckties," or "Lincoln gimlets." This process, not often described, was explained by a Major Nichols on the scene:

> The method of destruction is simple, but very effective. Two ingenious instruments have been made for this purpose. One of them is a clasp, which locks under the rail. It has a ring in the top, into which is inserted a long lever, and the rail is thus ripped from the sleepers [ties]. The sleepers are then piled in a heap and set on fire, the rails roasting in the flames until they bend of their own weight. When sufficiently heated, each rail is taken off by wrenches fitting closely over the ends, and, by turning in opposite directions, it is so twisted that even a rolling machine could not bring it back into shape.

There could be little argument over the systematic destruction of railroads or even the requisition of food on the Great March to Savannah, but it didn't end there. Destroying enemy equipment and living off the land were well-established practices of war, dating to prehistory, Sherman noted, and long practiced by the Confederates as well. But Yankee Bummers, especially General Judson Kilpatrick's cavalry (who would later jokingly dub the town of Barnwell, South Carolina, "Burnwell"), far exceeded these tactics. The Bummers were usually not honest decent youths from farms and cities, but impoverished, conscripted, devil-may-care adventurers

who were out to get all they could in a war they never made. Ironically, they were often Sherman's best, most loyal fighters as well,
unafraid of killing or dying. They interpreted Sherman's instructions to "forage liberally on the country" as "take whatever you
can." Few cases of murder or rape were ever documented, but the
Bummers terrorized Southerners rich and poor, looting mansion
and cabin alike and often destroying or setting on fire what they
didn't take. There were many instances of violence and destruction far exceeding Sherman's official admission that these troops
"did some things they ought not to have done." Official policy was
that foragers were not to trespass or enter private homes, but the
orders were often not obeyed and rarely enforced. People were
choked or beaten until they revealed the hiding places of family
valuables, which they sometimes hid in swamps and graveyards.
Bummers ripped feather mattresses apart searching for gold and
jewelry former slaves gladly pointed them to; they probed every
inch of gardens with bayonets to find buried treasure; they stole
women's clothing and lingerie for their army camp followers.
When such men left a house, it was at best a shambles, with windows broken, paintings slashed, pianos axed, liquor bottles empty,
and nothing of value remaining from floor to ceiling. Often they
could be seen leading off all the livestock. Wrote a Northern newsman: "It is not infrequently that an ancient hen is seen swinging
from the pommel of a saddle, and a brood of young chickens following the horse."

While most Union soldiers never thought of "taking trophies,"
an army euphemism for stealing, or violating civilians (a good
number, in fact, aided the victims of such atrocities with gifts of
food and blankets), to the helplessly enraged people of the South
all Sherman's Yankees seemed Bummers, "a huge horde of
thieves," "a plague of locusts," "fiends loosed from hell." In an official report Sherman, who once playfully called himself "an old
Bummer," estimated that in his Grand March through one-third of
Georgia the damage done to the state was fully $100 million. Only
$20 million of that had been of benefit to his army, he wrote, "the
remainder simply waste and destruction."

Sherman's Bummers at work during the March to the Sea. From *Battles and Leaders of the Civil War,* vol. 4, 1888.

Sherman was no more a Bummer or Genghis Khan than Grant was another Suvorov, but this hard soldier, who often slept on the ground or in trees among his troops and stayed up all night planning details of each battle, was among the first modern generals to justify making war against civilians, or at least not protecting them. He wrote in his memoirs:

> In the beginning of the war, I, too, had the old West Point notion that pillage was a capital crime, and punished it by shooting, but the rebels wanted us to detach a division here, a brigade there, to protect their families and property while they were off fighting [us]. . . . This was a one-sided game of war, and many of us . . . ceased to quarrel with our own men about such minor things, and went in to subdue the enemy, leaving minor depredations to be charged up to the account of the rebels who had forced us into the war, and who deserved all they got and *more.*

The depredations of course weren't "minor things" to the people suffering them, but Sherman truly believed that the crueler his men were the quicker the war would be over. He did write that "war at best is barbarism, but to involve all—children, women, old and helpless—is more than can be justified." Yet in his memoirs he says that he didn't restrain his army "lest its vigor and energy be impaired." Nothing could restrain them anyway, not even fellow foragers found with their necks slit by Southern partisans.

There are even a few anecdotes told about Sherman that illustrate his kindness. One time during the March to the Sea he occupied the house of a woman whose daughter was dying. The woman wept continuously because a Yankee general was living in her home. "The poor woman is distracted and cannot rest," Sherman said in leaving. "Either the army must move or she."

Mostly Uncle Billy winked at the wanton plundering of his men, rarely prosecuting the Bummers though issuing no official orders to encourage them. Occasionally he seemed proud of their foraging skills. "I've got a regiment that can kill, gut and scrape a pig without breaking ranks," he said at one point. He was full of convenient contradictions. "No doubt, many acts of pillage, robbery and violence were committed," he admitted one time. "But these acts were exceptional and incidental," he later claimed.

Exceptional and incidental indeed. Georgian Eliza Andrews wrote in her diary:

> About three miles from Sparta, Georgia, we struck the "burnt country", as it is so well named by the natives. . . . I almost felt as if I should like to hang a Yankee myself. There was hardly a fence left standing all the way from Sparta to Gordon. The fields were trampled down and the road was lined with carcasses of horses, hogs and cattle that the invaders, unable either to consume or carry away with them, had wantonly shot down, to starve out the people and prevent them from making their crops. The stench in some places was unbearable. . . . The dwellings that were standing all showed signs of pillage. . . . here and there long chimney stacks, "Sheridan's sentinels," told of homes lain in ashes. The infamous wretches! I couldn't wonder now that those

poor people should want to put a rope around the neck of every red-handed devil of 'em.

According to Confederate cavalryman Captain J. P. Austin, Sherman's Bummers respected nothing. "Ornaments were snatched from the persons of delicate females, and woe unto him who displayed a watch, fob, or gold chain; as he would be relieved of it in short order. Even houses of worship were not respected. The sacred vessels of the churches were appropriated by the drunken mob."

Infrequently, a Southern woman might outwit the scavenging Bummers. "Early in the morning . . . my mother secured two fine turkeys from the yard, and, slipping them into our house, put them separately in dark closets," recalled Allie Travis, a young woman from Covington, Georgia. "The darkness and solitude so awed them that they kept perfectly quiet, and so escaped Yankee rapacity."

This wasn't often the case. Another woman, Dolly Sumner Lunt Burge, specifically described a Bummer raid on her house in her wartime journal:

> Like demons they rush in! My yards are full. To my smokehouse, my dairy, pantry, kitchen, and cellar, like famished wolves they come, breaking locks and whatever is in their way. The thousand pounds of meat in my smokehouse is gone in a twinkling, my flour, my meat, my lard, butter, eggs, pickles of various kind—both in vinegar and brine—wine, jars and jugs are all gone. My eighteen fat turkeys, my hens, chickens, and fowls, my young pigs, are shot down and hunted as if they were rebels themselves. Utterly powerless I ran out and appealed to the guard: "I cannot help you, Madam, it is orders." . . . Sherman himself and a greater portion of his army passed my house that day. All day, as the sad moments rolled on, were they passing not only in front of my house, but from behind; they tore down my garden polings, made a road through my backyard and a lot field, driving their stock and riding through, tearing down my fences and desolating my home—wantonly doing it when there was no necessity for it.

On Sherman's army of dreaded bluecoats marched, torching their way through Georgia, whose bitter sons and daughters were often heard to cry out, "Why don't you go on over to South Carolina? They're the ones who started it all." No army ate better during the war. Fried chicken, roast pork, steak, ham and eggs—one such breakfast was cooked over a fire made of Confederate money. In order to conserve ammunition, the Bummers clubbed cattle to death, bayoneted hogs, strangled chickens. They left nothing but ashes, bones, and chicken feathers behind.

While the Georgians liked "pizen" better'n Yankees, freed slaves by the thousands carrying all their meager possessions—some twenty-five thousand in all from time to time—followed Sherman and his men on their march, idolizing the "Angel of the Lord," "the man that rules the world," on their way to a place called "freedom." The two vast wings of Sherman's army had only about 13,000 Confederate troops to contend with—mostly cavalry, state militia, and home guards who could do little more than harass them. One account claims only 102 Union soldiers were killed on the entire March to the Sea. Sherman kept their destination secret. For some two weeks as they marched deeper into Georgia his troops were dubbed the "Lost Army," Sherman having cut communications with the rear. There was little or no mention of his army made in the press, since no one was sure of its whereabouts from day to day. "Sherman's army is now somewhat in the condition of a ground mole when he disappears under a lawn," General Grant said. 'You can here and there trace his track, but you are not quite certain where he will come out until you see his head." Others were calling his audacious march foolhardy—until he emerged at Savannah on December 10.

Over eighteen thousand strongly entrenched Confederate troops faced Sherman now, leaving him to invest the city instead of attacking directly. Three days later, however, his men, charging across mine-laden rice fields under heavy fire, captured Fort McAllister, south of Savannah, the last obstacle to contact with the Union fleet, thus reopening Union communications and supply lines. The city was doomed. It was only a week more before Confederate general William Joseph Hardee evacuated his troops, afraid his woefully understrength army would be encircled and captured.

"I beg to present you, as a Christmas gift, the city of Savannah, with 150 heavy guns and plenty of ammunition, and also about 25,000 bales of cotton," Sherman wrote in his famous message to President Lincoln on December 22, which the president received on Christmas day. Wrote Lincoln in return: "Many, many thanks for your Christmas gift. . . . When you were about leaving Atlanta for the Atlantic coast, I was anxious, if not fearful; but feeling that you were the better judge, and remembering that 'nothing risked, nothing gained,' I did not interfere. Now, the undertaking being a success, the honor is all yours."

Soon Savannah's former slaves were singing songs of jubilee. Newsman Charles Coffin wrote of "how gloriously it sounded . . . the Freedmen's Battle Hymn . . . sung by five hundred freedmen in the Savannah slave-mart, where some of the singers had been sold in days gone by." The North rejoiced. With Sherman's triumph and Thomas's resounding victory at Nashville over Hood's Army of Tennessee six days before, peace seemed to be in the air. Sherman would regroup and march northward through the Carolinas, as everyone expected, his troops or the retreating enemy (the argument still rages) responsible for burning down two-thirds of the beautiful city of Columbia, the ferocity of his Bummers worse if possible, "the whole army burning with an insatiable desire to wreak vengeance upon South Carolina," as he put it.

"Hell was empty, and all its devils were in this devoted city, learning new deviltry from Yankee teachers," a Columbia preacher wrote.

"Here is where secession began and here, by God, is where it will end!" Federal troops were heard to say. Recalled Confederate cavalryman Austin:

> [Sherman] swept on with his army of sixty thousand men like a full developed cyclone, leaving behind him a track of desolation and ashes fifty miles wide. In front of them was terror and dismay. Bummers plundered and robbed everyone who was so unfortunate as to be within their reach. . . . Poor, bleeding South

Carolina! Her time had come. The protestations of her old men and the pleadings of her noble women had no effect in staying the ravages of sword, flame and pillage.

Charleston, the cradle of secession, was evacuated the day after Sherman occupied Columbia, and on February 18 the Stars and Stripes was again raised over the rubble that was Fort Sumter. Sherman's long, brilliant march would ensure his military reputation as one of the greatest American generals, although most Southerners would agree with General Wade Hampton that because of his army's depredations and his apparent approval of them he "disgraced the profession of arms." Later, however, reinstated Confederate general Joe Johnston wrote admiringly of Sherman's generalship as he led his Union army through the Carolinas, often through swamps considered impassable at that time of the year, his battalions of axmen cutting down whole forests and making log roads. "If his army goes to hell, it will courderoy the road," he said of Sherman. "I made up my mind there had been no such army since the days of Julius Caesar."

THERE WAS LITTLE GOOD NEWS down in Dixie while Sherman and his Bummers swept through Georgia and the Carolinas. Southerners did have some fun joking about the "battle of Kilpatrick's Pants" on March 9 in South Carolina. In this brief, intimate encounter "the boy general" Kilpatrick, at twenty-eight one of the Union's youngest and most heartless Bummers, was nearly captured in bed—in media res with an army camp follower, according to one version of the story. He only escaped Wade Hampton's Secesh cavalry by fleeing without his trousers. Even here, however, the Federals counterattacked and defeated the hapless Hampton.

More cheering and lasting comic relief were provided by news of the earlier Rebel raid on Vermont led by Lieutenant Bennett Young, one of the war's most far-flung and least-known actions, part of a daring plan that included a later abortive effort to burn down New York City on election day.

Sherman's men marching through the swamps in the Carolinas, January 1865. From *Harper's Pictorial History of the Civil War*, 1866.

But Bennett Young's raid worked, to a point. Beginning on October 10, 1864, Young and his associates, disguised in civilian clothes, had crossed the border by train from Canada two or three at a time and begun casing St. Albans, Vermont, ascertaining the number of weapons on hand, the habits of the villagers, and the best business days for St. Albans's three banks.

Wednesday, October 19, was chosen as the target date. Tuesday was market day in the little town on Lake Champlain, and the bank vaults were full. Because it was raining heavily, and because many townspeople were attending the state legislature at Montpelier and an important court at Burlington, the streets of St. Albans would be almost deserted.

It was a few minutes after three when Young raised his hand slightly, giving the signal for the raid. His men, twenty-two in all, began walking toward him, none of them appearing out of the ordinary. To the townspeople they were sportsmen, salesmen, or tourists staying in the local hotel; or perhaps they were visitors from Montreal, only fifty-five miles away. Nobody suspected that they were Confederate raiders in disguise; that their leader, Bennett Young, was a lieutenant in the Confederate army. No one dreamed Vermont, hundreds of miles away from any battlefield, would be the scene of a Civil War action.

Young, a tall, confident, dark-haired man, swaggered toward the St. Albans Bank, looking more like a depositor than the perpetrator of an immense illegal withdrawal. He was about to initiate one of the most arrogant schemes of what he considered the War to Suppress Yankee Arrogance.

Throwing off their overcoats to reveal their Confederate uniforms, the raiders took their assigned positions. Only twelve men would handle the three banks, while ten lookouts posted themselves on the main thoroughfare to herd all passersby toward the village green. Quiet and order were of the utmost importance because hundreds of able men were at work in nearby railroad shops.

"Cry for help and we'll kill all of you," the villagers were told.

But an old man, the town's jeweler, refused to obey. A Rebel ordered him onto the green, but he chose to believe that the lookout was no more than a common drunk.

"Oh, no," he laughed. "I guess you won't shoot me!"

The raider did shoot, but fortunately his bullet was deflected by the rock ribs of the crusty old New Englander. The jeweler, convinced now, hobbled over to the green, joining the other villagers and not speaking another word.

The St. Albans Bank was first on the Rebel schedule. Only one clerk was on duty. Young and another raider calmly approached the teller's cage. Suddenly Young leaned forward, brandishing his revolver. The teller leaped back into the conference room and shut the door. But before he secured the lock, Young and his companion had battered their way in.

"Who do you think you are?" the teller asked contemptuously. "What do you think you're doing?"

"We're Confederate soldiers," Young laughed, "and we're going to rob this bank. This city is now in the possession of the Confederate States of America!"

"There's no battle here. You're vandals."

"What are your troops doing in Georgia and the Shenandoah?" Young asked bitterly. "Burning homes, plundering, looting!" He smiled then. "All we're going to do is rob us a few banks and maybe blow out your brains."

The teller meekly stepped back from the revolver pressed against his temple and quietly watched as the raiders stuffed about $75,000 into their bags. "Give us a record of what you took," he asked politely when Young finished. "We have to lodge a claim with the government."

Young merely laughed and walked out. He crossed over to the Franklin County Bank, where two raiders had already entered. His comrades had waited until the bank was empty, inquiring about current prices, exchanging greenbacks for a few gold pieces. Then they signaled Young to join them.

"We're Confederate soldiers!" Young shouted to the tellers. "There's one hundred of us, so don't be trying anything!"

One teller broke for the door, but was caught. The other stood there shaking. His coworker again tried to break away, but angry Confederates collared him and locked him in the vault.

"It's airtight," the frightened teller shouted. "It's inhuman. He'll suffocate in there."

The raiders ransacked the bank, carefully went through every drawer and compartment, adding large packages of bills to their loot.

"It's inhuman," the teller kept repeating, pointing at the safe, "you can't do that," but when the Confederates were ready to leave, they locked him inside, too. They then raced toward the livery stables.

Seven other raiders were almost finished looting a third bank, the First National, as Young led his men in search of horses. The First National proved the easiest mark at first. Only one cashier was at work, and a retired general, ninety years old and deaf, was seated across the room reading a paper. The cashier offered no resistance, and the raiders filled their valises with bonds and treasury notes. Then a depositor entered and witnessed the robbery. He wrestled one of the Confederates to the ground. Seconds later, two eighteen-inch Confederate revolvers were pointed at the depositor's head. Just then the deaf old general hobbled forward to the rescue, having missed most of the robbery from behind his opened newspaper.

"Two against one is not fair play," he proclaimed.

The Confederates laughed and dashed out toward the mounts Lieutenant Young had acquired, which included horses stolen from startled riders in the street and two truck horses detached from a wagon. They rode out of St. Albans bareback, shooting up the town as they left, throwing bottles of Greek fire. Even then a few people still didn't understand what was happening.

"What are you people trying to celebrate?" the village photographer cried out.

"I'll let you know," Lieutenant Young answered and pumped two shots into the photographer's window. Letting out a Rebel yell, he then turned and headed his band of young soldiers toward the Canadian border, leaving the townspeople to put out the fires.

By now most of St. Albans was awakening to what had happened. The two tellers pounded and screamed until they were set free from their vault. Other victims had telegraphed emergency messages to the state capital and the Vermont militia was on its way via rail, while the *United States,* a side-wheeler loaded with troops, was steaming down from the north. Roads and bridges in the border country were put under heavy guard and a large posse was formed in St. Albans. The Confederate raiders had stolen $210,000 from the three sleepy St. Albans banks.

Meanwhile, Young's bareback raiders were moving as fast as their mounts could carry them, which was not very fast. Near Sheldon, Vermont, they were pleasantly surprised to come upon a farmer trotting alone on an excellent-looking horse. Young forced the farmer to dismount, leaving him with a sad, grass-chopping specimen stolen in St. Albans. But all was not over for the poor farmer. As he stood and stared dejectedly at the aged creature he had inherited, the St. Albans' posse opened fire on him, recognizing the horse and believing him to be a raider. Although he understood none of this, he finally realized that they were trying to kill him and scampered away, saving his life by hiding in a swamp.

Young's men, aided by the posse's distraction, rode on throughout most of the night, with the Vermonters doggedly trailing them. Young's plans did not call for stopping, but most of the Rebels became so chafed and sore from riding bareback that they had to rest at Stambridge, Quebec. There they abandoned what were probably the sorriest nags in history ever to carry a military expedition and gave their posteriors a well-deserved rest. The other callused and courageous men worked their way home, delivering $130,000 of the bank loot to their government in Richmond.

The Vermonters crossed into Canada, trying to apprehend the recuperating Rebels at Stambridge, but Canadian police took the Confederates into custody instead and refused to turn them over. A trial was held later in Montreal; but the Canadians, like the English, favored the Confederacy, and the raiders were only tried for violating Canadian neutrality. A jury freed them, declaring that they were soldiers acting under military orders, although the remaining $80,000 was returned to the Vermonters. Canadians sympathetic to the South mobbed Lieutenant Young's raiders when they were exonerated, and the Vermonters watched glumly as the raiders headed for home. It took a long while for all of Yankeedom to get over the fact that twenty-two Rebs, without horses and financed with only $400 from the Confederate secretary of war, had turned the state of Vermont into a state of chaos.

BUT THE ST. ALBANS RAID was an aberration. With Atlanta and Savannah in Union hands by Christmas and Sherman getting ready to move into the Carolinas, General Grant saw his grand strategy falling neatly into place piece by piece. Another early Christmas present came from that "little mountain of combative force," young Philip Sheridan. Since Grant had given him command of

the Army of the Shenandoah in August, Little Phil had won a series of battles at Waynesboro, Winchester, and Cedar Creek, eliminating the last major opposition in the Shenandoah Valley. Later,
when Lincoln met the victorious Sheridan, he would say that he
once thought a cavalryman should be at least six-feet-four high,
but "I have changed my mind—five foot four will do in a pinch."
The president, no ballet beauty himself, went on to describe
Sheridan as a graceless "brown chunky little chap, not enough
neck to hang him, and such long arms that if his ankles itch he can
scratch them without stooping."

Sheridan, a great favorite of Grant, rode horses almost as well
as his chief and probably smoked as many cigars as Grant and
Sherman combined. He, too, strongly believed in attacking, giving
'em hell—wars weren't won by digging in and waiting. Grant had
sent the former Indian fighter into the valley with forty-three
thousand men, over two times as many as the army under General
Jubal Early that had come close to taking Washington. "With quick
military instinct," wrote General Wesley Merritt in *Battles and
Leaders of the Civil War,* "[Grant] saw that the Valley was not useful
to the Government for aggressive operations. He decided that it
must be made untenable for either army. In doing this he reasoned
that the advantage would be with us, who did not want it as a
source of supplies, nor as a place of arms, and against the Confederates, who wanted it for both." General Sheridan was instructed
to clear the valley of Early and destroy it, to make barren the
breadbasket of Lee's army.

The pugnacious bulldog Sheridan—a little terror of a man who
in his youth had been suspended from West Point for a year after
attacking a cadet sergeant with a bayonet—clearly did the job.
During just a single two-day period in early October, he wrote in
an official report, "the whole country from the Blue Ridge to the
North Mountain has been rendered untenable for a rebel army. I
have destroyed over two-thousand barns filled with wheat and hay
and farming implements; over seventy mills filled with flour and
wheat; have driven in front of the army over four thousand head
of stock, and have killed and issued to the troops not less than

three thousand sheep." He did not torch towns and cities as Sherman's men did, except in a single case where all houses within a five-mile area were burned as retribution for the murder of a Union officer. As he said when he was done, however, "The crow that flies over the Valley of Virginia must henceforth carry his own rations with him."

In repulsing the surprise attack by Early and his Army of the Valley at Cedar Creek on October 19, the thirty-three-year-old Sheridan became a Northern hero almost as renowned and revered as Grant and Sherman. Sheridan was hurrying back from Washington, where he had been rather reluctantly consulting with Secretary of War Stanton, when he heard of "Old Jubal's" attack and finally galloped to the front nineteen miles away on his jet-black charger Rienzi. It was a breakneck ride rivaling Paul Revere's in American legend, and one of the most dramatic in military history. Major George A. Forsyth, who rode behind him, wrote:

> He turned his horse's head southward, tightening the reins of his bridle, and with a slight touch of the spur he dashed up the turnpike and was off. . . .On either side we saw, through the Indian-summer haze, the distant hills fairly ablaze with foliage and all over was the deep blue of cloudless Southern sky. . . . Then we came suddenly upon indubitable evidence of battle and Federal retreat while galloping over the open fields. . . . The general would wave his hat to the men and point to the front, never lessening his speed as he pressed forward. It was enough; one glance at the eager face and familiar black horse and they knew him, and swung their caps and broke into cheers as he passed among them. Shouldering their arms, they started after him for the front, shouting to their comrades further out in the fields, "Sheridan, Sheridan!" and pointing after him as they dashed onward. . . . His cheery shout of "Turn back, men, turn back! Face the other way!" as he waved his hat toward the front, had but one result: a wild cheer of recognition, an answering wave of the cap. . . . I think it is no exaggeration to say that, as he dashed on to the field of battle, for miles back the turnpike was lined with men pressing forward after him to the front.

They passed by the rows of corpses of fallen comrades laid out by the field hospital, "the great pile of flesh constantly growing higher" where bloody-aproned surgeons were still cutting off shattered arms and legs. They passed the walking wounded, those young and old who had lost their minds for hours or always. No one knows how Sheridan rallied them, these broken men who had retreated for miles; but he did, and they utterly destroyed the army of Lee's "Bad Old Man," which would never again really menace the Yankee army. "Face back," Sheridan is supposed to have shouted to his retreating men from his black and white fet-locked horse. "We're going back! We're going to raise them out of their boots! We'll make coffee out of Cedar Creek tonight!" Others say he used stronger language. "Come on back, boys!" one sergeant recalled him crying. "Give 'em hell, God damn 'em!" Colonel Rutherford B. Hayes, later the nineteenth U.S. president, testified that he said, "Boys turn back; face the other way. I am going to sleep in that camp tonight or in hell." Sheridan always denied he uttered such words, but he did his denying in puritanical times. In any case, the aggressive little general was celebrated throughout the North in song and story. His gelding Rienzi won fame comparable to Lee's mount Traveler and today stands stuffed in the Smithsonian Institution. Both rider and horse were immortalized in the romantic narrative poem "Sheridan's Ride" by popular Pennsylvania poet and artist Thomas Buchanan Read, whose best-known painting was also of the same subject. The singsong verse exaggerated Sheridan's and his horse's roles but was quoted everywhere, especially during Lincoln's campaign for reelection that fall. Four of the poem's seven stanzas follow:

Up from the South at break of day,
Bringing to Winchester fresh dismay,
The affrighted air with a shudder bore,
Like a herald in haste, to the chieftain's door,
The terrible grumble and rumble and roar,
Telling the battle was on once more,
And Sheridan twenty miles away. . . .

General Sheridan on his famous ride in the popular painting by T. Buchanan Read. From *Great Men and Famous Women*, 1894.

But there is a road from Winchester town,
A good, broad highway, leading down;
And there, through the flash of the morning light,
A steed as black as the steeds of night
Was seen to pass as with early flight.

As if he knew the terrible need,
He stretched away with the utmost speed;
Hills rose and fell—but his heart was gay,
With Sheridan fifteen miles away. . . .

Under his spurning feet, the road
Like an arrowy Alpine river flowed,
And the landscape sped away behind,
Like an ocean flying before the wind;
And the steed, like a bark fed with furnace ire,
Swept on, with his wild eyes full of fire;
But, lo! he is nearing his heart's desire,
He is snuffing the smoke of the roaring fray,
With Sheridan only five miles away.

The first that the General saw were the groups
Of stragglers, and then the retreating troops;
What was done,—what to do,—a glance told him both,
And, striking his spurs with a terrible oath,
He dashed down the line mid a storm of huzzas,
And the wave of retreat checked its course there, because
The sight of the master compelled it to pause.
With foam and with dust the black charger was gray;
By the flash of his eye, and his nostrils' play,
He seemed to the whole great army to say,
"I have brought you Sheridan all the way
From Winchester town, to save the day!"

As for old Early, a brilliant general who often acted as if he'd
been weaned on two lemons, he took the defeat rather bitterly.
Addressing his hungry, often shoeless troops, who had shown great
courage in the initial surprise attack against a superior force and
suffered some three thousand casualties (the North lost almost
twice as many), Early had this to say:

> I have the mortification of announcing to you that by your sub-
> sequent misconduct, all the benefits of [your early] victory were
> lost and a serious disaster incurred. Many of you, including some

commissioned officers, yielding to a disgraceful propensity to plunder, deserted your colors to appropriate the abandoned property of the enemy; and subsequently those who had previously remained at their posts, seeing their ranks thinned by the absence of the plunderers, when the enemy, late in the afternoon, with his shattered columns, made but a feeble effort to retrieve the day, yielded to a needless panic, and fled the field in confusion.

A great morale builder, Old Jubilee, when Confederate morale was at a low point everywhere—just what the South didn't need. Things were bad enough. Federal incursions had been made into Confederate territory all over the country, and Sheridan and Sherman were on their way back to join Grant at Petersburg, Sheridan the destroyer having turned the Virginia valley into a wasteland useful to no one. Everywhere Confederate soldiers just wanted to go home. A lowly private who left the Army of Tennessee summed it up best in a letter to his sister:

Dear Sister Lizzy:

i hev conkludid that the dam fulishness uv tryin to lick shurmin Had better be stopped. we hav bin gettin nuthin but hell & lots uvit ever sinse we saw the dam yankys & i am tirde uv it. shurmin has a lot of pimps that don't care a dam what they doo. and its no use tryin to whip em. if we dont git hell when shurmin starts again I muss my gess. if i cood git home ide tri dam hard to git thare. my old horse is plaid out or ide trie to go now. maibee ile start to nite fur ime damn tired uv this war fur nuthin. if the dam yankys Havent got thair yit its a dam wunder. Thair thicker an lise on a hen and a dam site ornraier.

YOUR BROTHER JIM.

4

Breakthrough: The Capture of Petersburg and Richmond

This is a sad business, colonel. It has happened as I told them in Richmond it would happen. The line has been stretched until it is broken.

—General Robert E. Lee, March 1865

THE BONE-CHILLING WINTER MONTHS OF 1865, one of the worst winters in memory, saw Lee's troops still holding out in their Petersburg Gibraltar of dirt and logs, with little action save sniping along the lines. Grant and his well-fed, well-clad men had reason to be happy looking back over the past year. Good news came from every direction. They had the only sizable fighting Confederate Army pinned down in front of them at Petersburg, a famished force facing Union divisions vastly superior in numbers, supplies, and morale. The Yankee army was over twice as large— 124,000 to 57,000—"an overwhelming superiority," Lee confided. People were calling Lee the "Great Entrencher"; one Northern journal dubbed "the chivalry" "the shovelry," because all they seemed to do was dig in deeper. Lee's soldiers were calling themselves Les Miserables. Besides the good news about Sherman,

Admiral Farragut standing in the rigging of his flagship *Hartford* during the important battle of Mobile Bay, August 5, 1864, in which he is said to have exclaimed, "Damn the torpedoes! Full speed ahead!" From *Great Men and Famous Women*, 1894.

Thomas, and Sheridan, every Billy Yank knew that the naval blockade of the South was virtually impregnable. The Federal navy had sunk the Confederate raider *Alabama* back in June and won the last significant naval battle of the war at Mobile, Alabama, in August under Admiral David Farragut, whose famous signal "Damn the torpedoes! Full speed ahead!" was on every Northerner's lips. Except for remote areas that didn't matter, the South was hemmed in everywhere.

Crumpling a newspaper in his hand one morning, Grant exclaimed, "Tell the President I have got them like that!" Grant's major concern now was that Lee would slip away somehow as the Gray Fox had so many times before. He wrote:

> I was afraid every morning that I would awake from my sleep to hear that Lee had gone, and that nothing was left but a picket line. He had his railroad by the way of Danville south, and I was afraid that he was running off his men and all stores and ord-

nance except such as would be necessary . . . for his immediate defense. I knew he could move much more lightly and rapidly than I, and that, if he got the start, he would leave me behind so that we would have the same army to fight further south—and the war might be prolonged another year.

To almost everyone's pleasure on both sides, Grant had even rid himself of the politician-general Benjamin Butler. "Butler the Beast," whose infamous Order Number 28 had declared that any New Orleans woman showing contempt for Yankee soldiers would be treated as a common prostitute. "Silver Spoon Butler," so named for the many silver spoons he and his men filched from wealthy New Orleans homes. "Notorious Ben Butler," the first politician to whom the term "baby kisser" was applied. The tricky, egotistical Butler was baselessly rumored to have a strong hold on Grant because he supplied him with liquor—for which, of course, Grant didn't need a supplier. Military men hated Butler. "I want simply to ask you how you can place a man in command of two army corps who is helpless as a child on the field of battle and as visionary as an opium-eater in council?" General Baldy Smith had once written to Grant.

Butler's downfall, like Burnside's, came with a great explosion. Leading an expedition to capture Fort Fisher near Wilmington, North Carolina, the day before Christmas, Butler instructed his men to pack an old barge, the *Louisiana*, with 235 pounds of fused gunpowder and explode it 830 yards from shore, certain that the fort and its garrison would be totally destroyed. It was to be, Butler said, "the biggest man made explosion in history," though Grant's engineers advised him that the explosion would "have about the same effect on the fort that firing feathers from muskets would have on the enemy." But Butler insisted on going ahead with what he called his "little experiment." Actually, he had suggested something similar to Grant a few weeks before—a plan to blow up Charleston with a ship loaded with 1,000 pounds of gunpowder. Both plots were inspired by an accidental British gunpowder explosion he had read about somewhere. This time Grant reluctantly went along with him, much to Grant's later regret. As someone put it, the mountain finally gave birth to the mouse. When the *Louisiana* exploded at two o'clock in the morning, nothing at all was damaged save the powder boat itself, and no one received so much as a scratch. The explosion didn't even startle the Rebels, who believed what they heard was the accidental explosion of the boiler in a Yankee gunboat, or a grounded gunboat of their own blown up to prevent it from falling into Yankee hands. "Oh, it was horrible," a Confederate prisoner later said in mock horror, telling his Yankee captors of the blast. "Woke up every man in the fort."

This gunboat plot was the first in a series of fiascos during the three-day action at Fort Fisher that featured Butler arguing with Admiral David D. Porter and everyone else about why everything went wrong. The expedition failed miserably, and ended with Butler withdrawing his assault force because he thought his losses had been too high. Later, on January 15, a second expedition, commanded by General Alfred Terry, would capture the fort under the same conditions Butler considered too dangerous.

Another large charge of gunpowder sealed General Butler's fate. On the first day of the New Year, Butler's work crews—mostly black troops—were busy finishing the Dutch Gap Canal, a canal being constructed to allow Union ships to bypass a large, dangerous bend in the James River that was commanded by Confederate batteries. The operation was supposed to end with the last remaining portion of the canal excavated by an explosion of six tons of gunpowder. The blast went off early that Sunday, but instead of clearing the ditch it refilled what had already been dug with more dirt, rock, and gravel. Four months of work had been for naught. The project was abandoned.

Why Grant approved a third Yankee Plan involving an explosion after the disastrous failures of the first two, he never satisfactorily explained. Clearly Yankees (though they were legendary mechanics) and gunpowder just did not mix—after Fort Fisher was finally taken, two drunken Federal sailors with blazing torches were searching a magazine in the fort for loot when they accidentally exploded thirteen thousand pounds of gunpowder, killing twenty-five men and injuring another sixty-six. In any event, Grant had clearly had enough of Butler—who was second in rank only to himself—and asked Washington to relieve him of command "because of a lack of confidence in his military ability, making him an unsafe commander for a large army." By January 7 such orders were issued by the secretary of war, Lincoln having won his second term and not so dependent anymore on Butler's political support. Butler, who was replaced by Major General Edward Ord, appeared unfazed by his military failures, telling one and all that he still enjoyed the president's confidence. A detailed plan he proposed to Lincoln involved him taking 150,000 black soldiers and digging an interoceanic canal across Panama on a thirty-mile strip of land that the United States would buy there. Lincoln, of course, had more important things on his mind.

Among these matters were the various peace feelers being made North and South. Old Francis P. Blair, the powerful Washington political figure, suggested a scheme designed to reunite the two sides by having a joint force invade Mexico and expel the French and their puppet emperor, Maximilian, whose presence there violated the Monroe Doctrine. Blair briefed Lincoln about the plan after traveling to Richmond and explaining it to Jefferson Davis. Though neither president liked the idea, both eventually agreed to peace talks aboard the Federal steamer *River Queen* off Hampton Roads, Virginia, on February 3.

President Lincoln, gaunt and tired—"the tiredest man in the world" and thirty pounds below his usual weight at this juncture in the long, bloody war—met with a delegation headed by the outspoken Confederate vice president, Alexander Stephens, chosen by Davis despite their political differences because Stephens and Lincoln had been friends in the U.S. Congress. Tired as he was, Lincoln wasn't without his usual sense of humor. When Little Alec, as the ninety-pound Stephens was called, came aboard the *River Queen* and finished shucking his several shawls, long muffler, and huge overcoat, Lincoln shook his old friend's hand and said, "Never have I seen so small a nubbin come out of so much husk." Stephens laughed, but wasn't to be outdone. Later during the four-hour conference he told a story about Illinois, Lincoln's home state. In an early Congress, Stephens said, no one was sure how to pronounce the state's name: was it Illi-*noy* or Illi-*nois?* Said old John Quincy Adams: "If one were to judge from the character of the Representatives in this Congress from that state, I should decide unhesitatingly that the proper pronunciation was 'All noise!'" It was Lincoln's turn to laugh at himself.

Lincoln told Secretary of State William H. Seward before the conference began that the South had to recognize Federal authority as a first step to any peace; there could be no "two countries" involved, as Davis wanted. Davis' peace commissioners tried to talk him out of this position, suggesting an armistice first, with the arrangements for reunion discussed later. Lincoln couldn't be swayed. When delegate Robert Hunter, president pro tempore of the Confederate Senate, remarked that England's King Charles I had bargained with armed rebels against his government—certainly a precedent for Lincoln making a treaty—Lincoln quipped that "all I distinctly recollect about the case of Charles I is that he lost his head, and I have no head to spare."

Despite the rapier repartee—and there was much more of it—the conference at Hampton Roads ended a failure. Lincoln returned to Washington, where he suggested a scheme to his cabinet whereby the United States would pay the slave states $400 million if they surrendered by April 1. When his cabinet unanimously rejected the plan, Lincoln remarked that if the war lasted a hundred days more, the over $3 million a day spent on it would amount to about $400 million, "besides all the lives [saved]." He dropped the scheme in the face of overwhelming opposition, but he hadn't heard the last of peace plans. The most important of these came from General Lee, who had recently assumed the rank of general in chief of Confederate armies. In a secret letter known only to Davis, he wrote to his counterpart Grant proposing a "military convention" to "arrive at a satisfactory adjustment of the present unhappy difficulties." Lee had been advised by General James Longstreet that Union general Edward Ord had assured him Grant would be in favor of such a peace overture. Grant made no mention of his feelings one way or the other, but referred the offer to President Lincoln, who sat down and wrote an order for Secretary of War Stanton to send back to Grant, writing it as if its author was Stanton. "He [Lincoln] instructs me to say," the order read, "that you are not to decide, discuss, or confer upon any political question. Such questions the President holds in his own hands, and will submit them to no military conferences or conventions. Meantime you are to press to the utmost your military advantages." Grant could accept the surrender of Lee's troops, the instructions further specified, but that was where his authority ended.

On March 4 Grant advised Lee of the gist of Lincoln's order. That same day the president delivered his second inaugural address, speaking in the very first paragraph of "insurgent agents" who had sought "to dissolve the union, and divide effects, by negotiation." Then Lincoln voiced his belief that "all knew" slavery "was, somehow, the cause of the war" and that it must be ended:

> Fondly do we hope—fervently do we pray—that this mighty scourge of war may speedily pass away. Yet, if God wills that it continue until all the wealth piled by the bondsman's two hundred and fifty years of unrequited toil shall be sunk, and until every drop of blood drawn by the lash shall be paid by another drawn with the sword, as was said three thousand years ago, so still it must be said, "The judgments of the Lord are true and righteous altogether."

Finally came the ending paragraph, healing words that would become an American psalm, a sacred poem to all but those like actor John Wilkes Booth, who stood close by in the crowd, wild thoughts pulsing in his brain:

> With malice toward none; with charity for all; with firmness in the right, as God gives us to see the right, let us strive on to finish the work we are in; to bind up the nation's wounds; to care for him who shall have borne the battle and for his widow, and his orphan—to do all which may achieve and cherish a just and lasting peace among ourselves, and with all nations.

Lee and all the South knew now of Lincoln's idea of a proper peace, and most reasonable people realized that Lincoln—"gentle, plain, just and resolute," as Walt Whitman called him—would be magnanimous once the war ended. But Jefferson Davis remained intractable, dreaming his grandiose dreams of a separate nation gloriously defeating the Yankees against overwhelming odds and driving them from the South, which would then return to its old ways of life. Many Southern fire-eaters fed on the same fantasies. Minister Joseph C. Stiles mounted the pulpit of Richmond's First Baptist Church and compared Richmond with the Dutch city of Leiden, besieged by the Spanish for *"eighty years."* The old lion demanded that Richmondites emulate Leiden's brave starving inhabitants, whom the Spanish besiegers had taunted as rat-eaters and dog-eaters. "We *are* rat-eaters and dog-eaters," the Leidenites had replied, "and as long as you can hear a dog bark or a cat meow, know that we will not surrender! And when the dogs and cats and rats are all consumed, every man will cook the flesh off his left arm that he will live longer to fight you with his right arm! And when we can do no more, we will not surrender; we'll *fire the city*, and with our men, women and children, perish in the flames!"

Whether Southerners would eat dogs, cats, and rats has never been proved (there are stories of Rebel soldiers hunting wharf rats, and one army purveyor was said to supply dog meat). But Jefferson Davis, apparently completely serious, did sing the praises of rat meat, if not self-cannibalizing. "I don't see why rats, if fat, are not as good as squirrels," he told a child who innocently asked how the Confederate army would be fed. "Our men did eat mule meat at Vicksburg," he added matter-of-factly, "but it would be an expensive luxury now." He might have said the same of horse meat boiled tender and fried in fat, long a wonderful wartime meal for many. In any case, soldiers and civilians alike were close to starvation in Petersburg and Richmond ever since Sheridan ravaged the Shenandoah and Fort Fisher had been captured, closing off the port of Wilmington. Firewood cost $5 a piece, coffee $45 a pound, butter $25 a pound, chickens $50 each. Meat was almost impossible to come by—there wasn't even enough for the armies in the field. Flour was so rare that it commanded $1,500 a barrel.

Most people couldn't afford to buy food at these prices. Confederate money was becoming worthless, with $100 in gold bringing $10,000 in Confederate currency, or "shinplasters." A soldier's whole monthly pay wouldn't buy him a pair of shoes. One journalist commented on the "unchanging expression of ineffable melancholy which the engraver has given" to the portraits of Confederate officials on the Confederate banknotes. According to a common joke, one needed a basket to carry one's money to market, only a wallet to bring home one's purchases. Of the Confederate army Major Cooke recalled years later:

> On the approach of spring 1865 we had possibly 33,000 men able to bear arms. . . . We were scarecrows, in fact, by that time. I never saw so many thin, hungry men, with sharp, pinched faces. Our clothing was disgraceful—no less. Soap had become a refinement unknown. Starved, dirty, ragged, unwashed, devoured by pests, afflicted with disease, the army stood firm. Scrofula, I remember, followed the shortage of soap. We lacked everything that men might need.

Lee's men were deserting from the front and rear of the lines. Sixty-thousand had left since the siege began; three thousand had surrendered in Washington alone that March. Lee found it necessary to issue General Order Number 8, which read in part:

> It having been reported that the evil habit prevails with some in the army of proposing to their comrades in jest to desert and go home, the commanding general earnestly warns those guilty of this practice against the danger they incur. The penalty for advising or persuading a soldier to desert is death, and those indulging in such jests will find it difficult on a trial to rebut the presumption of guilt arising from their words.

It was no laughing matter to Lee. He searched for ways to keep his troops from deserting and to replace those who had deserted. With his troops hungry, cold, and disabled, dying from disease and deserting, the Confederate Congress finally gave its approval to a bill introduced by Mississippi congressman Ethelbert Barksdale authorizing the use of armed slaves as Confederate soldiers, it being understood but not stated that they would later be made free by their states for their service. General Lee had supported the bill—debated for over five months—and the *Richmond Examiner* editorialized that it only overcame its powerful opposition, winning by just one vote, because "the country will not venture to deny to General Lee . . . *anything* he may ask for." But fantasies of 300,000 to 850,000 slaves fighting for their homeland never materialized, and there wouldn't have been more than five thousand rifles for them if they had come forth. Black troops were recruited, but the plan came too late and most slaves did not trust the implied offer of freedom. By the last days of March, however, some armed slaves were seen in Confederate uniforms marching through Richmond.

Though General Lee, severely reduced in supplies and numbers, still had a few tricks up his sleeve, he clearly saw the end in sight as early as late February; perhaps he had from the beginning. To his wife, suffering terribly from arthritis, barely able to move, the great caretaker wrote:

> After sending my note this morning, I received from the express office a bag of socks. . . . You will have to send down your offerings as soon as you can and bring your work to a close, for I think General Grant will move against us soon—within a week if nothing prevents—and no man can tell what may be the result . . . but trusting in a merciful God, who does not always give the battle to the strong, I pray we may not be overwhelmed. I shall, however, endeavor to do my duty and fight to the last. Should it be necessary to abandon our position to prevent being surrounded, what will you do? Will you remain or leave the city? You must consider the question and make up your mind. . . . It is a fearful condition and one must rely for guidance and protection upon a kind Providence. . . . Give much love to all. They are all hearts . . ."

Grant's headquarters at City Point, 1865. From *Harper's Pictorial History of the Civil War,* 1866.

While President Davis and his wife Varina were selling their carriage horses in Richmond to meet their expenses, President Lincoln, his wife Mary, and his son Tad were on their way aboard the steamer *River Queen* to meet General Grant again at City Point. As tired as he was, the "Railsplitter" managed to deftly cut a log in two with the boys in the Union camp. Two days later on March 25, the president was at the front viewing the results of the Confederate assault on Fort Stedman early that same morning.

General Lee had ordered the audacious full-scale assault as part of his plan to break out of Petersburg and lead his army to the Virginia–North Carolina border, where he thought he would unite with General Johnston in a force of close to one hundred thousand. Lee had finally convinced Jefferson Davis that the Confederate position at Petersburg was untenable and hoped, or desperately dreamed, that the new combined force might crush Sherman's army, then join with Confederate troops across the Mississippi and begin a new war. At worst, he thought, such a breakout would lead his army toward a food source and prolong the war for a time, perhaps winning better peace terms. Anticipating that Grant would soon begin his grand movement against the Confederate right—a move actually planned by Grant that same day for the twenty-ninth—he struck at Fort Stedman on the Union right. Fort Stedman stood close to Burnside's Crater, about 150 yards from the Confederate line. A slightly constructed earthwork, poorly maintained because it was constantly under fire, it had no value in itself but stood on the crest of an elevation called Hare's Hill, from which Lee figured he could pierce the Federal lines at the rear if he took the fort by surprise. From there his twenty thousand troops under General John B. Gordon could rush toward the Union military supply railroad Grant had constructed at City Point, one of the first such military railroads ever built. Ideally, this would cause Grant to panic and draw in both the left and right sides of his lines to protect the important railroad supply line, leaving Confederate generals Longstreet and Hill free to start southward without much opposition. Finally, the assaulting troops themselves would draw back suddenly and follow the others, giving all the Rebel troops a two-day start to join up with General Johnston before Grant could organize his army for pursuit.

It was an involved plan—basically relying on the Yankees to act almost as if they were in a trance—and employed specially chosen advance men who pretended to be Confederate deserters. At three o'clock in the morning these individual soldiers, followed by squad after squad of armed Rebels, began surrendering to Fort Stedman's pickets only fifty yards away from the fort. This was not unusual at the time, and the pickets thought little of it; but suddenly the "deserters" turned on the pickets and overpowered them, quietly sending them back to Confederate lines as prisoners. Meanwhile, as General Grant wrote, "our men [in the fort] were sleeping serenely, as if in great security."

At the same instant that the advance force captured Stedman's picket line, five thousand men in three strong columns emerged from the Confederate line and stealthily made their way toward the fort. With the pickets eliminated, the first column only had to make a rush of fifty yards to take Stedman completely by surprise, capturing all its sleepy five-hundred-man garrison. The second and third columns easily took the Union batteries on the left and right of the fort.

Lee's plan was working; the Rebels had made a gap one-quarter-mile wide into, though not through, the Union line. They even turned some of the Union guns upon the Yankees. But the support troops who were supposed to rush in and reinforce the three columns were for reasons unknown never pushed forward. Gordon's men were left unsupported and there just weren't enough of them to complete the plan. Union troops, rallying and changing position, forced the Confederates back to Fort Stedman, from which General Gordon withdrew when a Federal division attacked the fort at about 7:30. It only took about fifteen minutes more for the Federal line to be restored and the entire assault defeated. Many Confederates were taken prisoner and many were killed in the vicious cross fire while trying to get back to their own lines.

Lee's last great offensive chance—in fact, his last real offensive effort—was gone with the failure of the well-conceived, poorly executed plan. He rode dejectedly back from a crimson field where he had left some 4,000 killed, wounded, and captured—including about 10 percent of his infantry—compared with 1,150 Federal casualties. There was no open road to Johnston in his future. Things were darker now than they had ever been. The assault had not only won no time or ground for the Confederates, it had led to the Yankees carrying the Confederates' entrenched picket line—which, as Grant put it, "gave us but a short distance to charge over when our attack came to be made a few days later."

To Lincoln, looking at the dead and wounded of both sides huddled on the ground, the battle did not seem a victory. Here was none of the grandeur and sublimity of war others talked of. He was told that among the dead was a slight, frail, redheaded boy in gray. A bullet through his head, pale from his pain, he had not wanted to die. Crying, his last words were, "Mother, mother," repeated over and over. Perhaps the president remembered the Confederate boys sent to their death by General John Breckinridge, a former vice president of the United States, who had recently been appointed Confederate secretary of war. A year before, on May 14, 1864, Breckinridge had ordered 215 boy-soldiers from the Virginia Military Institute Cadet Corps into battle at New Market in the

Shenandoah. "They are only children," Breckinridge protested when an officer urged that he use the volunteer school boys, but after a moment, he gave the command: "Put the boys in and God forgive me for my orders." The eager youngsters helped carry the day, but 10 of the children died and 47 were wounded, some of them no more than fifteen, some possibly only fourteen. "What will be next—infants?" many may have thought, but the action was widely hailed as a glorious victory.

Lincoln would not have called it glorious or even a victory. While the surgeons and burial squads did their work now under a white flag of truce, the president's eyes filled with tears and he repeated that all-too-familiar phrase of the war, "Robbing the cradle and the grave." A guard with Lincoln later recalled: "I saw him ride over the battlefield . . . the man with the hole in his forehead and the man with both arms shot away lying accusing, before his eyes." Recalled a Union officer at the president's side, "He remarked that he had seen enough of the horrors of war, that he hoped this was the beginning of the end."

Four days later it would be. The day after the Stedman battle, Sheridan's cavalry from the Shenandoah crossed the James and swung wide around Lee's army, arriving unscathed at Harrison's Landing, swelling Grant's already far superior ranks to 125,000. "I fear now that it will be impossible to prevent a juncture between Grant and Sherman," Lee wrote to Jefferson Davis in Richmond, "nor do I deem it prudent that this army should maintain its position until the latter shall approach too near."

Lee was ready to pull out before Sherman came closer, but Grant attacked first, early on the morning of March 29, sending Sheridan with a great force of ten thousand horse soldiers and three divisions of infantry under General Warren to envelop the weak Confederate right flank southwest of Petersburg. Turning the Rebel right flank would threaten the Confederates' escape route to the west and deprive Lee of an essential supply of food for his men if the Southside Railroad was taken. Lee, anticipating the move, stripped his lines of all but ten thousand men—who were left to guard over ten miles of works—and late that night hastily sent out a huge column under Generals George Pickett and Fitzhugh Lee to meet the Union forces.

At the crossing of Quaker and Boydton Roads, running north to the Confederate works, the Union column under General Warren sharply clashed with Confederates pushed out from their line and forced them back into their entrenchments. Each side suffered over four hundred dead and wounded. Meanwhile, the Confederate column marched quicktime trying to reach the right flank fifteen miles away. Lee feared it would be too late. But torrential rains bogged down Warren's advance. The roads the Yankees advanced on were fit for the navy at points, were mortar beds and quicksand at others; men waded through mud up to their knees, horses had to be pulled out by their halters, heavy artillery had to be hauled over miles of quickly built log corduroy road. The route the Confederate column traveled was better, enabling it to make up for its late start and reach White Oak Road, just beyond the end of the entrenched Confederate line, on the morning of March 31.

Outnumbered five to one in the area, the Confederate troops fought valiantly and succeeded in halting the Union advance at White Oak Road and Dinwiddie Court House after the rain relented that morning. But General Pickett felt that the Federal force was far too large for his men to handle and fell back in the heavy rain to Five Forks, a retreat from the defenses of Petersburg that could make Lee's evacuation a certainty.

Lee realized this and on the morning of April 1 ordered General Pickett to "hold Five Forks at all hazards." The Confederate troops dug in deep at the essential crossroads, trying to reinforce the right flank on the siege line. Singing "Dixie" and "Annie Laurie" as they worked, they seemed in good spirits; but they were battered, tired, underfed soldiers, and their leadership in the field at this point left something to be desired. Pickett, Fitzhugh Lee, and several other hungry Southern generals—the entire Rebel high command—were said to be enjoying a leisurely repast of fresh shad that General Thomas Rosser had caught and baked far back in the rear just before Sheridan and Wallace attacked that afternoon, making them late to the field and rendering them unable to direct their troops properly at the very beginning of the Five Forks battle. They apparently thought it was too late in the day for a Yankee assault. Thus Warren's delays, the cause of his dismissal by Sheridan later, may actually have helped the Union cause, lulling Pickett into a false sense of security.

According to Grant, when the dismounted cavalry of Sheridan first went over the Confederate parapets at Five Forks, "the two armies were mingled together for a time in such a manner that it was almost a question which one was going to demand the surrender of the other." Sheridan's troops attacked from the front while Warren's infantry corps hit at the left flank, crushing the enemy. Sheridan himself spurred his charger Rienzi from regiment to regiment; he was all over the field, leaping earthworks, urging his troops on. A mounted Federal band joined in the encouragement, playing lively tunes until its instruments were destroyed by enemy bullets. Here was the magnetic Sheridan "in full swing and color," General Joshua Lawrence Chamberlain wrote, "carrying the pulse and will of men . . . transforming his men into his own mind and will."

Chamberlain himself, already a great hero of the Republic, played a striking role in the action. The distinguished Maine college professor, who spoke seven languages, was as brave as he was brilliant. Fighting in twenty battles during the war, he was wounded six times, twice so badly that the newspapers reported his death. Chamberlain would later win the Congressional Medal of Honor for his heroism at Gettysburg's Little Round Top. In 1864, Grant promoted him to brigadier general on the battlefield at Petersburg, wanting him to have the rank before he died from his wounds. But he didn't die; nor did he die at Quaker Road on March 29, when he was badly wounded leading his troops in an advance that helped make Sheridan's victory at Five Forks possible. At one point, dazed from his wounds, his left arm useless, his horse shot from under him, he actually pretended to be a Confederate general and led troops into the Federal lines, where they were taken prisoner. The brave Down-Easter then managed to hold Quaker Road with his men until Union artillery came up: "Now they come with headlong speed, horses smoking, battery thundering . . . into action while the earth flew beneath their wheels—magnificent, the shining terrible Napoleons." After the "splendid and terrible" victory full of killing that night, this teacher of language and religion wondered, "Was it God's command we heard, or His forgiveness we must forever implore?"

There, at Quaker Road, and for all the final days of the war Chamberlain fought brilliantly and valiantly, despite two cracked ribs, but even he could not rival Sheridan, who seemed like the spirit of war itself. With no regard for the furious fire at Five Forks, Sheridan took a red and white battle flag and waved it in the air, bullets riddling it as he led his troops forward over the swampy ground. "Come on, men!" shouted this epitome of a fighting general. "Go at 'em with a will! They're getting ready to run now! Now go for them! The cowardly scoundrels can't fight such brave men as mine! We'll get the twist on 'em boys, there won't be a grease spot left of 'em!" One time he saw a man shot in the jugular vein. "I'm killed!" the soldier cried. "No, you're not hurt a bit!" Sheridan the foreman, the driver, ordered. "Pick up your gun and get in there and fight!" So forceful was the command that the soldier, blood spurting from his throat, picked up his musket and charged forward a few yards before he fell dead of his wound.

Another time Sheridan encountered a wounded soldier heading toward the rear. "They've hit you, have they?" he cried. "Don't give it up just yet. Give the bloody rebels a round or two to remember you by. Down three or four of the rascals before you go to the hospital!"

Correspondent Cadwallader wrote that "no living soldier was ever more terrible in battle" than Sheridan. "Shoot every man down like a dog that tries to skulk from duty!" he shouted to his men on the field. In Cadwallader's opinion, "America never produced his equal for inspiring an army and leading them into battle. Absolutely fearless himself . . . he always raised the courage and faith of others to the level of his own. . . . [He was] flaming, fiery, omnipresent, and well-nigh omnipotent."

"Bullets were humming like a swarm of bees around our heads," one of Sheridan's officers said later, "and shells were cracking through the ranks. All this time Sheridan was dashing from one point of the line to another, waving his flag, shaking his fist, encouraging, entreating, threatening, praying, swearing, the very incarnation of battle."

There is no doubt about Sheridan's bravery that night, but another hero of the battle was General Warren, whose horse was shot from under him and whose aide was killed beside him as he led his troops forward through a sharp fusillade, inspiring his men to break through. Warren, however, got no thanks from Sheridan, who relieved him of his command for allegedly moving too slowly, a charge Grant had made against him at Spotsylvania and Petersburg. Sheridan's main allegation was that "General Warren did not exert himself to get up his corps as rapidly as he might have done, and his manner gave me the impression that he wished the sun to go down before dispositions for the attack could be completed." In truth, Warren did form his divisions without unnecessary delay, considering the situation, and he was cleared seventeen years later by a board of inquiry of this and most of Sheridan's other charges— but three months after, as Cadwallader wrote, his disgrace had "driven him to a premature grave." Why Sheridan made the charges still remains something of a mystery, unless it was because he was piqued about Warren's tardiness on several other occasions or annoyed that Grant had sent Warren to assist him, instead of General Wright, in the first place. In any case, after a brilliant, decisive victory, made by perfectly executing Sheridan's plans, Warren—an excellent if too conservative general who had been delayed by mud, high waters, and other factors beyond his control—received among the strangest orders ever received by a victorious general: "Major General Warren, commanding Fifth Corps, is relieved from duty, and will report at once for orders to Lieutenant General Grant, commanding armies U.S. By command of Major General Sheridan." When he meekly asked Sheridan if he wouldn't reconsider this harsh order that would certainly ruin his military career,

Sheridan shouted, "Reconsider, hell! I don't reconsider my decisions! Obey the order!"

Warren had helped win the victory before he was dismissed. And a brilliant, decisive victory it was. As Grant recalled, "The enemy finally broke and ran in every direction, some six-thousand prisoners, besides artillery and small arms in large quantities, falling into our hands." This figure is disputed, and there is no record of the Confederate casualties, but at least half of the ragged Confederate force of ten thousand was captured, most of them by Warren's seventeen thousand troops, who did the bulk of the Union fighting. The Federals had an estimated one thousand casualties. Not only had the Yankees seized the Five Forks area and split Pickett from the main Confederate army, they had almost completely encircled Petersburg south of the Appomattox River. One Rebel general called Five Forks "the Waterloo of the Confederacy." A jubilant Grant saw a chance to "end matters right here" and immediately ordered a full-scale assault on the severely weakened Confederate siege lines for the next day. President Lincoln, waving captured battle flags Grant sent to him aboard the *River Queen*, almost dancing with joy, cried out "Victory! This means victory! This *is* victory!"

General Lee, on receiving news of the rout, lost control of himself, which he rarely did, and displayed real anger in the field. The next time he would lead the troops himself, he said sharply, and he ordered one of his generals to have all stragglers, officers as well as enlisted men, gathered up and put under guard. But he knew there wouldn't be any next time as he sat down to telegraph Secretary of War John C. Breckinridge that he would immediately have to evacuate Richmond because Union troops were forcing the Confederates to abandon the defense of Petersburg. A copy of the telegram, which arrived at the Confederate War Department at 10:45 A.M., was delivered to Jefferson Davis at St. Paul's Episcopal Church, where Davis was attending Sunday services. The minister had just read Zechariah 2:13—"The Lord is in his holy temple; let all the earth keep silence before him"—to his kneeling congregation. Then the Reverend Charles Minnigerode looked up to see a sexton come down the aisle and tap Davis on the shoulder, handing him the message Lee had so long imagined sending and Davis had so long pretended he would never receive. Informing Davis that Grant had broken the Confederate lines, it ended: "I advise that all preparations be made for leaving Richmond tonight. I will advise you later, according to circumstances." President Davis, his face gray with pallor, rose from his knees, hat in hand, and walking quickly, quietly, but rather unsteadily, left the church.

The Federal grand assault had begun at daybreak; it was 4:40 A.M. when the signal gun sounded. The night before, bands on both sides of the lines had played and soldiers sang, fraternizing as they did many times during the yearlong siege—Southerners belting out "Dixie," the Yankees "Hail Columbia"—boys competing with each other. Now they would compete to the death.

Through the gray, dense fog, over fourteen thousand Federals steadily advanced along the lines. For the first time, balls from Union batteries—closer to the city now—crashed through the streets of Petersburg. Preceding the attack had come the heaviest bombardment of the war, including even Gettysburg. Miles of cannon, field guns, and mortars—every gun the Union had—relentlessly blasted the Rebels along the whole fifty-three-mile line, including north of the James. "It was a stream of living fire," a Union soldier wrote later, "the shells screamed through the air in a semi-circle of flame." It looked like a terrible lightning storm to some, like the sky lit by the aurora borealis to others. The ground shook and shuddered.

Thin as the Rebel lines were—each soldier had to defend a five-foot length—the assault by the Second, Ninth, Sixth, and Twenty-fourth Corps was hardly a walk in the park. As at Cold Harbor, men with their names on slips of paper pinned to their uniforms, their last letters home safe in their pockets, ran into blistering fire from the Confederate trenches. "Well, goodbye, boys—this means death," attackers were heard to say as they advanced. In little more than ten minutes, over twelve hundred men in General Wright's Sixth Corps were dead. "Tell my wife I love her," one soldier requested. "After all this," a dying veteran managed. "The cards beat the players," quipped still another. Shooting, stabbing, and clubbing, Yankee soldiers leaped into the elaborately designed trenches, the labyrinth of bombproof shelters, rifle pits, and batteries. In hand-to-hand fighting men were bayoneted, their heads smashed with rifle butts. Would this be another Cold Harbor, a Union slaughter? Men began to wonder, advancing into the heavy Confederate fire sweeping the field. The unlucky were killed in an instant; Bibles and playing cards stopped bullets for others. General John Parke's men got caught in the Confederate works to the east and couldn't move any further, suffering over one thousand casualties while holding off the Rebels. But suddenly the weakened Confederate lines broke in several places before the huge wedge of Union troops. The Federals "saw daylight." To the west came the most crucial break—Wright's men seized Confederate entrenchments around Fort Fisher after vicious hand-to-hand fighting. A brigade held the captured trenches while the rest advanced into the open, where they joined with linebreakers from General Ord's command and elsewhere, moving toward Petersburg, wildly shouting, tossing their caps in the air. "The Rebels were swept away and scattered like chaff before a tornado," an Eleventh Corps officer recalled. The Union drive was successful almost everywhere; Lee's line was now broken in half.

It was about this time, 7 A.M., that one of Lee's most valued lieutenants, General Ambrose Powell (A. P.) Hill, was killed. Watching the battle from Petersburg, Lee had turned to Hill and said, "How is this, General? Your men are giving way." Hill rode off with a single aide to check the situation and encountered an advance patrol of two Union soldiers in a small woods or cornfield outside the city. "We must take them," Hill told his aide, but the two Pennsylvanians extended their rifles. "If you fire, you'll be swept to hell," the aide bluffed, "our men are here—surrender!" "Surrender!" Hill cried, but the two Yankees fired. Hill died, shot through the heart. The legendary general had fought in almost all the great battles of the war. Southern poet Daniel B. Lucas later wrote of him: "'Twas time to go, for all was gone— / 'Twas time to die, for all was done!" Said Lee, tears in his eyes, on hearing of Hill's death: "He is at rest now and we who are left are the ones to suffer."

By morning's end Grant was so elated—a rare emotion for him to show—that he penned a quick letter to his wife:

> I am now writing from far inside what was the Rebel fortifications this morning but what are ours now. . . . Altogether this has been one of the greatest victories of the war. Greatest because it is over what the Rebels have always regarded as their most invincible army and the one used for the defense of their capital. We may have some more hard work but I hope not.

Grant's elation meant Lee's depression, and the Gray Fox must have remembered his remark to an aide after Five Forks: "This is a sad business, colonel. It has happened as I told them in Richmond it would happen. The line has stretched until it is broken." Now the long line was broken in pieces and would never be put together again. Lee's last hope was that his men would hold a number of inner fortifications until he could escape by crossing the Appomattox River, the only route left to him. At first it didn't look like this was going to happen. Union forces were winning skirmishes everywhere. At Gravelly Ford. At Scott's Crossroads. Columns under General Nelson Miles struck Confederate troops at Sutherland's Station; overrunning the Rebel left flank there at the Ocean Methodist Church, they scattered the defenders and took possession of the Southside Railroad, Lee's last supply line into Petersburg. But the Sutherland Rebels did hold their position until almost dusk and obstinate Confederate troops were holding out at Fort Gregg, an enclosed work outside of Petersburg. Some Rebel commanders told their men to fight to the death. Colonel Theodore Lyman wrote home of a die-hard Confederate captain who ordered his men to surrender to no one: "He himself fought to the last, and was killed with the butt end of a musket, and most of his men were slain in the work."

At Fort Gregg, Maryland captain John Chew's men faced Union troops from General John Gibbon's corps. Fort Gregg was a mixed garrison of troops from Virginia, Louisiana, North Carolina, and Mississippi. The fort, situated next to Fort Whitworth, stood in the path of the Federals marching on Petersburg from the rear. It had to be held long enough to give Lee time to make his planned escape that night. At about one o'clock Union troops assaulted the fort, which stood some two hundred yards behind the lines, but the Rebel fire was so fierce and accurate that they were forced to withdraw. Again a charge was made, the Union troops suffering great casualties in the fusillade that met them. Still they swarmed up the parapet, brave assailants met by stubborn defenders who drove them back. Three more charges were made through the afternoon, each featuring intense hand-to-hand combat, the Rebels even throwing rocks. Finally, the Union's superior numbers told in the "desperate battle," as Grant called it. The Union troops took the crest and carried the fort, the Rebels in nearby Fort Whitworth immediately evacuating. In buying Lee time to evacuate, only 30 of the fort's 250 defenders survived. Over 500 of the Union assailants lay dead or wounded.

Lee had his chance to escape now, but "with that Sunday's sun," a reporter wrote, "the hope of the Rebels set, never to rise again." By nightfall all of the Confederate line had broken under Grant's incessant hammering, never to be repaired. The Federal troops celebrated as they moved on, looting tents and huts, one man wrapping a Rebel flag around himself like a toga, another donning the coat of a fallen Confederate officer. All around them were Confederate dead, barefooted thirteen-year-old boys beside barefooted old men. Captured were former strongholds like Fort Mahone and Sedgwick, respectively called Fort Damnation and Fort Hell for the savage unrelenting fire they had poured on Union troops over the long siege. Petersburg itself had been entered at 4:30 P.M., when the First Michigan Regiment raised its colors over the courthouse. Over 63,000 Federals and 18,000 Confederates had participated in the daylong battle, the Union suffering 3,361 casualties and Southern casualties unrecorded but probably totaling over 2,000. Thousands of Confederate soldiers were captured—not less than 12,000, according to Grant.

The occupation of Petersburg, April 1865. From *Harper's Pictorial History of the Civil War,* 1866.

That evening of April 2 President Lincoln, who had watched some of the fighting at the front from a safe distance, telegraphed General Grant congratulations on his great victory: "Allow me to tender to you, and all with you, the nation's grateful thanks for this additional and magnificent success." Grant had invited the president to visit with him at Petersburg in the morning.

With Lee stumbling west in retreat on the far side of the Appomattox River, Lincoln came to meet Grant at the home of Thomas Wallace on Market Street, which Grant had sequestered and made his temporary headquarters. According to one of Grant's aides, Lincoln "dismounted in the street and came in through the front gate with long and rapid strides, his face beaming with delight. He seized General Grant's hand as the general stepped forward to greet him, and stood shaking it for some time and pouring out his thanks and congratulations. . . . I doubt whether Mr. Lincoln ever experienced a happier moment in his life."

This did not stop the house owner's young son from pointing at the president and indignantly asking his father why he let "that man" come into his home. "I think it would not do to try to stop a man from coming in who has fifty thousand men at his back," his father replied.

Grant had military matters on his mind while he talked with President Lincoln. "As we would occasionally look around the corner we could see the streets and the Appomattox bottom . . . packed with the Confederate army," he wrote in his *Memoirs*. "I did not have artillery brought up, because I was sure Lee was trying to make his escape, and I wanted to push immediately in pursuit. At all events I had not the heart to turn the artillery upon such a mass of defeated and fleeing men, and I hoped to capture them soon." This does not sound much like the man some called "Butcher Grant." It is also early evidence of the change in Grant from the general who espoused total war to the compassionate victor he was to become.

Sitting there quietly with Lincoln, Grant must have mused about the encounter he had that morning with a man he strongly suspected of being an enemy agent. He later wrote:

[The man represented himself as] an engineer of the Army of Northern Virginia. He said that Lee had for some time been at work preparing a strong enclosed entrenchment, into which he would throw his army when forced out of Petersburg, and fight his final battle there; that he was actually at that time drawing his troops from Richmond and falling back into this prepared work. [The man's] statement was made to General Meade and myself. . . . I had already given orders for a movement up the south side of the Appomattox River for the purpose of heading off Lee; but Meade was so impressed by this man's story that he thought we ought to cross the Appomattox there at once and move against Lee in his new position. I knew that Lee was no fool, as he would have been to have put himself and his army between two formidable streams like the James and Appomattox Rivers, and between two such armies as those of the Potomac and James. . . . It would only have been a question of days . . . if he had taken the position assigned to him by the so-called engineer, when he could have been obliged to surrender his army. Such is one of the ruses resorted to in war to deceive your antagonist. My judgement was that Lee would necessarily have to evacuate Richmond, and that the only course for him to pursue would be to follow the Danville Road.

For about an hour and a half Grant and Lincoln sat on the porch of the Wallace house waiting for word that Richmond had fallen. Newly freed slaves filled the small yard, where they stood staring with awe at their great—supernatural to some—liberators. When no news came, Grant, all business, apologized and left the president, riding off to organize his men to pursue and destroy Lee's retreating army. Lincoln remained for a while in a strangely silent Petersburg, where not a woman was seen in the streets and the only men—aside from the jubilant Union Tenth Corps, led into Petersburg by a unit of black soldiers—were the old and ailing. Then he rode back to City Point, still waiting for word from Richmond.

Chaos had reigned in Richmond ever since President Davis received Lee's momentous telegram in church the previous day. On that quiet Sunday morning, which a Federal officer near the city described as "one of the most perfect days that had dawned on earth since the creation," word soon spread quickly about the evacuation. Wrote Alfred Guernsey a year later: "Never since the Babylonians learned that Cyrus had penetrated their walls, or when the dwellers in New Carthage assembled in the theatre were told that the Vandals of Genseric were upon them, was there a greater surprise than at Richmond on that bright April Sabbath when it was made known that within a few hours the city was to fall into the hands of the Yankees." Most people just wouldn't believe it. *Richmond Examiner* editor Edward A. Pollard wrote later:

> The report of a great misfortune soon traverses a city without the aid of printed bulletins. But that of the evacuation of Richmond fell upon many incredulous ears. . . . There were few people in the streets; no vehicles disturbed the quiet of the Sabbath; the sound of the churchgoing bells rose into the cloudless sky and floated on the blue tide of the beautiful day. How was it

Confederate president Jefferson Davis at the start of
the Civil War. From *Meet General Grant*, 1929.

possible to imagine that in the next twenty-four hours this
powerful city, a secure possession for four years, was at last to
succumb?

A tight-lipped Davis had left the church and walked quickly to
his office, where he studied Lee's latest telegram, the third of six
he sent to War Secretary Breckinridge or Davis that day. This one
read in part: "I THINK IT IS ABSOLUTELY NECESSARY THAT WE SHOULD
ABANDON OUR POSITION TONIGHT. I HAVE GIVEN ALL THE NECESSARY OR-
DERS ON THE SUBJECT TO THE TROOPS, AND THE OPERATION, THOUGH DIF-
FICULT, I HOPE WILL BE PERFORMED SUCCESSFULLY." Davis wrote back
objecting to such a quick evacuation. Many arms and supplies
would be lost to the enemy, the Confederate president protested;
but Lee, who had warned him for months of the coming storm, did

not even answer his telegram. He angrily tore it to bits, telling an aide, "I am sure I gave him sufficient notice!" He repeated his dire warning in a message to Breckinridge:

> IT IS ABSOLUTELY NECESSARY THAT WE SHOULD ABANDON OUR POSITION TONIGHT, OR RUN THE RISK OF BEING CUT OFF IN THE MORNING. I HAVE TAKEN EVERY PRECAUTION THAT I CAN TO MAKE THE MOVEMENT SUCCESSFUL. IT WILL BE A DIFFICULT OPERATION, BUT I HOPE NOT IMPRACTICABLE. PLEASE GIVE ALL ORDERS THAT YOU FIND NECESSARY IN AND ABOUT RICHMOND. THE TROOPS WILL ALL BE DIRECTED TO AMELIA COURT HOUSE.

By 4:00 P.M. the mayor of Richmond announced that the Confederate government was moving to Danville, 140 miles south, where Davis thought Lee would proceed with his army after reaching Amelia. Davis remained in his office, consulting with other Confederate officials, ordering documents to be burned, others to be packed, deciding who in the government would go, how they would get there. Evacuation was a fact, not a rumor now, no good news having come from Lee. "As the day wore on," Pollard recalled, "clatter and bustle denoted the progress of the evacuation and convinced those who had been incredulous of its reality. The disorder increased each hour. The streets were thronged with fugitives making their way to the railroad depots; pale women and little shoeless children struggled in the crowd; oaths and blasphemous shouts smote the air."

Davis left his office at about 5:00 P.M. and walked to the executive mansion, where he and his wife packed a few personal possessions, heading for the Richmond & Danville Railroad depot two hours later. Hundreds of people crowded the station—some with money, jewels, and gold sewn in their clothes, others carrying all their valuables in suitcases they could barely lift, many more with just the clothes upon their backs. All pleaded to get on board any train south, but most were turned away and had to return home or join the refugee columns streaming out of the city. Slave dealer Robert Lumpkin, trying to leave with fifty chained slaves, was refused passage and had to turn his coffled slaves loose in the street—at a loss, he claimed, of $50,000. Davis himself waited to

This Currier and Ives print shows the evacuation of Richmond across the James River on April 2, 1865. From the Library of Congress.

leave on his special train until eleven o'clock that night, he and his cabinet staying until the last possible minute on the chance of hearing good news from General Lee. Again nothing but bad news came. They finally departed, "silence reigning over the fugitives" until the Rebel "government on wheels" reached Danville, Virginia, the next afternoon.

"Blue-black is our horizon, a storm of woe impending," Mrs. Chesnut wrote in her diary. "Dismay reigned supreme," recalled Confederate captain Clement Sulivane, who directed the evacuation of trains, wagons, buggies, and people on foot heading into "a quiet night, with its millions of stars." But it was a night quiet only up in the heavens. Down in Richmond in the night streets, Guernsey wrote:

> Disorder grew fiercer and fiercer till it rose to tumult and riot. All the rascality of the city seemed let loose, and surged around every spot where there was a chance of pillage. There were numerous stores and warehouses filled with goods worth a prince's ransom. These were broken open and their contents borne away with scarcely a pretense of opposition. The poorest scoundrel in the city was for a moment a richer man than he had ever hoped to be.

Richmond had suffered death and great hunger for over four years, which explained in large part why some good citizens finally joined the rabble, "the vilest of the vile," looting the city. "It's every man for himself and the devil for us all tonight!" one looter cried as the mob swept through the streets. The ranks of rampaging men and women included former masters and former slaves, thieves, prostitutes, and army deserters. To these looters were added convicts freed from the city penitentiary when all the prison guards there were ordered to help herd Union prisoners of war out of Richmond from the infamous Libby Prison. Nothing escaped the pillagers. One old woman pushed a sofa down the street. Warehouses were raided for their huge quantities of flour, meat, sugar, and coffee; people were enraged that these foods had never (for some still unknown reason) been distributed to them or to Lee's starving army. But shoe stores, clothing stores, haberdashers, even candy stores were also cleaned out. "It was finally . . . proposed to maintain order in the city by two regiments of militia, to destroy every drop of liquor in all warehouses and stores and to establish a patrol through the night," Pollard recalled. But as quick as the militiamen broke into the streets, looters were beside them grabbing casks and cases of the best Southern whiskey. Saloon keepers and store owners gave up trying to resist both militia and mob. The menacing, snarling mob fought among itself for the best pickings. Some who couldn't carry cases away, or were so drunk they could barely carry themselves, filled pitchers, buckets, boots, and hats with liquor. They even knelt down and lapped it up from the gutters. Then, Pollard wrote,

> the militia slipped through the hands of their officers, many joining the rabble, and in a short while the whole city was plunged into mad confusion and indescribable horrors. It was an extraordinary night; disorder, pillage, shouts, and revelry. . . . In the now dimly lighted city could be seen black masses of people . . . swaying to and fro in whatever momentary passion possessed them. . . . Confusion became worse confounded; the sidewalks were sparkling with broken glass; stores were entered at pleasure and stripped from top to bottom; yells of drunken men, shouts of roving pillagers, wild cries of distress from women and children filled the air and made night hideous.

New horrors came with morning. During the night the departing rear guard of Lee's army, commanded by General Richard Ewell, followed foolish orders and torched four tobacco warehouses, trying to keep the valuable tobacco out of Yankee hands. These and warehouses of army stores were burned despite the objections of Richmond's mayor Joseph Mayo, who realized the consequences. The great blaze combined with flames from fires spread by looters or started by the torches they carried; it spread unchecked—there were no firefighters to halt its progress—claiming hundreds of buildings as the wind hurled it along its path. More warehouses went up; so did the Gallego flour mill, the largest in the world and the tallest building in the city. The red army of fire whipped through street after street in Richmond's business district, claiming banks, insurance companies, newspaper offices, hotels, and private residences. No effort was made to stop its progress. To the roar and crackle of the flames were added the explosions of Confederate arsenals stocked with shells and cartridges, the shells exploding high in the air and the cartridges rattling like musket volleys fighting some great battle of their own. Powder magazines went off with deafening roars, houses rocked like ships at sea in a storm. Ten thousand shells were bursting every minute, one eyewitness recalled, the city wrapped in a cloud of black smoke. It was as if all the world's artillery was locked in battle, another observer reported. When the three-quarters of a million shells in the main arsenal went off, the explosion shook the city with earthquake force, ripping doors off hinges miles away.

To this madness was added the earthshaking explosions of the magazines of the Confederate ironclads, which Admiral Raphael Semmes ordered to be blown up on the north side of the James River. Finally, the last bridge out of Richmond was blown by the last of Lee's retreating soldiers.

Editor Pollard, hardly a great fan of Davis, recalled:

> In this mad fire, this wild, unnecessary destruction of their property, the citizens of Richmond had a fitting souvenir of the imprudence and recklessness of the departing Administration. Morning broke on a scene never to be forgotten. . . . The smoke

and glare of fire mingled with the golden beams of the rising sun. . . . The fire was reaching to whole blocks of buildings. . . . Its roar sounded in the ears; it leaped from street to street. Pillagers were still busy at their looting, and in the hot breath of the fire were figures as of demons contending for prey.

The Rebels were all gone at daylight and the Yankees faced a city of flames as they prepared to enter Richmond that Monday morning. Every unit, every man wanted to be the first to set foot in the former capital of the Confederacy; one officer marveled that so few were killed in the excitement. Luckily, the Confederates retreated so hastily that they had no time to pull out the small flags that marked the numerous torpedoes, or land mines, buried along their line. The torpedoes were carefully removed by the Federal advance guard; only one Union soldier lost his life to the minefields before Richmond.

Who the first was to enter the city would be a subject of controversy for many years, almost as much argued as who fired the first shot at Fort Sumter. But most witnesses say that it was a squad of Massachusetts cavalry, forty men in all, from General Godfrey Weitzel's command who rode in first, led by Majors Atherton Stevens and Eammons Graves. These scouts trotted leisurely down the streets at about 7 A.M., buildings ablaze and collapsing on each side of them, and were the first to hear the fearful cry "the Yankees have come!" recorded in Mrs. McGuire's diary. "I saw them unfurl a tiny flag," wrote Mrs. Mary Fontaine, "and I sank on my knees, and the bitter, bitter tears came in a torrent." "Oh, it is too awful to remember," cried another woman. No one resisted the Yankees, the crowd of looters fleeing down side streets, and they rode untouched into the public square. There Major Stevens raised the first Yankee flags—guidons of the Fourth Massachusetts Cavalry—from the Capitol. Soon after, these were taken down and the Stars and Stripes was raised in their place.

About fifteen minutes later General Weitzel led an unbroken line of troops up Main Street. A regiment of thundering black Union cavalry "as if moved by an irrepressible impulse . . . drew their sabres and broke into wild shouts," Guernsey noted. But there was no violence except for the flames around them. Federal bands played "Yankee Doodle," "Rally Round the Flag," "The Battle Cry of Freedom," and the old favorite "The Girl I Left Behind Me." Former slaves, "completely crazed," virtually the only welcomers, shouted that the day of jubilee had finally come; they handed their liberators food and drink, danced and sang, offered to carry Union packs and rifles. "They rushed around us, hugged and kissed our legs and horses, shouting hallelujah and glory," Weitzel remembered. "Sweeter music never reached the human ear" than the news of their freedom. "These hands do no more slave work," cried one old woman.

At 8:15 Weitzel accepted Mayor Mayo's surrender at City Hall and quickly got down to work, deeply affected by the terrified crowd of burned-out, homeless people huddling in the public square with their saved possessions, ranging from bedding and children's toys to costly furniture and mirrors. He ordered young Colonel Edward Ripley to take charge of the city and to stop the conflagration and the general pillage still going on, giving Ripley *"carte blanche* to do it your own way." Ripley issued immediate orders instructing the occupying army that its primary duty was to save the city. All looters, civilian or soldier, would be summarily punished; no soldier would enter any private home uninvited; all law-abiding citizens would be treated with respect. Ripley even saw to it that special guards, including a black cavalryman, and an ambulance were stationed outside the Franklin Street house of the ailing Mrs. Robert E. Lee, whose arthritis had forced her to stay behind, confined to her rolling chair. A year later, the Reverend John Leyburn praised the conduct of the Federal troops in his *Harper's* magazine article, "The Fall of Richmond": "Very agreeable was the disappointment at the liberation of the victorious army. The fact was that with few exceptions, the troops behaved astonishingly well, and were remarkably courteous and respectful. Some cases of outrage were committed in the suburbs, but every attempt of the sort in the city of which I heard was followed by condign punishment." There was to be no repeat of Atlanta or Columbia here. Libby Prison soon filled to overflowing with both Rebel and Yankee looters.

But Leyburn also wrote of the "sea of flames" around him, the "showers of blazing sparks," the "thunder of exploding shells" that "might have awakened the dead" as "the earth seemed to writhe in agony." The great Richmond fire still had to be fought. Detachments of Union troops, supplemented by every able-bodied man found on the streets, were assigned to fight the blaze and the city fire department was finally pressed into action. For over six hours they fought the conflagration in the intense heat, pumping the fire engines, forming bucket brigades, and demolishing buildings to create firebreaks the flames couldn't leap over. It was impossible to extinguish the holocaust, but these defensive actions at least contained the fire until the wind shifted that afternoon, sweeping the flames back toward the devastated area where they had originated and where the fire all but died for want of fuel. By that time fully one-third of Richmond had been destroyed, including the entire business section. The Capitol had been looted, valueless Confederate bonds of huge denominations blowing across the lawn. Some nine hundred buildings ranging from homes to banks and factories were burned to the ground or survived as nothing but gutted shells. So great was the devastation that *Richmond Examiner* editor Pollard, wandering around the city, could scarcely tell where he was.

To this smoldering ruin of a city the next day, April 4, came President Lincoln and his son Tad. They were guarded by just the president's bodyguard, four officers, and twelve sailors with rifles. According to most accounts, the crowd that greeted Lincoln consisted only of freed slaves and Union soldiers. One former slave knelt at the president's feet, calling him the Messiah and Father Abraham. "Don't kneel to me," Lincoln told him. "You must kneel to God only and thank him for your freedom." But the old man explained himself, saying he'd been "so many years in the desert without water, it's mighty pleasant to be lookin' at last on our spring of life."

The freed blacks were jubilant, singing, dancing in the streets, throwing themselves on the ground, casting hats and clothing, but

President Lincoln visiting Richmond after its fall. From *Harper's Pictorial History of the Civil War*, 1866.

no whites greeted the president except one strange young woman with an American flag draped over her shoulders. In fact, Lincoln's bodyguard William Crook later recalled that he saw a white man in a second-floor window pointing what seemed to be a gun at the president. Crook quickly stepped in front of Lincoln and the would-be assassin was just as quickly gone. All of the little parade to the center of Richmond was by foot and nerves were unsteady, but Lincoln remained calm and imperturbable. Reporter Charles Coffin wrote:

> No carriage was to be had, so the President, leading his son Tad, walked over to General Weitzel's headquarters—formerly Jeff Davis's mansion, the White House of the Confederacy. The walk was long and the President halted a moment to rest. "May de good Lord bless you, President Linkum!" said an old Negro, removing his hat and bowing, with tears of joy rolling down his cheeks. The President removed his own hat and bowed in silence. It was a bow which upset the forms, laws, customs and ceremonies of centuries of slavery.

President Lincoln smiled, and then as always his face saddened when he glimpsed more of the destruction, the hundreds of homeless people squatting on the city streets. Inside the mansion all that was left of the Confederacy was the Davis's little dog. Entering Jefferson Davis's office, Lincoln sat in the Confederate president's chair, stretching out his long legs, haggard and weary but laughing, almost president of all the United States again, apparently giving no thought to his possible assassin, thoroughly enjoying himself while out on the crimson fields of Virginia Grant pursued Lee to the end. It was to be one of the last of Lincoln's great pleasures in life. In eleven days he would be dead of another assassin's bullet. He had dreamed of it a few days before at City Point:

> Before me was a catafalque, on which rested a corpse wrapped in funeral vestments. Around it were stationed soldiers who were acting as guards; and there was a throng of people, some gazing mournfully upon the corpse, whose face was covered, others weeping pitifully. "Who is dead in the White House?" I demanded of one of the soldiers. "The President," was his answer; "he was killed by an assassin!" Then came a loud burst of grief from the crowd, which awoke me from my dream.

5

The Last Long March: Westward to Appomattox

Resuming, marching, even in the darkness marching . . .
The unknown road still marching.

    —Walt Whitman, "A March in the Ranks Hard-Prest,
    and the Road Unknown," 1865

O~N THE DARK, MOONLESS NIGHT~ of April 2 and into the next morning, while the city was burning, General Lee's exhausted Army of Northern Virginia escaped by five different routes from Richmond and Petersburg. Lee himself led the main force of less than fifteen thousand infantry. "Fighting all day, marching all night, with exhaustion and hunger claiming their victims at every mile of the march, with charges of infantry at the rear and of cavalry on the flanks, it seemed the war god had turned loose all his furies to revel in havoc," wrote General Gordon, commanding Lee's rear guard, remembering how he urged his men on.

The Southern troops were demoralized even before they began the last desperate march. Before his battalion, stationed in the James River defenses, left Richmond at midnight on April 2, Major Robert Stiles had tried to calm and strengthen his men by reading from the Soldier's Psalm, the Ninety-first: "Thou shall not be afraid for the terror by night, nor for the arrow that flieth by day;

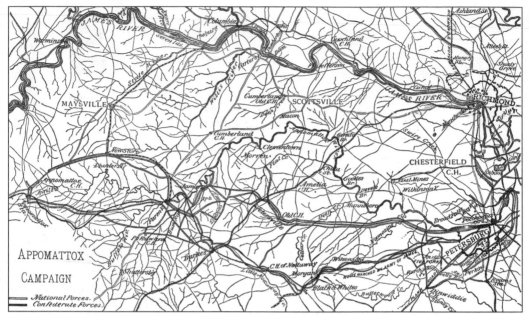

Map of the Appomattox campaign. From *Personal Memoirs of U. S. Grant*, 1886.

. . . A thousand shall fall at thy side, and ten thousand at thy right hand; but it shall not come nigh thee." But he had never seen the troops so anxious: "Their blanched faces and staring eyes turned backward upon me spoke volumes of nervous demoralization. . . . I felt that a hare might shatter the column."

Stiles's battalion had just crossed the James when one after another Admiral Semmes's ironclads exploded. "It seemed as if the very dome of heaven would be shattered down upon us," he recalled years later. "Earth and air and the black sky glared in the lurid light. Columns and towers and pinnacles of flame shot upward to an amazing height, from which, on all sides, the ignited shells . . . burst as if bombarding heaven."

The explosions unnerved the men even more and Stiles began feeling the pressure himself. "No Confederate soldier who was on that fearful retreat can fail to recall it as one of the most trying experiences of his life," he wrote. "Trying enough in the mere fact that the Army of Northern Virginia was flying before its foes, but . . . incomparably trying in the lack of food, rest and sleep." The general nervousness was a dangerous thing, he noted. At one point a powerful black stallion spooked and pulled the rail he was tied to out of a heavy rail fence, dragging it with him as he galloped down the road crowded with troops, "mowing them down like the scythe of a war chariot." Thinking this was a charge of enemy cavalry, an agitated trooper fired his musket. "On the instant," Stiles recalled, "three or four battalions, mine among them, began firing into each other. I was never more alarmed. Muskets were discharged in my very face, and I fully expected to be shot down; but after the most trying and perilous experience, the commanding officers succeeded in getting control of their men."

Many, if not most, of the Rebel soldiers were similarly unnerved or dispirited. One soldier on the march claimed:

> The Confederacy was considered as "gone up," and every man felt it his duty, as well as his privilege to save himself. I do not mean to say that there was any insubordination whatever; but the whole right of the army was so crushed by the defeats of the last few days that it straggled along without thought. So we moved in disorder, keeping no regular column, no regular pace. . . . There were not many words spoken. An indescribable sadness weighed upon us.

Yet despite fear, pain, weariness, hunger, and wholesale desertions, Lee's army still had amazing spirit. Grant knew capturing Richmond, the soul of the Confederacy and the South's most important munitions maker, wasn't enough—the Army of Northern Virginia itself had to be beaten. Though it was stumbling in retreat, Union commanders remembered that of the thousands of Rebel prisoners taken just a few days ago at Five Forks not even a hundred would take the oath of allegiance to the Union. They had been promised they could go home if they would just take the oath and fight no more, but the overwhelming majority refused and bitterly cursed the relative handful of "cowards and traitors" who did. It was wise to expect that many such men marched in the army the Union forces pursued. There was a lot more fighting to be done.

Grant had decided he would try to get ahead of and cut off Lee and his exhausted troops rather than chase and overtake them from behind. His two intercepting columns moved west in parallel lines on the south side of the Appomattox River, which flows eastward some 137 miles from Appomattox County to Richmond and Petersburg. The larger column, composed of the cavalry, Sheridan's Fifth Corps, and the corps of Generals Horatio Wright and Andrew Humphreys, kept close to the river. The smaller column, consisting of three divisions of the Army of the James led by General Ord, marched along the Southside Railroad. The soldiers carried extra rations for the forced march, eliminating waits for supply trains, and they were expected to cover thirty miles a day. "Your legs must do it, boys!" their officers kept shouting to them. "Your legs must do it!"

On the other side of the Appomattox, Lee's weary column slugged along, picking up troops that had come on different routes from Richmond and Petersburg, including the divisions of General Longstreet, General Mahone from the Bermuda Hundred, the colorful, one-legged General Richard "Old Baldhead" Ewell, General Custis Lee, and fragments of divisions led by Generals Henry Heth, Cadmus Wilcox, and Gordon. Local defense troops from Richmond also joined Lee, as did Richmond artillerists and even a so-called naval battalion. Almost all these units were woefully undermanned.

Lee's army had a one-day head start on Grant's and could not be seen on the opposite side of the river. But his lead quickly dwindled, as would be expected of an army of starving men burdened by an artillery train drawn by animals barely able to pull it.

Despite their head start, the slower Confederate army, Lee riding tirelessly beside its wagons, was attacked as early as April 3 by Sheridan's superior cavalry, which played a critical role in harrying the Rebels throughout the retreat. They were always hovering around, a Confederate soldier recalled, "like ill-omened birds of prey, awaiting their opportunity." Sheridan had disobeyed Grant's

The flamboyant General
George Armstrong Custer.
From the National Archives.

orders to move south with his men and join General Sherman in
North Carolina (because "I wanted my cavalry to be in at the
death"), but Grant seemed glad that he had; in any case, he never
reprimanded Little Phil. Sheridan's cavalry's action on the third
was made by a brigade of a division led by General George Armstrong Custer, whose name would one day, for better or worse, become better known than any Civil War leader save Lincoln, Lee,
and Grant. In the popular imagination Lee's last stand at Appomattox against the Yankees would never rival Custer's last stand at
the Little Bighorn against the Indians, later depicted in over 50
Hollywood movies.

The legendary Custer, last in his class at West Point, looked
like he had stepped off a stage or out of the pages of a romantic
novel. He would have stood out anywhere in his brown velveteen
breeches piped with gold, long boots, blousy crimson shirt and
matching velveteen jacket covered with gold braid. His curly golden
hair (at West Point they had reprimanded him and dubbed him
"Fanny" for its length and sparkle) flowed well over his shoulders

and was topped by a huge, broadbrim slouch hat. His blond mustache matched his hair. Around his neck, wrote one of Sheridan's staff officers, he wore "a long flowing ribbon [scarf] of brilliant red cashmere or silk. . . . He was scarcely more than a boy in years, but was a man of tremendous energy and immense physical power. His great height and striking countenance . . . gave him the appearance of one of the Vikings of old."

It was a wonder that this blue-eyed boy general with his long hair flying behind like a golden flag as he rode into battle hadn't been picked off by some enemy sharpshooter. There was no more flamboyantly dressed target in either Civil War army, not even "Beauty," the daring Rebel general Jeb Stuart, who had been mortally wounded a year ago emptying his pistols at Yankee cavalry. Custer had been in the thick of things since the first battle of Bull Run, always attired in variations of the same bravura uniform, commanding his troops successfully at Gettysburg and through the Virginia Shenandoah campaign, honorary field promotions having advanced him from lieutenant to the rank of general by the time he was only twenty-three, the youngest general in the Union army. Like Sheridan, he was no great student of war. He was loud, rowdy, and often cruel and unthinking; but he remained always a brave warrior, a great cavalryman noted for his daring charges whose men often imitated him in dress—wearing bright red scarves—and hell-for-leather demeanor.

A brigade of Custer's cavalry under Colonel William Wells attacked General Fitzhugh Lee's cavalry near Namozine Church on April 3 in the first of many such harassing rearguard actions that would plague Lee's retreat. Estimated casualties totaled seventy-five for both sides, and Confederate general Rufus Barringer was captured nearby during the skirmish. Thereafter, Sheridan regularly raided Lee's columns and "Old Curly" Custer struck up bands to attack them. Sheridan's wild, lawless scouts, often disguised as displaced persons or Confederate soldiers, went so far as to ride among the Rebels and gather intelligence about their future moves. Lee soon became aware of his desperate situation. General Chamberlain wrote:

His hope now was to get to the Danville railroad junction . . . and possibly a clear road to Danville or Lynchburg. So he pushed the heads of his flying columns along the roads running between the Southside railroad and the Appomattox River, a path traversed by many and difficult streams, only to find at every crossing some hot vanguard of Sheridan or Humphreys or Wright or Griffin, or at last of Ord; and at each time, too, after fighting more or less severe, . . . stretching on with ever increasing desperation. . . . There was blood at every bridge and ford. Yet higher up road and river stretched the two armies; one with the frenzy of a forlorn hoper; the other with the energy of fierce resolve.

As they retreated the Rebels left behind brave men buried on the wayside, dying men, the walking wounded, even some deserters, according to Chamberlain, who "declared they were not white, but colored—a claim not often set up in that section of the Republic." As the Yankees pushed on at double-quick march they stopped only to make bonfires of abandoned guns and munitions that might be used once more against them. Their cavalry kept harassing Lee's stumbling columns, hitting them in one spot, then withdrawing, only to thrust at them again a few miles up the road.

Wrote Confederate General Gordon:

On and on, hour after hour, from hilltop to hilltop, the lines were alternately forming, fighting and retreating, making one almost continuous shifting battle. Here, in one direction, a battery of artillery became involved; there, in another, a blocked ammunition train required rescue. And thus came short but sharp little battles which made up sideshows of the main performance, while the different divisions of Lee's lionhearted army were being broken and scattered or captured. . . . The road and fields swarmed with the eager pursuers, and Lee now and then was forced to halt his whole army, reduced to less than 10,000 fighters, in order to meet these simultaneous attacks. Various divisions along the line of march turned upon the Federals, and in each case checked them long enough for some other Confederate commands to move on. . . . It was impossible for us to bury our dead. . . . We could do nothing for the unfortunate sufferers who were too severely wounded to march, except leave them on the road-side with canteens of water.

On April 4 Lee's retreating army skirmished with the Yankees at Tabernacle Church (Beaver Pond Creek). Lee reached the little redbrick town of Amelia Court House, a station on the Richmond & Danville Railroad, that same morning, but had wasted precious time. For one thing, it took another twenty-four hours before the last of his troops arrived there. More importantly, the rations he expected to find at Amelia for his troops—who had started out three days earlier with food enough for one day—weren't anywhere to be found. During the last days on the Petersburg-Richmond line Lee had anticipated the Confederate retreat and ordered that the Commissary Department in Richmond collect 350,000 rations and store them at Amelia Court House. The rations had been collected, but no one is sure what happened to them after that. The order could have been lost at Richmond during the confusion of the evacuation, or the food may never have been unloaded at Amelia from the train carrying it.

In any case, not a piece of hardtack was to be found, although plenty of artillery pieces and ammunition had been unloaded. Lee was devastated; "completely paralyzed" for a few moments, according to one of his officers. He realized he would lose the whole day's lead he'd gained on Grant, for now he had to send foraging parties out to search for food in an already ransacked countryside. When the wagons returned at the end of the day, they were all but empty.

"Not finding the supplies ordered to be placed at Amelia Court House," Lee observed later, "24 hours were lost in endeavoring to collect in the country subsistence for the men and horses. The delay was fatal and could not be retrieved." On the morning of April 5 there was no breakfast for his troops and he was forced to put these feeble, starving men on the march again, testing the limits of human endurance. Because of the foraging delay, he could no longer retreat along the Richmond & Danville Railroad, this route already being blocked by Sheridan's fast-moving forces. Jefferson Davis, waiting anxiously for Lee at Danville, would not hear from him for another twenty-four hours, but Davis had clearly vowed the day before to maintain the struggle. In a general proclamation he told the citizens of the new capital and all the South:

> It would be unwise even if it were possible, to conceal the great moral, as well as material interest to our cause that must result from the occupation of Richmond by the enemy. It is equally unwise and unworthy of us, as patriots engaged in a most sacred cause, to allow our energies to falter, or our efforts to become relaxed, under reverses however calamitous.

Davis prepared to fix up an executive office, but most of Lee's troops had already faltered from hunger. Now their spirits were faltering, and the sacred cause seemed a lost cause. Lee turned them toward Farmville, where he had rations ordered via railroad from Lynchburg to feed his starving men. Whether the food would get there was at best uncertain.

As he marched on, Lee hoped that his cavalry could "secure the rear of his column from interruption," as he wrote to General Gordon, whose troops were his rear guard. Lee's first column was led by General Longstreet, while the middle, with the bulk of the wagons, was headed by General Richard Anderson. Before Gordon came Old Baldhead Ewell with the Richmond garrison. The columns moved at a painfully slow pace, barely half a mile an hour, the famished men further encumbered by dying animals that could hardly drag the wagons over the rough roads. Confederate cavalry led by Generals Fitzhugh Lee and Rosser did attack Union cavalry under George Crook, assaulting them as they returned from burning Confederate wagons at Painesville. In the running fight that started north of Amelia Springs and pushed through and beyond Jetersville there were 250 casualties, but no side could be called a victor. Lee continued on toward Farmville, where he planned to obtain the desperately needed rations and then head south to the Danville route, finally following it to Johnston's army in North Carolina.

The fiery Sheridan was convinced that Lee's army was doomed; he urged Grant to get up to the scene of the action and went to extreme lengths to convince him. Wrote Grant in his *Memoirs*:

I received a second message from Sheridan on the 5th, in which he urged more emphatically the importance of my presence. This was brought to me by a scout in gray uniform. It was written on tissue paper, and wrapped up in tin-foil such as chewing tobacco is folded in. This was a precaution taken so that if the scout should be captured he could take this tin-foil out of his pocket and putting it into his mouth chew it. It would cause no suspicion at all to see a Confederate soldier chewing tobacco.

The morning after he received this secret message at Nottaway Court House on the Southside Railroad, Grant set out to meet Sheridan, guided by the scout dressed as a Confederate colonel. He traveled with only a few of his staff and fourteen cavalrymen. It was a foolish journey for Grant to make with such a small escort on unknown roads, and if the Confederates had captured him in this wilderness, Union fortunes might well have been reversed. Horace Porter kept his gun cocked, suspecting that the scout might be in the pay of the Confederates, but he proved loyal and trustworthy. Still the sixteen-mile ride through the woods was lonely and hazardous, wrote correspondent Sylvanus Cadwallader, along for the ride, and all "farm houses, possible ambush, junctions and crossings of roads were approached with caution."

After convincing amazed Union sentries that he was indeed General Grant, the general in chief and his party finally reached Sheridan's Jetersville headquarters, a small log cabin in the middle of a tobacco patch. Sheridan, "not a little profane in expressing his opinion," according to Cadwallader, pulled out his maps and explained to Grant that General Meade's plan to move to the right flank would give Lee the chance to escape and put the Federal forces in the rear of him. "We then together visited Meade, reaching his quarters about midnight," Grant wrote. "I explained to Meade that we did not want to follow the enemy; we wanted to get ahead of him, and that his orders would allow the enemy to escape, and besides that, I had no doubt Lee was moving right now. Meade changed his orders at once. They were now given for an advance on Amelia Court House, at an early hour in the morning."

Lee's troops had moved out during the night, as Grant expected. Meade's men soon encountered them that morning, fighting a series of actions involving heavy casualties. "There was as much gallantry displayed by some of the Confederates in these little engagements as was displayed at any time during the war," Grant later wrote.

Some of the Union troops pursuing Lee had been marching thirty-five miles a day and were bone weary. "Our troops had a very difficult country to overcome," Chamberlain recalled later, "broken, tangled and full of swamps. They had to cross streams by wading armpit deep, and then push on to strike the rear of the [Confederate] ranks." But unlike the Rebels, the Federals had not been without food for four days, and even the most pessimistic among them sensed that victory was at hand.

Lee's columns, raided continuously by Union cavalry, had huge gaps between them as they marched through Rice's Station toward Farmville, where Lee planned to cross the Appomattox River to its northern bank and move west to Lynchburg. It was a broken army now, its pieces the forms of men, muskets and wagons and animals littering the road of retreat. Hundreds of soldiers hadn't the strength to carry their muskets and stuck them, bayonets fixed, into the ground, marching on weaponless.

At Rice's Station (or Depot) General Longstreet's vanguard of Confederate soldiers, leading Lee's strung-out army, found itself far ahead of the rest of the troops. By noontime a gap of over five miles separated Longstreet's command from General Anderson's forces and General Ewell's men, following Anderson. At this point, according to Chamberlain, Southern strategy left much to be desired. He later wrote:

> There was some unaccountably poor generalship that day in the Confederate army. Longstreet held his troops all day at Rice's Station waiting for Anderson and Ewell and Gordon, who had been held back to cover the wagon trains. . . . If Lee had abandoned all surplus artillery and camp equipage and retained only his ammunition and hospital wagons, and established temporary depots of supplies at important railroad stations, he might have been able to move rapidly enough to make a successful junction with Johnson at Danville or at least, to reach the [Blue Ridge] mountains of Lynchburg.

But as it was, Anderson's and Ewell's wagons were ordered on a detour to cross the Appomattox River. The stage was now being set for the battle that has ever since been widely regarded as the last major engagement of the Civil War and the death knell of Lee's Army of Northern Virginia. Just ahead of Anderson were two branches of Sayler's Creek, itself a small tributary of the Appomattox that ran through a shallow valley. All day Sheridan's Union cavalry had been slashing at the weary Southern columns, looking for an opening; and now Custer, spotting the detoured wagon train, found one. Custer's men, sabers swinging, poured into the gap, killing the drivers, cutting horses loose, and setting the wagons on fire. Four hundred wagons were destroyed and hundreds of prisoners taken. As the Federal riders attacked, the gap widened and Ewell tried to save the remaining wagons, ordering those behind him to proceed on a road forking north. On coming to the fork in the road, however, Gordon's troops, the Confederate rear guard, followed the wagons—as they had throughout the retreat—instead of joining Ewell and Anderson. This left the Army of Northern Virginia split into three segments: an isolated Gordon heading toward the Appomattox; Ewell and Anderson a distance off to the north; and Lee and Longstreet waiting unaware at Rice's Station five miles away.

Ewell and Anderson's thousands were in danger from all sides. General Sheridan had just ordered up Horatio Wright's Sixth Corps when a lone Custer cavalryman—Ohioan William Richardson, who had been taken prisoner briefly during the wagon raid and escaped in a wild ride through hostile troops—advised Little Phil that Custer had cut the wagon train completely in two and was pressing the Confederates hard. Sheridan knew he had the enemy completely surrounded. When Anderson's brigades moved three-quarters of a mile down the road, they found Union cavalry blocking their path; Wright's corps was assaulting the rear of Ewell's troops. "The corps was massing into the fields at double-quick," wrote Confederate private W. L. Timberlake later, "the battle lines, blooming with color, growing longer and deeper at every moment, the batteries at a gallop coming into action. We knew what it all meant."

These were men terribly outnumbered and understrength; hunger was still Grant's greatest ally. They had not eaten in days except for handfuls of parched corn stolen from feed for the horses and the few scraps that their foraging parties had gathered; more than once whole companies of them were ordered into the woods to browse like animal herds on the tender shoots of trees bursting into bud. It was a wonder they could fight at all. Yankee infantry and cavalry came at them on the run from four directions, bugles blaring. There seemed no hope, yet they fought back savagely at first.

Fighting with Custis Lee's division, part of Ewell's forces, the Confederate battalion headed by Major Stiles was in the thick of things. Alongside them was the Naval Battalion of about two thousand men, headed by Admiral John Tucker. "The soldiers called them 'Aye, Ayes,'" Stiles later wrote, "because they responded 'Aye, aye' to every order, sometimes repeating the order itself and adding, 'Aye, aye it is, sir!' *Starboard* and *larboard* were their terms for left and right flank."

But there wasn't much else to smile about during the battle of Sayler's Creek, which included three separate engagements at Hillsman Farm, Lockett's Farm, and Marshall's Crossroads. Stiles recalled how his men "rushed bareheaded with unloaded muskets" after a retreating Federal line of infantry only to have the Union artillery open fire on them. The standard-bearer was killed and "his brother, a lieutenant, stepped over his body . . . taking hold of the staff. *He* was shot through the brain and fell backward." Five men were killed trying to hold on to the colors.

The fighting became bestial. "By the time we had settled into our position," Stiles wrote, "we were attacked simultaneously, front and rear, by overwhelming numbers, and quicker than I can tell it the battle degenerated into butchery and a confused melee of brutal personal conflicts. I saw numbers of men kill each other with bayonets and the butts of muskets, and even bite each other's throats and ears and noses, rolling on the ground like wild beasts."

Soon after, Stiles watched helplessly as one of his soldiers killed his best friend:

I had cautioned my men against wearing captured "Yankee over-coats," especially in battle, but had not been able to enforce the order perfectly—and almost at my side I saw a young fellow of one of my companies jam the muzzle of his musket against the back of the head of his most intimate friend, clad in a Yankee overcoat, and blow his brains out. I tried to strike the musket barrel up, but alas, my sword had broken in the clash and I could not reach it. I well remember the yell of demoniac triumph with which that simple country lad of yesterday clubbed his musket and whirled savagely upon another victim.

Stiles also witnessed the death of a boy he had especially tried to reassure back when he read his men the Soldier's Psalm—"A thousand shall fall at thy side, and ten thousand at thy right hand; but it shall not come nigh thee"—at the beginning of the long march:

A good many had been wounded and several killed when a twenty-pounder Parrott shell struck immediately in my front, on the line, nearly severing a man in twain, and hurling him bodily over my head, his arms hanging down and his hands almost slapping me in the face as they passed. In that one awful moment I distinctly recognized young Blount, who had gazed in my face so intensely Sunday night. But for that particular paralysis which in battle some times passes upon a man's entire being—excepting only his fighting powers—the recognition might have been too much for me.

Stiles finally saw that nothing more could change the result of the battle:

I could not let myself degenerate into a mere fighting brute or devil, because the lives of these poor fellows were . . . in my hands, though there was nothing I could do just then to shield or save them. Suddenly, by one of those inexplicable shiftings which take place on a battlefield the fighting around me almost entirely ceased and . . . the slaughter seemed to be pretty much over. I concluded I would try to make my escape.

This he did, but he ran straight into a Federal force and was captured.

So many Confederates were killed and captured in the disastrous battle that Lee, watching from a hilltop, turned to an aide and told him, "That half of our army has been destroyed." Even the most battle-hardened Rebel veterans were confused, dazed, and helpless. It was at this point, for example, that General Ewell was heard to make a strange remark related to nothing at hand, unless it was hunger: "Tomatoes are very good; I wish I had some." Wrote a Union sergeant: "The Rebels lost all formation and went across country, our boys chasing up and gathering them in." Union troops were shouting "There's Phil! There's Phil!", pointing at Sheridan and throwing their hats up in the air, cheering and dancing. Barrels of worthless Confederate money abandoned in the Rebel escape were tossed into the air by Billy Yanks, or burned in their campfires. The ground was so matted with discarded Confederate muskets that someone's horse stepped on one and it discharged, killing a Union officer.

Before the smoke of thousands of muskets and artillery pieces had cleared, at least eight Confederate generals surrendered at Sayler's Creek, including the one-legged Ewell himself, Lee's eldest son Custis, Eppa Hunton, Montgomery Corse, Dudley DuBose, Seth Barton, James Simms, and Joseph Kershaw. Lee was wrong: close to one-third, not one-half, of his already decimated army was destroyed. Still, some 8,000 Confederates were killed or captured, while Federal losses numbered about 1,180. When Lee saw the few survivors struggling down the road, he exclaimed, "My God! Has the army dissolved?" Already some of his own officers were advising him to face up to the hopelessness of the situation. Prominent among them was Brigadier General Henry Wise, who as governor of Virginia in better times had demanded that Southerners not be deterred by even "a red river of blood." Now he was telling Lee: "To prolong the struggle is murder, and the blood of every man who is killed from this time forth is on your head."

General Gordon, who had taken the wrong turn at the beginning of the battle, managed to get some of his men out, but even he left seventeen hundred prisoners. After fighting a savage battle at Perkinson's Mills, near the mouth of Sayler's Creek, where his march had stalled when a bridge collapsed, Gordon realized that it was futile to resist any longer. "He gave us orders to save ourselves," one of his men wrote, "showing us the way by galloping his horse down the hill and fording the creek." Then he marched with what was left of his forces the few miles toward Farmville on the south bank of the Appomattox. There he would join up with Longstreet and Lee, who had found themselves blocked by General Gibbon's Twenty-fourth Corps at Rice's Station and after some skirmishing had withdrawn in the dark to Farmville.

That night, having won the race to Farmville, Lee slept in a sparsely furnished room at the Prince Edward Hotel, happy at least that his starving troops had received their first rations in four days. But everyone was not fed, and most of the forty thousand rations of bread and eighty thousand of meat were abandoned by morning, left uneaten because the supply trains had to be moved out of danger when Federal cavalry was spotted coming from the east over a bridge that had not been destroyed as ordered. The supplies were captured the next day at Pamplin's Depot.

It was now Lee's plan to strike west for Lynchburg. He ordered supplies sent from Lynchburg to a Southside Railroad depot called Appomattox Station, just a few miles from the little town of Appomattox Court House, figuring he could pick up the food and rest his weary troops there if he moved swiftly enough. But to accomplish this all the bridges across the Appomattox had to be destroyed, making it impossible for the Federals to cross that unfordable river without a long delay.

On the morning of April 7 Lee's men began their march, this time heading north across the Appomattox from Farmville, on a route that would take them about twenty-five miles through many hamlets and villages until they reached Appomattox Station and the supplies awaiting them. From there it was only twenty miles or so to Lynchburg and the protecting mountains.

But time and luck ran out on them. Sheridan's fast-moving cavalry captured an Appomattox River wagon bridge before it could be destroyed, putting out fires as they advanced. In another action costing twelve hundred casualties, the Union Second Corps under General Humphreys secured High Bridge before it could be fired. In all, General William Mahone's rearguard division succeeded in destroying only four of the twenty-one bridges spanning the river. Union forces poured over them in hot pursuit of Lee's army.

Mahone's men, after failing in their bridge-burning mission, tried to redeem themselves with a stubborn stand near Cumberland Church, three miles to the north of Farmville. Digging in on high ground, they held out from 2 P.M. until nightfall, repulsing two Union attacks that cost 655 Federal casualties and 255 Confederate. Even near the end the bodies were still piling up like cordwood, one enlisted man was heard to say. Despite the valiant stand against vastly superior forces, Lee had lost irreplaceable hours before being able to resume his last march under cover of darkness.

Grant had arrived at Farmville on the afternoon of April 7 in his mud-spattered clothes, carrying no baggage and exhausted from his ride to meet Sheridan the day before. Resting on the porch of the Prince Edward Hotel, he heard a message from Sheridan advising him that a lone Union cavalry scout had spotted several freight cars of rations waiting for Lee's army at Appomattox Station. Sheridan was sure he could reach the rail station, twenty-five miles away, by the following day and beat Lee to this cache of precious provisions. Grant was also advised that fiery Confederate general Dick Ewell, no easy man to keep down, had told his captors when taken at Sayler's Creek that the Rebel cause had been lost ever since the Confederates left Richmond and he hoped Lee would surrender. Ewell had added, Grant later wrote in his *Memoirs*, "that for every man that was killed after this in the war somebody is responsible, and [such deaths] would be very little better than murder." Then there was President Lincoln's reply to Sheridan's report after the battle of Sayler's Creek, in which Sheridan predicted that "if the thing is pressed I think Lee will surrender." Lincoln had sent a message to Grant urging him to "let the thing be pressed."

Considering these factors, Grant finally glanced up at General Gibbon and quietly said, "I have a great mind to summon Lee to surrender." No more than a few moments passed before he took pen in hand and wrote a brief message to the Confederate commander:

> The results of the last week must convince you of the hopelessness of further resistance on the part of the Army of Northern Virginia in this struggle. I feel that it is so, and regard it as my duty to shift from myself the responsibility of any further effusion of blood by asking of you the surrender of that portion of the Confederate State's army known as the Army of Northern Virginia.

The short note was written at 5 P.M. and entrusted to General Seth Williams, the adjutant general, who would have a messenger carry it to Lee under a flag of truce. For a while Grant waited on the broad piazza, watching a torchlight parade his jubilant troops spontaneously made while passing him on their way over the Appomattox. The men were waving their torches and caps, singing "John Brown's Body" while marching to the music of brigade bands, cheering the man on the porch who was leading them to victory, leading them home. "The night march had become a grand review, with Grant as the reviewing officer," Horace Porter wrote. Then Grant went to bed in the same room Lee had slept in the night before, only to be awakened at midnight by an officer carrying Lee's answer to his message.

General Lee, north of the Appomattox, had not received the surrender request until 9:30. After studying it, he showed the letter to General Longstreet, who dismissed it with a cautious "Not yet." Lee agreed. Replying to Grant, he advised: "General: I have received your note of this date. Though not entertaining the opinion you express of the hopelessness of further resistance on the part of the Army of Northern Virginia, I reciprocate your desire to avoid useless effusion of blood, and therefore, before considering your proposition, ask the terms you will offer on condition of its surrender."

Lee, only a few miles ahead of his pursuers, was on the road heading toward the little village of Appomattox Court House when he received Grant's answer to his letter on the mild sunny afternoon of April 8. Grant wrote the reply at Farmville that morning before he and his party began moving north of the Appomattox River, instead of south along the enemy line of retreat, so that there would be less delay in his correspondence with Lee. Still the note took all day to reach its destination. It read:

General R. E. Lee, Commanding C.S.A.:

Your note of last evening in reply to mine of the same date, asking the conditions on which I will accept the surrender of the Army of Northern Virginia, is just received. In reply I would say that, peace being my great desire, there is but one condition I would insist upon—namely, that the men and officers surrendered shall be disqualified for taking up arms against the Government of the United States until properly exchanged. I will meet you, or will designate officers to meet any officers you may name for the same purpose, at any point agreeable to you, for the purpose of arranging definitely the terms upon which the surrender of the Army of Northern Virginia will be received.

This was no "Unconditional Surrender" Grant dictating terms. Lee was being offered a surrender as generous as any that could be offered to a defeated army. The only nonnegotiable condition was that the Confederates definitely surrender. But something of the old gray fox may still have remained in Lee. In any case, he tried for more despite the vastly superior numbers at his back and throat. His answer to Grant read:

General:

I received at a late hour your note of today. In mine of yesterday I did not intend to propose the surrender of the Army of Northern Virginia, but to ask the terms of your proposition. To be frank, I do not think the emergency has arisen to call for the surrender of this army, but, as the restoration of peace should be the sole object of all, I desired to know whether your proposals would lead to that end. I cannot, therefore, meet with a view to surrender the Army of Northern Virginia; but as far as your proposal may affect the Confederate States forces under my command, and tend to the restoration of peace, I should be pleased to meet you at 10 A.M. to-morrow on the old stage road to Richmond, between the picket-lines of the two armies.

The important switch here was that Lee was trying for a general peace settlement, one including all Confederate forces ("the Confederate States forces under my command"), Lee having been general in chief of all Confederate armies since February. Grant had been suffering from a blinding headache when he received this latest letter—"one of his sick headaches," as General Meade put it, "which are rare but cause him fearful pain, such as almost to overcome his iron stoicism." All day he had futilely tried to shake the migraine, using old home remedies like bathing his feet in hot water and mustard and applying mustard plasters to his wrists and the back of his neck. He had hardly been able to ride that afternoon of April 8, and even sprawled out on the sofa in the white farmhouse at Curdsville selected as headquarters for the night he found no relief from the excruciating headache brought on by the fatigue, anxiety, and lack of food and sleep over the last few days. Around him staff officers bunked on the floor; others pounded away on an old piano all evening. Grant got little sleep, and the letter he received from Lee near midnight made him feel worse. After reading the letter he held his head in his hands and said, "It looks as if Lee still means to fight."

According to correspondent Cadwallader, who was present, General Rawlins was much angrier than Grant about Lee's latest proposal. Cadwallader recalled Rawlins saying:

> Lee did propose, in his heart, to surrender. He now tries to take advantage of a single word ["peace"] used by you [in Grant's last letter] as a reason for extending such easy terms. He now wants to entrap us into making a treaty of peace. You said nothing about that. You asked him to surrender. He replied by asking what terms you would give if he surrendered. You answered, by stating the terms. Now he wants to arrange for peace—something beyond and above the surrender of his army—something to embrace the whole Confederacy, if possible. No, Sir! No, Sir! Why it is a positive insult; and an attempt in an underhanded way, to change the whole terms of the correspondence.

Rawlins raved on, sarcastically repeating Lee's words: "'He *don't think the emergency has arisen!*' That's cool, but another falsehood.

That emergency has been staring him in the face for forty-eight hours. If he hasn't seen it yet, we will soon bring it to his comprehension! He has to surrender. He shall surrender. By the eternal, it shall be surrender and nothing else!" Rawlins also reminded Grant that Lincoln had forbidden him to negotiate a general peace.

Grant spent much of the night tossing about and pacing the yard outside the farmhouse, knowing he could not meet with Lee under these circumstances, considering what to write in reply. The latest news from the field had been encouraging, except for an internecine feud that broke out between his own weary infantry and artillery troops. The infantry, complaining that artillerymen were endangering them by reckless driving on the road, retaliated by clubbing offending artillery horses with swords and rifles in one of the oddest "battles" of the Civil War.

In the real war to the south, Sheridan's cavalry was in front of Lee, blocking the all-important road to Lynchburg, while the Sixth and Second Corps were close behind the Confederates. Sheridan, as he predicted, had reached Appomattox Court House before Lee did. On that afternoon of April 8 he sent Custer's cavalry division charging in like a thunderbolt to seize Appomattox Station and the four trains of provisions, including bacon, meal, and hardtack, that had finally arrived for the Confederate troops. Taking the four-thousand-man Rebel detail completely by surprise before they could unload the cars into their wagons and ambulances, Custer's riders, several of them former railroad men, quickly moved the trains back out of reach. Pushing on with the main body of his troops, Custer attacked the Rebel wagons and an artillery train with twenty-five guns, scattering the Confederate defenders into the woods.

The Confederates were effectively boxed in now. There was no escape to the north, and Yankee infantry faced them from the west. "Lee couldn't go back, he couldn't go forward, and he couldn't go sideways," a Union soldier observed. But Lee's *best chance* was to fight his way west along the Lynchburg road, to try and break through against cavalry in that direction. Sheridan, however, had anticipated this, and ordered up the Fifth Corps and divisions from the Army of the James to support him. By the morning of April 9 these troops, having marched all night, had arrived. Some had been inspired by the promise of rations, after going more than a day without food. Others grew terribly tired of twenty- and thirty-mile marches, as a Yankee trooper admitted, "but wanted to be there when the Rebels found the 'last ditch' of which they had talked so much for years."

Contemplating the situation back at headquarters, Grant felt a little better, but his migraine still raged. "General," Horace Porter said, trying to console him, "I never knew you to be ill that you did not receive some good news. I have become a little superstitious regarding these coincidences, and I should not be surprised if some good fortune overtook you before night." Grant only smiled feebly and said: "The best thing that can happen to me today is to get rid of the pain I am suffering." But he sat down early that morning of April 9 to answer General Lee's letter, keeping especially in mind Rawlins's warning about Lincoln's strict orders, sent via Stanton's dispatch of March 3, that he could only discuss the surrender of the Army of Northern Virginia, not an overall peace settlement. He wrote:

> General:
>
> Your note of yesterday is received. I have no authority to treat on the subject of peace. The meeting proposed for 10 A.M. to-day could lead to no good. I will state, however, that I am equally desirous for peace with yourself, and the whole North entertains the same feeling. The terms upon which peace can be had are well understood. By the South laying down their arms, they would hasten that most desirable event, save thousands of lives, and hundreds of millions of property not yet destroyed. Seriously hoping that all our difficulties may be settled without the loss of another life, I subscribe myself, etc.

Grant, migraine and all, was off to Sheridan's front soon after he answered Lee. Even as he rode, what would prove to be the last bloody, forlorn battle of the war in Virginia was taking place that Palm Sunday of April 9.

The night before, Lee and his generals had decided to make one last escape attempt. At dawn on that hot, cloudless morning the ragged remnants of General Gordon's Second Corps and Fitzhugh Lee's cavalry formed their line of battle at Appomattox Court House. Lee, despite his ongoing negotiations with Grant, and his feeling that all was lost, felt obligated to make this final effort to break through the closing Union pincers and fight his way along the Lynchburg road running through the little town.

Wrote a Confederate soldier: "It was a bleak and misty morning, and after the line was formed for the charge, the men, who shivered in the coolness, built a fire of fence rails. . . . Nearby was a field piece that was to be fired as a signal for the line to advance." The piece sounded and the Confederates began at a quickstep, raising their voices in the "old-time yell." Ahead sat Sheridan under his battle flag. "Weird-looking flag it is," Chamberlain wrote, "fork-tailed, red and white, the two bands that compose it each charged with a star of the contrasting color: two eyes sternly glaring through the cannon-cloud. Beneath it, that storm-center spirit, that form of condensed energies, mounted on the grim charger Rienzi . . . both rider and steed of an unearthly shade of darkness terrible to look upon, as if masking some unknown powers." The Confederates advanced into the ring of men and steel around them, the first muskets firing, and Sheridan galloped back and forth directing his men and officers. At first, Sheridan's cavalry troops lost ground. "Now smash 'em, I tell you, smash 'em!" Sheridan cried. But the Rebels pressed on, broke into a double-quick march, an irresistible rush, sensing victory. Then Little Phil's dismounted cavalry seemed to step to the side like a curtain opening to reveal a long line of the infantry Sheridan had sent for that night—Ord's troops, whose commander later shouted to them, "Your legs have done it, my men! Your legs have done it!" The Confederates let out the last bone-chilling, defiant Rebel yell of the long chase and charged this seemingly endless wall of blue.

General Chamberlain described the last charge from the time his brigade came on the field:

> At cavalry speed we pushed through the woods, right on Sheridan's battle flag gleaming in an open field. Right before us our cavalry was stemming the surges of the old Stonewall Brigade

[which had fought with Stonewall Jackson], desperate to beat its way through. . . . For a moment it is a glorious sight: every arm of the service in full play—cavalry, artillery, infantry—then a sudden shifting scene as the cavalry . . . sweeps like a stormcloud beyond our right to close in on the enemy's left and complete the fateful envelopement. . . . In a few minutes the tide is turned. . . . Their last hope is gone—to break through our cavalry before our infantry can get up. Neither to Danville or Lynchburg can they cut their way. . . . It is the end! They are now giving way, but keep good front, by force of old habit. Halfway up the slope they make a stand with what perhaps they think a good omen—behind a stone wall.

But not the Stonewall Brigade, not Lee and all of Lee's hungry horses and all of Lee's hungry men could put the Army of Northern Virginia back together again in this vast amphitheater of broken, bloody ground where the Appomattox River finally became a rivulet or a trickle. A despondent Lee looked out over the field: "How easily could I be rid of this, and be at rest! I have only to ride along the line and all will be over! But it is our duty to live." He had already sent a reply to Grant's last letter, indicating that he would consider the surrender of his army now, provided the terms were acceptable, writing:

General:

I received your note of this morning on the picket-line, whither I had come to meet you and ascertain definitely what terms are embraced in your proposal of yesterday with reference to the surrender of this army. I now ask an interview, in accordance with the offer contained in your letter yesterday, for that purpose.

When Grant received Lee's letter from a Confederate courier at about noon, his migraine suddenly disappeared. He had what he wanted. This was surrender, and—if things moved quickly enough—without a really bloody final slaughter, which he had promised Lincoln he would try to avoid. He sat down on the grassy bank by the roadside, wrote a brief reply to Lee explaining where he would be, and pushed forward to Appomattox Court House.

Now, surveying the impending disaster on the battlefield, waiting for a reply from Grant, Lee sent his aide Colonel C. S. Venable out to General Gordon to ask "if we might still break through the countless hordes of the enemy who hemmed us in." Gordon, up on the front line, replied, "Tell General Lee I have fought my corps to a frazzle, and I fear I can do nothing unless I am heavily supported by Longstreet's corps."

As Longstreet, facing an attack from the east by the Union Second Corps, was in no position to help, there was nothing more to be done. "When I bore Gordon's message back to General Lee," Venable recalled, "he said: 'Then there is nothing left me but to go and see General Grant, and I would rather die a thousand deaths.'"

Lee had no choice except surrender. As General Meade later wrote to his wife: "Lee's army was reduced to a force of less than ten thousand effective armed men. We had at least fifty thousand around him, so that nothing but madness would have justified resistance." But Colonel Venable remembered the "wild words" of "passionate grief" the officers around Lee uttered:

> Said one, "Oh, general, what will history say of the surrender of the army in the field?" Lee replied, "Yes, I know they will say hard things of us, they will not understand how we were overwhelmed by numbers. But that is not the question, colonel: the question is, *Is it right to surrender this army?* If it is right to surrender this army. If it is right, then *I* will take *all* responsibility."

With that, Lee sent out from Gordon's lines young cavalry captain R. M. Sims bearing a white flag (a red-bordered towel belonging to Sims actually had to make do) with a request for a cease-fire until he could meet General Grant and discuss surrender terms. A Union officer led Sims to General Custer, but Sims angrily refused to give the truce flag to another Federal officer, who wanted it as a war souvenir. "I'll see you in hell first," he told the man. "It is humiliating enough to have to carry it and exhibit it, but I'm not going to let you preserve it as a monument of our defeat."

An instant before the cease-fire went into effect Confederate guns sounded in the distance. According to Chamberlain,

Just then a last cannon-shot from the edge of town plunges through the breast of a gallant and dear young officer in my front line— Lieutenant [Hiram] Clark of the 185th New York—the last man killed in the Army of the Potomac, if not the last in the Appomattox lines. Not a strange thing for war—this swift stroke of the mortal, but coming after the truce was in, it seemed a cruel fate.

Grieving Union soldiers gathered around Clark's body, as they did over the body of Private William Montgomery of the 155th Pennsylvania, a fifteen-year-old who had also lost his little life in the last artillery fire. It was about ten o'clock and a truce had been agreed upon until one in the afternoon. Since dawn over seven hundred men had been killed, possibly many more, and Lee had requested the truce not a moment too soon. For Sheridan was still eager to fight, poised and more than ready to shoot, slash, and club the enemy in a last savage bloodbath that might have been another Cold Harbor. "Damn them, I wish they had held out an hour longer and I would have whipped hell out of him," he later told Colonel Orville Babcock, who was on his way to General Lee with Grant's reply to Lee's last letter. To another officer he raised a clenched fist in protest, fuming, "I've got 'em—got 'em like that!"

But except for war lovers like Sheridan and Custer, there was at the moment as little anger left on both sides as there was rejoicing. One Union infantryman remembered "how we sat there and pitied and sympathized with those courageous Southern men who had fought for four long and dreary years all so stubbornly, so bravely and so well, and now, whipped, beaten, completely used up, were fully at our mercy—it was pitiful, sad, hard, and seemed to us altogether too bad."

Nor did most of the Union officers exhibit the killer instinct Sheridan displayed. Said Confederate general Gordon, who arranged the terms of the battlefield truce with him:

Truth demands that I say of General Sheridan that his style of conversation and bearing, while never discourteous, were far less agreeable and pleasing than those of any other officer of the Union army whom it was my fortune to meet. I do not recall a word he said that I could regard as in any degree offensive, but there was an absence of that delicacy and consideration which was exhibited by other Union officers.

As for Grant himself, he did not want another slaughter field from which many embittered Rebels would escape, possibly to fight the war elsewhere. "My campaign [now]," he explained, "was not Richmond, not the defeat of Lee in actual fight, but to remove him and his army out of the contest, and, if possible, to have him use his influence in inducing the surrender of Johnston [in North Carolina] and the other isolated armies."

Grant's messenger Babcock finally found General Lee about half a mile from Appomattox Court House resting under a scrub apple tree. This was the seed of the perennial tale in which Lee surrenders to Grant in the shade of the orchard, handing him his ornate dress sword—a story that for a time even inspired a cottage industry of souvenirs made from the trees in the orchard. As Sylvanus Cadwallader put it:

> Gaudy lithographs were printed by the hundreds of thousands, representing these two eminent military men as meeting under the umbrageous boughs of a large apple tree, both hat in hand, Grant rather erect, with one hand extended to receive Lee's sword, and Lee rather bowed and in the act of presenting his sword, hilt forward, to Grant, whilst staff officers, lines of battle, squadrons of cavalry, batteries of artillery, and all the paraphernalia of war, were pictured in the background. No such meeting . . . ever occurred. . . . Yet not less than a car load of charms, trinkets and keepsakes have been sold which were manufactured from the famous apple tree.

In fact, the original apple tree was chopped down by entrepreneurial Yankee soldiers less than an hour after the surrender, every twig and leaf of it and its very roots cut up into mementos, only a huge hole in the ground remaining where it stood.

As Grant said, "Like many other stories, [the apple orchard tale] would be very good if it was only true." In truth, Lee, of course, never surrendered in the apple orchard and he never relinquished his sword to Grant, who was miles away at the time. Horace Porter remembered what really happened:

Lee was lying down by the roadside on a blanket which had been spread over a few fence rails on the ground under an apple tree, which was part of an orchard. The circumstance furnished the only ground for the widespread report that the surrender occurred under an apple-tree. Babcock dismounted upon coming near, and as he approached on foot, Lee sat up, with his feet hanging over the roadside embankment. The wheels of the wagons in passing along the road had cut away the earth of this embankment and left the roots of the tree projecting. Lee's feet were partly resting on these roots. One of his staff officers came forward, took the dispatch which Babcock handed him and gave it to General Lee.

The dispatch read:

General R.E. Lee, Commanding C.S. Army:

Your note of this date [April 7th] is but this moment [11:50 A.M.] received in consequence of my having passed from the Richmond and Lynchburg road to the Farmville and Lynchburg Road. I am at this writing about four miles west of Walker's Church, and will push forward for the purpose of meeting you. Notice sent to me on this road where you wish the interview to take place will meet me.

After reading the note Lee asked Babcock to write General Meade and extend the truce until Grant could be reached. Then he headed toward Appomattox Court House along with his military secretary, Colonel Charles Marshall, and Babcock to find a meeting place as Grant had requested. He was dressed smartly in his best hat and uniform of Confederate gray, three golden stars on his low collar, wearing new elegant gauntlets, with his shining boots tipped with glittering golden spurs. At his side he wore the long sword, its hilt studded with jewels, presented to him by the State of Virginia on a much happier day. To his staff officers who watched him start out early that morning he had remarked, "If I am to be General Grant's prisoner today I must look my best."

6

The Surrender

A *hundred, hundred months have passed* . . .
O, don't you cry, Susannah!
And Lee upon the steps stood fast
Nor heard the North's hosanna.

He looked to where his army lay
Through all the warming weather.
He stood without a word to say,
And struck his hands together.

—McKinlay Kantor, "Appomattox," 1935

A WORRIED GENERAL CHAMBERLAIN, "intensely waiting," afraid the truce would soon end and "murder" would commence, finally saw both legendary generals pass through his lines toward Appomattox that last day. First came Lee:

A commanding form, superbly mounted, richly accoutered, of imposing bearing, noble countenance, with expression of deep sadness overmastered by deeper strength . . . [Then] not long after, by another inleading road, appeared another form . . . plain, simple and familiar . . . but as much inspiring awe as Lee in his splendor and his sadness. It is Grant. Slouched hat without cord . . . high boots mud-splashed to the top . . . no sword . . . sitting his saddle with the ease of a born master; taking no notice

of anything, all his faculties gathered into intense thought . . .
He seemed greater than I had ever seen him—a look as of
another world about him. . . . Staff officers were flying about crying, "Lee surrenders!"

But General Lee was a half hour ahead of Grant even at the
surrender. With the ten or so houses of the small village of Appomattox Court House finally in sight, Lee on his dapple gray Traveler directed his secretary Colonel Marshall to ride ahead and find
a suitable place for the momentous meeting between General
Grant and himself. Marshall rode with Babcock down the hamlet's
single street, which he found virtually deserted until he came
upon a good-natured resident named Wilmer McLean out for a
stroll, advising him that General Lee needed a convenient room in
any house nearby.

Major McLean, a prosperous retired wholesale grocer, quickly
led them into the sitting room of the closest vacant house, but this
was found to be small and meagerly furnished. McLean then conducted them to the best house in town, a two-story brick dwelling
with a comfortable colonnaded porch shaded by trees, a flower garden and lawn in front, and the family farm in the back. It was
McLean's own home, and perhaps he hadn't initially volunteered
it because he just didn't want any military men on the premises.
For McLean, ardent Southern patriot though he was, had had
enough of war. By some strange coincidence the old gentleman's
previous home had been an estate called Yorkshire near Manassas
Junction in northern Virginia, the house and farm requisitioned for
use as General Beauregard's headquarters during the first battle of
Bull Run in 1861. There regiments camped on the farmland, his
barn was used as a hospital, and the place was frequently fired
upon by the Yankees, one shell actually dropping down the chim-
ney and exploding in a kettle of stew cooking in the fireplace,
serving it indiscriminately to all in the room. Major McLean soon
packed up and moved his family farther south to a new house in
Appomattox Court House. "Here," he assured them, "the sound
of battle, will never reach you." As Confederate officer William
Miller Owen put it: "McLean removed from Manassas after the
battle, with the intentions of seeking some quiet nook where the

The McLean house at Appomattox, where "the Surrender" took place. From *Personal Memoirs of U. S. Grant*, 1886.

alarms of war could never find him; but it was his fortune to be in at the war's beginning and in at its death."

McLean's well-kept house west of the courthouse was approved by Marshall, and soon he, Babcock, and Lee entered the first room left of the front door. There they sat for about a half hour, conversing pleasantly, waiting for General Grant.

Grant, in the meantime, was riding at a trot toward Appomattox Court House with Horace Porter and the rest of their party. This was the energetic Grant—"an intermittent energy," his aide Adam Badeau had called him, "immensely powerful when awake, but passive and plastic in repose." As usual, the only thing kempt about him was his horse, the well-kept thoroughbred Cincinnati. Despite the truce, Porter worried about Grant's safety:

> The road was filled with men, animals, and wagons, and to avoid them and shorten the distance we turned slightly to the right and began to "cut across lots," but before going far we spied men

conspicuously in gray, and it was seen that we were moving toward the enemy's left flank, and that a short ride farther would take us into his lines. It looked for a moment as if a very awkward condition of things might possibly arise, and Grant would become a prisoner in Lee's lines, instead of Lee in his. Such a circumstance would have given rise to an important cross-entry in the system of campaign book-keeping. There was only one remedy—to retrace our steps and strike the right road, which was done without serious discussion.

On finally reaching Appomattox Court House, Grant spotted Generals Sheridan and Ord among other Union officers.

"Is Lee over there?" Grant asked, pointing down the street.

"Yes, he's in that brick house," Sheridan replied.

"Well, then, we'll go over," said Grant.

It was 1:30 when Grant entered the McLean house alone, leaving his officers waiting in the front yard. Babcock let him into the parlor and he and Lee greeted each other, shaking hands before they sat down, this being the first time they had spoken to each other or met face-to-face during the entire course of the war.

They were quite a contrast. Lee was six feet tall, erect and elegant, with neatly groomed silver-gray hair and beard, and wearing his dazzling gray uniform with multicolored sash, his ceremonial sword encased in a leather scabbard worked in gold. On the table where he sat was a matching gray felt hat and new long buckskin gauntlets.

Grant, strikingly his opposite physically, stood some four inches shorter, a few inches less if you counted his stoop-shouldered posture. His baggage was still lost and he wore the same mud-spattered boots and uniform he had been wearing for the past three days. There was no sword—this too still lost—the only lethal weapons he carried were his cigars. "He had on a single-breasted blouse made of dark-blue flannel," Porter recalled, "unbuttoned in front, and showing a waistcoat underneath. He wore an ordinary pair of topboots, with his trousers inside, and was without spurs." Porter observed that except for the four stars on his shoulder straps his uniform looked like that of any ordinary private soldier. He had gone through a hard time and looked it, someone remarked.

Another member of his staff, Colonel Amos Webster, wrote that the whiskered "Grant, covered with mud in an old faded uniform, looked like a fly on a shoulder of beef." Even Grant himself later noted, "I must have contrasted very strangely with a man so handsomely dressed, six feet high and of faultless form." He had, in fact, worried about his mud-spattered appearance while approaching Appomattox, fearing he would offend General Lee.

If any offense was taken, Lee didn't show it. The two adversaries—one old, slender, and patrician; the other young, stocky, and pedestrian in appearance—sat about ten feet apart in the sitting room, Grant at a round marble-topped table in the center, Lee beside a small, square marble-topped table by the front window, his secretary Colonel Marshall standing at his side. Grant made it a point not to gloat over his victory. He recalled:

> What General Lee's feelings were I do not know. As he was a man of much dignity, with an impassable face, it was impossible to say whether he felt inwardly glad that the end had finally come, or felt sad over the result. . . . But my own feelings, which had been quite jubilant on the receipt of his letter, were sad and depressed. I felt like anything rather than rejoicing at the downfall of a foe who had fought so long and valiantly, and had suffered so much for a cause, though that cause was, I believe, one of the worst for which a people ever fought.

So, postponing the inevitable for a few moments, letting Lee down softly, Grant began chatting about army days in Mexico with his old enemy.

"I met you once before, General Lee," he said, "while we were serving in Mexico, when you came over from General Scott's headquarters to visit Garland's brigade. . . . I have always remembered your appearance, and I should have recognized you anywhere."

"Yes," replied Lee, "I know I met you on that occasion, and I have often thought of it and tried to recollect how you looked, but I have never been able to recall a single feature."

If the answer was something of a put-down, the self-effacing Grant didn't take offense then or later in his *Memoirs*. "Well, he'll surely remember me from here on," he might have thought at the moment, "he'll remember me mud-spattered uniform and all."

In any case, the two generals in chief talked a bit more from their separate tables about Mexico and the glory days when both wore blue, until Grant asked Lee if he might invite inside his staff officers waiting in the yard.

Babcock waved in Generals Sheridan, Rawlins, Merritt, Williams, John Barnard, Ingalls, and Ord, Colonels Ely Parker, M. R. Morgan, Horace Porter, Adam Badeau, and Assistant Adjutant General Colonel Theodore Bowers, who would do the necessary paperwork at a wooden table set up by the window. Over the years many others claimed they were present at the surrender, including the flamboyant General Custer and correspondent Sylvanus Cadwallader, but whatever the number, Lee shook hands with or bowed to each of them, "in a most courteous, condescending and yet affable manner," according to the imperturbable Ely Parker. The staff officers took whatever seats they could find or stood erect in the sixteen-by-twenty-foot parlor, most of them standing behind Grant in Thomas Lovel's fairly accurate painting of the surrender. Lee, with only Colonel Marshall at his side, was vastly outnumbered even here, about eight to one, though Grant did everything he could to spare him any humiliation.

The Union officers had walked in softly, according to Porter, "very much as people enter a sick-chamber when they expect to find the patient dangerously ill." General Lee, however, showed no sign of his poor health, maintaining his usual happy blending of courtesy and dignity. "He betrayed no haughtiness or ill-humor on the one hand," Cadwallader wrote, "nor affected cheerfulness, forced politeness, nor flippancy on the other. He was a gentleman—which fully and wholly expresses his behavior." Lee did not change his expression an iota during the greeting ceremony until Colonel Parker was introduced to him. Porter wrote:

> Parker was a full-blooded (Seneca) Indian, and the reigning Chief of the Six Nations. When Lee saw his swarthy features he looked at him with evident surprise, and his eyes rested on him for several seconds. What was passing in his mind probably no one ever knew, but the natural surmise was that he first mistook Parker for a Negro, and was struck with astonishment to find that

the commander of the Union armies had one of that race on his personal staff.

Another story has Lee saying Parker is the only real American in the room and Parker replying "We are all Americans." This may be true, but the fact remains that Parker was hardly treated as an American all his life, suffering prejudice both in the military and after Grant made him commissioner of Indian affairs when he became president. In any case, astonished or not, Lee wanted to get down to business at this point; the conversation had grown so pleasant that the purpose of the meeting had almost been forgotten. "I suppose, General Grant," he said, according to Colonel Porter's account, "that the object of our present meeting is fully understood. I asked to see you to ascertain upon what terms you would accept the surrender of my army." According to one Southern account, he said: "I am here to ascertain the terms upon which you will accept the surrender of the Army of Northern Virginia; but . . . I am not willing to discuss, even, any terms incompatible with the honor of my army."

"The terms I propose," Grant replied in his same even, pleasant manner, "are those stated substantially in my letter of yesterday—that is, the officers and men surrendered are to be paroled and disqualified from taking up arms again until properly exchanged, and all arms, ammunition, and supplies are to be delivered up as captured property."

Lee must have felt great relief, for both he and several of his staff had thought it entirely possible that Grant would demand the imprisonment of all his army. As Cadwallader wrote: "The belief had seemed widespread among Confederate officers that the United States government had pledged itself to grant no amnesties for treason, and that 'they must all hang together, or hang separately.'" But Lee showed no delight or surprise at the good news. Nodding quickly in assent, he said, "Those are about the conditions I expected would be proposed."

Grant wanted to talk about the pleasant prospects of peace now, and his hope that this meeting would lead to an end to the war and any further loss of life—but Lee wanted to get these favorable surrender terms on paper. "I would suggest," he told Grant, "that you commit to writing the terms you have proposed, so that they may be formally acted upon."

"Do I understand you to accept my terms?" Grant asked.

"I do," Lee said, and North and South were wed again, though it would long be a stormy marriage—up until recent times.

Grant began writing in his manifold order book, carbon paper between the yellow pages, puffing on his pipe instead of his usual cigar as he rapidly scrawled in pencil the terms he had proposed and several more just as generous. The document read:

> Appomattox Ct. H., Va.
> April 9, 1865

General R. E. Lee,
Commanding C.S.A.
General:

In accordance with the substance of my letter to you of the 8th instant, I propose to receive the surrender of the Army of Northern Virginia on the following terms, to wit: Rolls of all the officers and men to be made in duplicate, one copy to be given to an officer to be designated by me, the other to be retained by such officer or officers as you may designate. The officers to give their individual paroles not to take up arms against the Government of the United States until properly exchanged; and each company or regimental commander to sign a like parole for the men of their commands. The arms, artillery and public property to be parked and stacked, and turned over to the officers appointed by me to receive them. This will not embrace the side-arms of the officers, nor their private horses or baggage. This done, each officer and man will be allowed to return to his home, not to be disturbed by U.S. authority so long as they observe their parole and the laws in force where they reside.

U.S. GRANT, LIEUTENANT-GENERAL

The "properly exchanged" term in this historic letter simply meant that the surrendered Confederate soldiers could not return to fight until a Union prisoner was exchanged for each of them, an event both Lee and Grant knew would never take place. When Grant finished the letter, he scanned it with Parker, made several corrections, and handed his order book to General Lee, who wiped his steel-rimmed spectacles clean, crossed his legs, and read the two pages slowly and carefully.

"General, is that satisfactory?" Grant asked when Lee finished reading.

"Yes, I am bound to be satisfied with anything you offer," Lee replied. "It is more than I expected."

As well it should have been, for the last two sentences of the document, especially the final one, went far beyond the limits Lincoln had set for Grant in negotiating a surrender, though Lincoln would have agreed with them. Whether Grant acted generously on the spur of the moment, or had previously considered these last terms, is not certainly known, but they would have far-reaching effects. The final sentence amounted to a general amnesty for all Confederate troops, who would never have to worry about being tried for treason or reprisals of any kind for fighting against the U.S. government. Less important politically, but more important at the moment, was the provision that Lee's officers could keep their side arms, private horses, and baggage, often the only possessions these soldiers had left in their war-torn world. No wonder Lee turned to Grant and said, "This will have a very happy effect upon my army."

But there was even more to come; Lee fought for his men to the end. "There is one thing I would like to mention," the Gray Fox asked after a short pause, probably knowing the answer. "The cavalrymen and artillerymen own their own horses in our army. . . . I would like to understand whether these [enlisted] men will be permitted to take their private property."

"You will find that the terms as written do not allow this," Grant replied. "Only the officers are permitted to take their private property."

Lee read over the second page of the letter. "No," he admitted, "I see the terms do not allow it; that is clear."

But General Grant could see the disappointment in his face. "Well, the subject is quite new to me," he mused. "Of course I did not know that any private soldiers owned their animals, but I think this will be the last battle of the war—I sincerely hope so—and

Facsimile of the original terms of Lee's surrender as written by General Grant.
From *Personal Memoirs of U. S. Grant*, 1886.

until property of the [?]

Government of the United States and each Company or Regimental Commander sign a like parole for the men of their minor Commands.

The Arms, Artillery and public property to be parked and stacked and turned over to the officer appointed by me to receive them. This will not embrace the side Arms of the Officers, nor their private horses or baggage. This done each officer and man will be allowed to return to their homes not to be disturbed by United States Authority so long as they observe their parole and the laws in force where they may reside.

Very respectfully
Lieutenant [?]

that the surrender of this army will be followed soon by that of all the others, and I take it that most of the men in the ranks are small farmers, and as the country has been so raided by the two armies, it is doubtful whether they will be able to put in a crop to carry themselves and their families through the next winter without the aid of the horses they are now riding. So I will arrange it this way: I will not change the terms as now written, but I will instruct the officers I shall appoint to receive the paroles to let all the men who claim to own a horse or mule to take the animals home with them to work their little farms."

In addition, for those without horses, Grant would request all transportation companies in the area "to facilitate in every way the return of these men to their homes." The usually undemonstrative Lee couldn't help but show his appreciation of such considerate provisions. One could hardly think of Grant as a butcher now; his magnanimous surrender terms and his impeccable deportment made the rugged, unkempt commander—the stubborn Unconditional Surrender Grant—seem as accommodating, and gentle, and gracious as the most chivalrous of the chivalry, a mirror image of Lee himself. "This will have the best possible effect on the men," Lee told Grant, handing back the document. "It will be very gratifying and will do much toward conciliating our people."

Grant passed the historic document to Colonel Bowers to make a fair copy in ink, but a flustered Bowers spoiled three new sheets of paper before turning the job over to the impassive Seneca chief Parker, who promptly made a clean copy in a handwriting much better than anyone else's on Grant's staff. Grant then checked the letter, folded it, and sealed it in an official envelope addressed to General Lee, who broke the seal and read it again. Colonel Marshall, meanwhile, had as instructed prepared Lee's brief letter of surrender, which Lee signed and handed to Grant:

HEADQUARTERS, ARMY OF NORTHERN VIRGINIA,
April 9th, 1865

GENERAL: I received your letter of this date containing the terms of surrender of the Army of Northern Virginia as proposed by you. As they are substantially the same as those expressed in your letter of the 8th instant, they are accepted. I will proceed to designate the proper officers to carry the stipulations into effect.

> Very respectfully, your obt servt
> R. E. LEE, GENERAL

It was about three o'clock on that Palm Sunday afternoon when Lee signed the formal surrender letter ending four years of war in Virginia. Lee did not give over his jeweled sword to Grant, as legend has it. "The much talked of surrendering of Lee's sword and my handing it back, this and much more that has been said about it, is the purest romance," Grant recalled later. He did not even glance at Lee's letter, but handed it to Parker for safekeeping, explaining that the letter was only a formality; Lee's spoken word was good enough for him. Almost twenty-eight thousand men were to be surrendered and the paroles, printed on a slow army press, would not be ready until late the next day. All read the same as the parole of General Lee and his staff:

> We the undersigned prisoners of war belonging to the Army of Northern Virginia, having been this day surrendered by General Robert E. Lee, C.S.A., commanding said army, to Lieut. Genl. U.S. Grant, commanding Armies of the United States, do hereby give our solemn parole of honor that we will not hereafter serve in the armies of the Confederate States, or in any military capacity whatever, against the United States of America, or render aid to the enemies of the latter, until properly exchanged, in such manner as shall be mutually approved by the respective authorities.
>
> Done at Appomattox Court House, Virginia, this 9th day of April, 1865.
>
> > R.E. Lee, Genl
> > W.H. Taylor, Lt Col AAG
> > Charles S. Venable, Lt Col & AAG
> > Charles Marshall, Lt Col & AAG
> > H.E. Peyton, Lt Col & A & Inspt Genl
> > Giles B. Cooke, Maj & AA & IG
> > H.E. Young, Maj AAG Judge Adv

A few more details remained to be settled. "I have a thousand or more of your men as prisoners, . . ." Lee told Grant, "a number of them officers whom we have required to march along with us for several days. I shall be glad to send them into your lines as soon as it can be arranged, for I have no provisions for them. I have, indeed, nothing for my own men. They have been living for the last few days principally on parched corn, and we are badly in need of both rations and forage. I telegraphed to Lynchburg, directing several train-loads of rations to be sent on by rail from there, and when they arrive I shall be glad to have the present wants of my men supplied from them."

Apparently Lee was unaware that Sheridan had captured the Lynchburg supplies the night before. "I should like to have our men sent within our lines as soon as possible," Grant told him. "I will take steps at once to have your army supplied with rations. . . . Of about how many men does your present force consist?"

Lee was unable to say. "My losses in killed and wounded have been exceedingly heavy, and, besides, there have been many stragglers and some deserters," he explained. "All my reports and public papers, and, indeed, my own private letters, had to be destroyed on the march, to prevent them from falling into the hands of your people . . . so that I have no means of ascertaining our present strength."

"Suppose I send over twenty-five thousand rations. Do you think that will be a sufficient supply?" Grant asked, knowing Sheridan had captured far more.

"I think it will be ample," said Lee, who hadn't eaten a thing himself that day, "and it will be a great relief, I assure you."

Lee was not in the mood for any small talk. Rising and bowing in his courtly manner, he prepared to leave, Colonel Marshall falling in behind. It was a little before four o'clock—the historic meeting had lasted about two and a half hours—when he shook hands with General Grant and left the room. Out on the porch, Porter observed him waiting for his orderly to bring Traveler, noticing no one around him, sadness overwhelming him as he stood there and "smote his hands together a number of times in

Position of the Confederate army when the surrender was announced. From *Harper's Pictorial History of the Civil War,* 1866.

an absent sort of way." Just as he mounted Traveler, Grant and his officers stepped down from the porch and removed their hats respectfully. Lee returned the salute and rode away.

As Robert E. Lee moved slowly, dejectedly through his lines to his tent, grim Confederate veterans thronged around him, hats raised, bronzed faces bathed with tears, "reaching up a thousand hands to wring his own, to touch his horse or Lee himself," in the words of Major Cooke. They cried, they cursed, they babbled untranslatable words from the heart. "We don't blame you, but the people's hopes are dead!" one man cried. "Farewell, General Lee, I wish for your sake and mine that every Yankee on earth was sunk ten miles in hell!" vowed another. "God bless you, we'll fight 'em again!" shouted still another. "Blow Gabriel, blow!" a ragged veteran cried, throwing away his musket. "My God, let him blow, I am ready to die!"

"Men," Lee said, head bare, eyes swimming, "I have done for you all that it was in my power to do. You have done all your best.

Leave the rest to God. Go to your homes and resume your occu-
pations. Obey the laws and become good citizens as you were soldiers. My heart is too full to say more." The next day he would
thank them formally by writing General Order Number Nine,
which became known to generations as Lee's Farewell Address, a
document many copied and had General Lee sign:

> After four years of arduous service, marked by unsurpassed
> courage and fortitude, the Army of Northern Virginia has been
> compelled to yield to overwhelming numbers and resources.
>
> I need not tell the brave survivors of so many hard fought
> battles, who have remained steadfast to the last, that I have con-
> sented to the result from no distrust of them.
>
> But feeling that valor and devotion could accomplish noth-
> ing that would compensate for the loss that must have attended
> the continuance of the contest, I determined to avoid the use-
> less sacrifice of those whose past services have endeared them to
> their countrymen.
>
> By the terms of the agreement officers and men can return
> to their homes and remain until exchanged. You will take with
> you the satisfaction that proceeds from the consciousness of duty
> faithfully performed, and I earnestly pray that a Merciful God
> will extend to you His blessing and protection.
>
> With an increasing admiration of your constancy and devo-
> tion to your country, and a grateful remembrance of your kind
> and generous consideration for myself, I bid you all an affec-
> tionate farewell.
>
> R.E. Lee
> General

Even before Lee had passed into his own sad ragged ranks the
Union camps exploded with joy at the news of the surrender. Officers near the McLean house almost immediately began searching the parlor for souvenirs. McLean's home was "bombarded"
still again, though it was a much gentler bombardment. General
Ord paid him $40 for Lee's table; he later offered it to Mrs. Grant,
who said Mrs. Ord should have it. Sheridan paid $20 for Grant's
table, and presented it to General Custer's pretty wife. Brass
candlesticks, a stone inkstand, and a child's doll were only a few

of the souvenirs or holy relics carried off. Upholstery from chairs and sofas was cut to ribbons and cane-bottomed chairs cut into strips and handed out to soldiers in the yard as mementos of what would later be officially dedicated as the Surrender Grounds. These same soldiers stripped the McLean garden of flowers to press and carry in their wallets all their lives. The joyous souvenir hunting made it impossible for the surrender parlor to be preserved exactly as it was that historic afternoon when four years of war and gore were ended in Virginia. Sylvanus Cadwallader, who sketched the outside of the house for a nation of readers, wrote that the "craze for mementos" resulted in "sharp contention between the families of the distinguished officers" over the McLean furniture. He probably would have substantially agreed with members of the McLean family who later denied that any articles were sold and claimed that the Union officers looted the house. Cadwallader wrote:

> Numerous offers were made for the chairs in which Grant and Lee sat, but Major McLean steadily refused to part with them. It seems that a couple of cavalry officers, finding they could not obtain the chairs by any other means, seized then by force and carried them away. They tried to induce McLean to accept pay for them; but he flung the "greenbacks" on the floor indignantly. Sometime after the chairs were carried off a cavalryman rode up, thrust a ten dollar "greenback" into McLean's hands, and exclaimed as he rode away: "This is for the Major's chair." Search was made for the chairs, and the officers who confiscated them, but neither could be found.

Among the first to celebrate the surrender was General Meade in his camp a few miles east. So sick that he had been confined to his ambulance most of the week, Meade nevertheless leaped on his horse and galloped off bareheaded, raising both arms in the air, crying, "It's all over, boys! Lee's surrendered! It's all over!" Staff officers waving hats and swords joined him and two squads of cavalry followed, all of them shouting as they galloped along the road. Veteran soldiers lost all control, throwing everything they could lift in the air.

Wrote General Regis de Trobriand:

All at once a tempest of hurrahs shook the air along the front of
our line. . . . Mad hurrahs fill the air like the rolling of thunder,
in the fields, in the woods, along the roads, and are prolonged in
echo. . . . All the hopes of four years at last realized; all the fears
dissipated, all perils disappeared; all the privations, all the suf-
ferings, all the misery ended; the intoxication of triumph; the joy
at the near return to the domestic hearth—for all this, one single
burst of enthusiasm did not suffice. So the hurrahs and cries of
joy were prolonged . . .

One infantryman wrote that the cheers went on for over half
an hour: "Men shouted until they could shout no longer," others
sang hymns, many unabashedly cried. Another soldier wrote:

The air is black with hats and boots, coats, knapsacks, shirts and
cartridge boxes, blankets and shelter tents, canteens and haver-
sacks. [Men] fall on each others necks and laugh and cry by
turns. Huge, lumbering, bearded men embrace and kiss like
schoolgirls, then dance and sing and shout, stand on their heads
and play at leapfrog with each other. . . . All the time, from the
hills around, the deep-throated cannon give their harmless thun-
ders, and at each hollow boom the vast concourse rings out its
joy anew that murderous shot and shell no longer follow close
the accustomed sound.

It was these same deep-throated cannon Grant heard as he
rode away from the McLean house to his headquarters tent at
about 4:30 P.M. Grant was so deep in his thoughts about the surrender that he had completely forgotten to tell the War Department or Lincoln about it. When Porter jogged his memory he dismounted off the road and scrawled a telegram to Secretary of War
Stanton: "GENERAL LEE SURRENDERED THE ARMY OF NORTHERN VIRGINIA
THIS AFTERNOON ON TERMS PROPOSED BY MYSELF. THE ACCOMPANYING
ADDITIONAL CORRESPONDENCE WILL SHOW THE CONDITIONS FULLY. U.S.
GRANT, LIEUTENANT-GENERAL."

General Grant knew Lincoln would be happy with the terms,
that Washington and all the country would erupt with joy, but still
the celebratory guns seemed wrong to him. This was not the spirit

of Appomattox; it did not respect the fallen dead and the vanquished foe. Grant turned to an aide and told him to send officers out with orders to have the firing of salutes stopped at once. "The war is over," he said, "the Rebels are our countrymen again, and the best sign of rejoicing after the victory will be to abstain from all demonstrations in the field."

The cannon stopped, but of course the simple joy of victory, the joy of knowing that one would sleep that night and wake up in the morning, the joy of knowing one was going home alive—the celebration of that joy could not be commanded silent, could not be repressed even by those who tried. "As the armies were enemies no longer, there was no need of martial array that night, nor fear of surprise, nor call to arms," wrote *New York Times* reporter William Swinton. Chamberlain wrote:

> The soul-draining bugle-call "Lights Out!" did not mean darkness and silence that momentous evening. Far into the night gleamed some irrepressible camp fire and echoed the irrepressible cheer in which men voiced their deepest thought. . . . At last we sleep—those who can. And so ended that 9th of April, 1865—Palm Sunday—in that obscure little Virginia village now blazoned for immortal fame. Graver destinies were determined on that humble field than on many of classic and poetic fame. And though the issue brought bitterness to some, yet the heart of humanity the world over thrilled at the tidings.

7

News from Heaven

All, all are jubilant.

—Secretary of the Navy Gideon Welles, April 10, 1865

IT RAINED THE NEXT DAY in Appomattox, but on that April 10 morning at nine o'clock General Grant and his staff rode out to confer with General Lee again on a knoll overlooking both their lines, Lee galloping out alone to meet him when Grant arrived a little early. This meeting in the drizzling rain had been arranged at McLean's the day before and the two generals withdrew to discuss privately matters Grant knew exceeded his authority from Lincoln but which he felt morally bound to pursue. He did tell Horace Porter and the rest of his staff the gist of the conversation.

Porter recalled years after the event that both generals in their half-hour talk had expressed a hope that the war would soon be over. Lee told Grant there was no reason good relations could not be restored between North and South—not even the issue of slavery, which most Southerners no longer supported. He believed that all remaining Confederate armies should surrender, "as nothing could be gained by further resistance in the field," but he refrained from promising Grant that he would try to influence Jefferson Davis or anyone else about such a surrender. Porter insisted

207

that Grant never asked Lee to consult with President Lincoln concerning the terms of reconstruction. "After the conversation," he wrote, "the two commanders lifted their hats and said good-bye. Lee rode back to his camp to take a final farewell of his army, and Grant returned to McLean's house, where he seated himself on the porch until it was time to take his final departure."

Later, on April 20, Lee did write Jefferson Davis, urging the fleeing president to cease all hostilities:

> From what I have seen and learned, I believe an army cannot be organized or supported in Virginia, and as far as I know the condition of affairs, the country east of the Mississippi is morally and physically unable to maintain the contest unaided with any hope of ultimate success. A partisan [guerrilla] war may be contained, and hostilities protracted, causing individual suffering and the devastation of the country, but I see no prospect by that means of achieving separate independence. . . . To save useless effusion of blood, I would recommend measures be taken for suspension and the restoration of peace.

It will probably never be known whether Grant asked Lee to visit President Lincoln, as Colonel Marshall—Porter to the contrary—insisted that Lee told *him*. But Lee almost certainly advised Grant that his campaign in Virginia was "the last organized resistance which the South was capable of making—that . . . there was no longer any [Confederate] army which could make a stand." This Grant told his biographer John Russell Young years later, and it was the prevalent opinion North and South when the two commanders said good-bye that last time. Many more men would die after Appomattox, there were still armies in the field and Davis's government remained at large, but for all practical purposes the Civil War was over.

When Lee left Grant and rode back to camp he came upon a Union general, an old adversary of many battles. "Don't you know me, General Lee?" the man asked. "I'm George Meade."

"Oh, is that you, Meade?" Lee replied. "How did you get all that gray in your beard?"

"I'm afraid you're the cause of most of it," Meade laughed. The two rode together for a distance, across the ravine separating the Union forces from the shattered remains of the Confederate army. Meade ordered his color-bearer to unfurl the Stars and Stripes, riding past cheering men, including one proud and bitter Confederate veteran who cried out, "Damn your old rag! We are cheering General Lee!"

More typical were the Southerners who came over to the Federal lines to visit with their old adversaries. "We were glad to see them," Union private Theodore Gerrish recalled. "We received them kindly, and exchanged pocket knives and sundry trinkets, that each could have something to carry home as a reminiscence of the great event." However, a friendly wrestling match between a Billy Yank and a Johnny Reb is said to have resulted in the final death at Appomattox. The winner, according to the traditional tale, was General Lee's cook, Confederate champion Captain Joel Compton.

Lee had his general pass to leave now. Dated Appomattox Court House, Virginia, April 10, 1865, it was signed by Grant and read:

> All officers commanding posts, pickets or detachments will pass General R.E. Lee through their lines north or south on presentation of this pass. General Lee will be permitted to visit Richmond at any time, unless otherwise ordered by competent authority, and every facility for his doing so will be given by officers of the United States Army to whom this may be presented.

A Confederate soldier who saw Lee leaving wrote, "We who live today shall never see his like again, and whether our posterity does is problematical."

General Robert E. Lee, who would always be in the South of that day the Lancelot of all knights, the courtliest knight that ever bare shield, the kindliest man that ever strake with sword, the goodliest person that ever came among press of knights. The gray knight, the great patriarch, Uncle Robert, left Appomattox aboard the faithful Traveler toward eleven o'clock, attended by a single servant. Fatigued and bent over slightly, no longer ramrod straight in the saddle, he was on his way to Richmond and his ailing wife, who had aged as much as he had during the war, face gaunt, hair white—from the fields of war into the vales of peace.

Grant the great commoner chatted pleasantly on the McLean porch with passersby and General "Pete" Longstreet, who had been an attendant at his wedding, among other old Southern friends. "Why do men fight who were born to be brothers?" Longstreet later mused on recalling the meeting. Grant refused to go back to Richmond, according to his wife's memoirs, because he didn't want to distress the people there and add to their despair. The Union commander departed at about noon for City Point, where Julia waited for her "Victor," and then on to Washington to see President Lincoln for the last time before his assassination. Neither he nor Lee would be present at the formal Appomattox surrender ceremony that Grant had insisted upon, which was scheduled for April 12. Even as the two generals went their separate ways from Appomattox, the greatest celebration in the history of the country was in full swing.

PEACE! THE BLOODSHED ENDED!

WHOLE REBEL ARMY SURRENDERS!

VICTORY!

PEACE!

So read newspaper headlines across the nation. The celebrating had begun the evening before in Washington when Grant's telegram was received, a cable that brought "news from Heaven," as New England poet James Russell Lowell put it in a letter to a friend, Harvard professor Charles Eliot Norton. Barely mentioned were the casualties of the Appomattox campaign: 1,316 Union dead, 7,750 wounded; 1,200 Confederate dead, 6,000 wounded. The tidings of joy spread from great city to tiny rural hamlet as reporters wired their stories through the night, often with a glass or bottle of whiskey in hand.

In Richmond, despite Grant's orders, guns boomed and shattered windows. In Washington a five-hundred-gun dawn salute was ordered by Stanton; howitzers sounded from the Navy Yard, flares and fireworks lit the sky. There was no work that Monday except on the premises of Ebenezer Scrooges. All government offices were closed, and the whole city seemed to have taken to the streets from early morning on. Bands playing "Yankee Doodle," "Rally 'Round the Flag Boys," "Marching Through Georgia," and a dozen more popular songs marched down Pennsylvania Avenue, followed by crowds of people singing and cheering and waving flags.

A group of Treasury workers marched to the White House and serenaded President Lincoln with "Praise God from Whom All Blessings Flow" and "The Star-Spangled Banner" while he tried to eat his breakfast. Toward noon a crowd of over three thousand gathered at the White House and cheered wildly, especially when young Tad waved one of his collection of captured Confederate battle flags from a window. Without making a formal speech, a tired President Lincoln joked with the revelers and asked their three bands to join together and play "Dixie" because, although the South had always claimed it, "yesterday . . . we fairly captured it" and "it is one of the best tunes I have ever heard." Then he led the crowd, waving his big hands, in three cheers for General Grant and his men.

It was the same all over the North. "All, all are jubilant," wrote Secretary of the Navy Gideon Welles in his diary for the day. In Chicago bells pealed and a one-hundred-cannon salute awakened the city; throngs of people surged through the streets with torches. In New York City a gathering of twenty thousand businessmen sang "Praise God," the psalm of thanksgiving; flags waved from windows in mansions and tenements—the entire supply of flags in the city was said to be sold out. GOOD NEWS! LEE AND THE WHOLE REBEL ARMY SURRENDER! one newspaper headline screamed. Diarist George Templeton Strong wrote for his Monday, April 10, entry: "Lee and his army have surrendered. Gloria in excelsis Deo! They can bother and perplex none but historians henceforth, forever. There is no such army anymore. God be praised!"

Sometimes the celebrating went too far. "Dear Wife," wrote I. Shoger, a mud-marcher with Sheridan's army. "[We] got the news

The last photo of Lincoln, made April 10, 1865, by
Washington photographer Alexander Gardner. Only
one copy was ever made from the accidentally broken
negative. From *Meet General Grant*, 1929.

of Lee's capture . . . you aught to have seen the excitement. The
dispatch was redd by Genl. Sherman in front of the [Smithfield]
Court house. Our band was at the head of the collume, we playd
all the National airs, the soldiers threw up thair hats and chreed
with all thair might. They got a negro on a blanket and threw him
ten feet [in the air]."

GLORIOUS NEWS IS RECEIVED, blared another headline. Throughout the land cannons sounded, shotguns blasted, pistols cracked,

men galloped wildly on horses, wagons full of people raced down the streets cheering, church bells and cathedral bells and school bells rang out wildly and unceasingly, flag-bedecked riverboats sounded their whistles, fire engines blanketed with flags roared and whistled down grand avenues and dirt roads, saloon keepers poured free beer for everyone until they ran out of it. Anything that could make noise, from bands and firecrackers to women banging on pots and pans and burly men banging with sledge-hammers on giant boilers, was brought out into the streets. Never did so many flags wave in the nation's history, even though half the country wasn't waving any. Enemies shook hands and strangers hugged each other. Those against the war and those for the war all joined in rejoicing that the war was over, and all cried that Monday as they celebrated. People from every walk of life—from doctors and lawyers to foundry workers and porters—shouted: "The war is over! Hurrah for Grant! Hurrah for Lincoln! The boys are coming home!" No longer was America a house divided or a slaughterhouse. No longer did "the evil of slavery stain America's escutcheon," as General Theodore Gates put it, "she stood before the world in the sublime majesty of a nation free in fact, as well as theory."

It lasted all that day: the shouting and singing and dancing in the streets, the torchlight parades and bonfires, the men and women marching, turning somersaults and walking on their hands, standing upright atop their horses, swinging from trees and lamp-posts. It lasted into the next day until the exhausted celebrants finally turned to more somber forms of thanksgiving like Grand Illumination Night in Washington, when thousands of people put lighted candles in their windows.

Back in Appomattox Court House one final ceremony had to be performed. General Grant had insisted upon it against Confederate wishes—a formal surrender, the traditional laying down of arms. The official ceremony was essential, Grant had held, lest any of the country ever forget. To some such a ceremony seemed divisive, but as it happened it became the crowning glory of the spirit of reconciliation fostered at Appomattox, a surging tide of brotherhood that would begin to ebb when Lincoln died three days later of his assassin's bullet.

Grant had set the formal surrender for the morning of Wednesday April 12 and selected the Union hero Brigadier General Joshua Chamberlain to command the ceremony. Lee had appointed the brave Georgian General John B. Gordon to lead the column of Confederate troops across the valley from their broken encampment and up the road leading through Appomattox, where erect Union soldiers lined each side of the street. Behind Gordon in the gray column that chill gray morning were the two hundred survivors of the once mighty Stonewall Brigade, and behind their ragged unit marched thousands more men.

Remembering the spectacle, Chamberlain wrote:

> On they come with the old swinging route step and swaying battle-flags . . . crowded so thick, by the thinning out of men, that the whole column seemed crowned with red. . . . Before us in proud humiliation stood the embodiment of manhood: men whom neither toils nor sufferings, nor the fact of death, nor disaster, nor hopelessness could bend from their resolve; standing before us now, thin, worn, and famished, but erect, and with eyes looking level into ours, waking memories that bound us together as no other bond—was not such manhood to be welcomed back into a Union so tested and assured?

General Gordon at the head of the tramping column seemed to ride "with heavy spirit and downcast face," his officers grim, expecting the worst humiliation from Chamberlain, Rebel bullet holes ventilating his Yankee coat. But then Gordon heard from the Union lines the order for the marching salute, a bugle sounding the same order, the clatter of thousands of Union muskets raised to the shoulder in the "carry" salute to a respected enemy. Gordon knew immediately what this meant and turned toward Chamberlain, wheeled smartly, "making with himself and his horse one uplifted figure," raised his sword and as the horse dipped brought his sword down to his boot tip, saluting Chamberlain before he shouted an order for all the advancing Confederates to return the Union tribute to their courage. It was "honor answering honor,"

Chamberlain said. "On our part not a sound of trumpet more, nor roll of drums; not a cheer, nor word, nor whisper of vain-glorying, nor motion of man standing again at the order, but an awed stillness rather, and breath-holding, as if it were the passing of the dead."

With each unit that passed came the memory of terrible battles in which both victor and vanquished had fought: Bull Run . . . Shiloh . . . Gettysburg . . . Chickamauga . . . The Wilderness . . . Cold Harbor . . . Five Forks. There were tears on both sides. "Many of the grizzled veterans wept like women," a Confederate officer recalled. "My own eyes were as blind as my voice was dumb." Then came the most painful part of the ceremony for the worn, half-starved men in gray. Wrote Chamberlain:

> They fix bayonets, stack arms, then, hesitatingly, remove cartridge-boxes and lay them down. Lastly, reluctantly, with agony of expression—they tenderly fold their flags, battle-worn and torn, blood-stained, heart-holding colors, and lay them down, some frenziedly rushing from the ranks, kneeling over them, clinging to them, pressing them to their lips with burning tears. And only the Flag of the Union greets the sky!

After the last parole, a bitter Confederate officer, apparently made mad by the war, told Chamberlain, "You may forgive us, General, but we won't be *forgiven*. There is a rancor in our hearts which you little dream of. We *hate* you, sir!" But most were consoled by the ceremony and would stand upon their honor. "I fear we would not have done the same by you had the situation been reversed," said one Rebel officer. Said a North Carolinian: "I will go home and tell Joe Johnston we can't fight men such as you. I will advise him to surrender." Still another officer pointed to the Stars and Stripes. "We had our choice of weapons and of ground and we have lost," he said. "Now that is my flag, and I will prove myself as worthy as any of you."

By the next day the nearly twenty-eight thousand Confederates were paroled and departing the battlefield. "A strange and somber shadow rose up ghostlike from the haunts of memory or habit and rested down on the final parting scene," Chamberlain remembered. "How strange the undertone of sadness even at the release from prison and from pain! It seems as if we had put some precious part of ourselves there which we are loath to leave. When all is over . . . the long lines of scattered cartridges are set on fire and the lurid flames wreathing the blackness of earthly shadows give an unearthly border to our parting."

Recalled Confederate soldier Barry Benson: "So Blackwood and I left the army, our army, left them there on the hill with their arms stacked in the field all in rows, never to see them anymore. . . . We crossed the road into the field into the thickets and in a little while lost sight of all that was left of the army." Confederate Carlton McCarthy wrote: "Comrades wept as they gazed upon each other and with choking voices said farewell. And so—they parted. Little groups of two or three or four, without food, without money, but with the satisfaction that proceeds from the consciousness of duty faithfully performed, were soon plodding their way homeward."

Behind them they left comrades in the field hospitals. Hundreds, thousands who would never make the journey home alive. An observer at nearby Burkesville Hospital wrote:

> Three thousand men were lying in this squalid suffering. In one row were five men lying on a hard floor . . . all dying. Two of them were conscious and were able to gasp out last words for wife or mother which were quickly written down. . . . In a small room were three hopeless cases, placed there that they might breathe their last in peace apart from the noise and excitement— one with a shell wound through both his hips, another with an arm and shoulder carried away, and the other with his jaw and face terribly shattered and his tongue half gone.

But the lucky ones could not look back. They headed home down dusty roads and through green pastures filled with blue chicory, dandelions, Queen Anne's lace, purple crown vetch, hawkweed, all the lovely escapes or weed flowers of the country. Absent were the hundreds of thousands who had fallen on ten thousand such fields. With some went comrades crippled, blinded, made insane or almost so; they would be joined by others like them along

the way, by men with their names and addresses pinned to them
so that they could be delivered by kind strangers to their homes,
by men released from prison camps whose eyes bulged out and
whose skeletons had worked through. No simple country lads of
yesterday were going home—the country lads were all dead in one
way or another.

Chamberlain, who was looking on, would later write: "Over all
the hillsides in the peaceful sunshine, are clouds of men on foot or
horse, singly or in groups, making their earnest way, as if by the instinct of an ant, each with his own little burden, each for his own
little house."

Many burdens were far from little, but they weren't soldiers
anymore; they were no longer armies. "The charges were now
withdrawn from the guns," Horace Porter recalled, "the camp-fires
were left to smoulder in their ashes, the flags were tenderly
furled—those historic banners, battle-stained, bullet-riddled . . .
with scarcely enough left of them on which to imprint the names
of the battles they had seen—and the Army of the Union and the
Army of Northern Virginia turned their backs upon each other for
the first time in four long bloody years."

After Appomattox:
A Chronology

April 11, 1865. President Lincoln urges "a righteous and speedy peace" in his last public speech.

April 12. Mobile, Alabama, becomes the last major city of the South to fall to Federal troops, at a cost of 1,578 casualties when, as Grant would later write, "its possession was of no importance."

April 13. Lincoln halts the drafting of soldiers for the Union army.

April 14. On this Good Friday President Lincoln is mortally wounded by assassin John Wilkes Booth at Ford's Theater in Washington. On the same day the U.S. flag is raised again over Fort Sumter in Charleston, South Carolina, where the war began four years before.

April 15. Lincoln dies of his wound and Vice President Andrew Johnson assumes the presidency. With Lincoln died his generous reconstruction plans for the South. "The songs of victory are drowned in sorrow," one Northern newspaper observed.

April 18. Generals Sherman and Johnston sign a "memorandum or basis of agreement" calling for an armistice by all armies in the field. The agreement also establishes conciliatory reconstruction policies. Six days later President Johnson rejects the agreement as going beyond Sherman's authority.

April 20. In a letter to Jefferson Davis, Lee urges the Confederate president to end all fighting and not to encourage guerrilla warfare.

April 21. John S. Mosby disbands his famous Confederate rangers, most of whom surrender to the Federals.

April 26. John Wilkes Booth is shot and killed in a barn on the farm of Richard Garrett south of the Rappahannock River in Virginia. Whether a Federal soldier killed him or the shot was self-inflicted will never be established. "Useless, useless," were his last words.

Later that day, General Johnston surrenders his army of thirty thousand men to General Sherman under roughly the same terms Grant gave to Lee. This time President Johnson accepts the surrender.

April 27. The overcrowded riverboat *Sultana,* her boiler defective, explodes north of Memphis on the Mississippi River while carrying some 2,000 Union soldiers home from Southern prisoner of war camps. Estimates of the death toll range from 1,238 to 1,900 in one of history's worst maritime disasters.

May 4. Confederate forces in Alabama, Mississippi, and Louisiana are surrendered by General Richard Taylor to General Edward Canby.

May 9. General M. Jeff Thompson, commander of the Missouri-Arkansas region, begins negotiations to surrender his troops two days later.

May 10. Federal troops capture the fleeing Jefferson Davis, his wife, and several members of his staff in a woods near Irwinville, Georgia. Davis is not dressed as a woman, as legend has it, but is wearing a long raincoat and shawl to protect himself against the heavy rain. He will never be tried, though charged with treason, but will be imprisoned for two years, briefly in chains, before being released on $100,000 bail. He dies in 1889, at age eighty-one.

In a public proclamation President Johnson declares that "armed resistance to the authority of this Government . . . may be regarded as virtually at an end."

May 13. The battle or skirmish of Palmito Ranch is fought in Texas on the banks of the Rio Grande. Confederate troops under Colonel John R. I. P. ("Rest in Peace") Ford win this last significant battle of the Civil War, the Union suffering considerable casualties. In the battle Indiana private John Jay Williams becomes the last soldier to be killed in action in a Civil War battle, according to many sources. He is the last of at least 620,000 Union and Confederate soldiers to die in battle—one out of every fifty Americans. As historian James M. McPherson points out, when civilian deaths are added to this figure, "the toll of Civil War dead probably exceeds that of all other American wars put together." In addition to the hundreds of thousands of deaths, there are at least 470,000 wounded on both sides—well over one million casualties in all.

May 22. Three Confederate soldiers who refused to accept Lee's surrender fire upon five hundred Federal troops at the Floyd, Virginia, courthouse. After a six-mile chase they are trapped in a graveyard and killed by one synchronized round of three hundred shots when they refuse to stop firing. They are buried where they fell, each of them the last soldier to be killed in the Civil War.

May 23–24. The Grand Review of the Armies is held in Washington, D.C. Two hundred thousand troops from the Army of the Potomac, the Army of the Tennessee, and the Army of Georgia pass in a last review as huge crowds line the streets and cheer.

May 27. Minor skirmishing occurs at Switzlar's Mill in Chariton County, Missouri.

President Johnson proclaims a general amnesty to those who rebelled against Federal authority. However, those who held high rank in the Confederate government and military must apply for special individual pardons, as must those who own over $20,000 of property. General Lee later signs the special oath of allegiance to regain his citizenship, but Secretary of State Seward gives the document to a friend as a war souvenir and the document is never recorded. Thus, Lee is not officially a U.S. citizen again for another century—when his citizenship is restored by a special act of Congress in 1975.

June 2. General Edmund Kirby Smith officially approves the surrender made by Lieutenant General Simon Bolivar Buckner on May 26 of all Confederate forces west of the Mississippi. This was the last large body of Southern troops to surrender. However, some elements of these troops (notably General Joseph Shelby's one-thousand-man Iron Brigade) cross over into Mexico and settle there rather than submit to "Yankee rule."

June 23. Brigadier General Stand Watie surrenders his battalion of Cherokee, Cree, Seminole, and Osage Indians in the Oklahoma Territory. This was the last sizable surrender of the war.

June 28. The last shot of the war is fired by the C.S.S. *Shenandoah* in the Arctic Ocean at a Yankee whaler. When her captain, James Waddell, learns that the war is over, he sails her to England, where her Confederate Jack is lowered at 10 A.M. on November 6, 1865, the last official Confederate flag to be lowered.

December 18. After approval by twenty-seven states, the Thirteenth Amendment to the Constitution is declared in effect by Secretary of State Seward, abolishing slavery in the United States.

April 2, 1866. President Johnson proclaims the end of the war: "Now, therefore, I, Andrew Johnson, President of the United States, do hereby proclaim and declare that the insurrection which heretofore existed in the States of Georgia, South Carolina, Virginia, North Carolina, Tennessee, Alabama, Louisiana, Arkansas, Mississippi, and Florida is at an end and is henceforth to be so regarded." On August 20 he adds Texas to the list, its government finally having formed by that time, declaring, "I do further proclaim that the said insurrection is at an end and that peace, order, tranquility, and civil authority now exist in and throughout the whole of the United States of America."

October 12, 1870. Robert E. Lee, age sixty-three, who has long suffered from a heart condition, dies at his Lexington home. Lee had spent the years after the Civil War as president of Washington College (later Washington and Lee University), avoiding all politics, and never writing his wartime memoirs. His last words are variously said to be "Tell General Hill that he must come up," or "Strike the tent!"

July 23, 1885. Ulysses S. Grant, age sixty-three, dies from throat cancer after a long, painful illness. Grant had served two disastrous terms as president of the United States from 1868 to 1876. His administrations were marked by political corruption, many of the most corrupt officials being military men he had appointed to high political office. His failures continued as a businessman when his brokerage firm of Grant and Ward went under. But his genius for war, and his great bravery and energy, showed again with his writing of the *Personal Memoirs of U. S. Grant,* an excellent book published by Mark Twain. Grant had dictated it while he lay dying to make his family financially secure, and earned $350,000 in royalties for his survivors. Grant's last words were: "I am a great sufferer all the time. . . . All that I can do is pray that the prayers of all these good people may be answered so far as to have us all meet in another and better world. . . . I cannot speak even in a whisper . . ."

L'Envoi

Word over all, beautiful as the sky,
Beautiful that war and all its deeds of carnage must in time
    be utterly lost.
That the hands of the sisters Death and Night incessantly softly
    wash again, and ever again, this soil'd world;
For my enemy is dead, a man divine as myself is dead,
I look where he lies white-faced and still in the coffin—I
    draw near,
Bend down and touch lightly with my lips the white face in the
    coffin.

—Walt Whitman, "Reconciliation," 1865

Selected Bibliography

Other useful books, pamphlets, and periodicals are mentioned in the text. Newspapers and magazines consulted include the *Richmond Examiner,* the *Charleston Mercury,* the *New York Times,* the *New York Leader,* the *New York Tribune,* the *New York World,* the *New York Herald,* the *New York Illustrated News,* the *Washington Star,* the *Philadelphia Inquirer, Frank Leslie's Illustrated Newspaper, Harper's Weekly,* and the *Atlantic Monthly.*

Adams, Charles Francis. *Lee at Appomattox.* Boston: Houghton Mifflin, 1902.

Appomattox Court House, Handbook 109. Washington, D.C.: Division of Publications, National Park Service, U.S. Department of the Interior, 1980.

Badeau, Adam. *Military History of Ulysses S. Grant, from April, 1861 to April, 1865.* 3 vols. New York: Appleton, 1882.

Boritt, Gabor S. *Why the Confederacy Lost.* New York: Oxford University Press, 1992.

Burge, Dolly Sumner Lunt. *A Woman's Wartime Journal.* Atlanta: Cherokee Publishing, 1994.

Bushong, Millard K. *Old Jube: A Biography of General Jubal A. Early.* Shippensburg, Pa.: Beidel Printing, 1955.

Butler, Benjamin F. *Butler's Book.* Boston: Thayer Co., 1892.

Cadwallader, Sylvanus. *Three Years with Grant.* New York: Knopf, 1955.

Catton, Bruce. *The Army of the Potomac: A Stillness at Appomattox.* New York: Doubleday, 1953.

————. *Grant Takes Command.* Boston: Little, Brown, 1969.

————. *This Hallowed Ground.* New York: Doubleday, 1955.

Chamberlain, Joshua Lawrence. *The Passing of the Armies.* New York: Putnam, 1915.

Chesnut, Mary Boykin. *Mary Chesnut's Civil War.* New Haven: Yale University Press, 1981.

Commager, Henry Steele. *The Blue and the Gray.* New York: Bobbs-Merrill, 1950.

Connelly, Thomas Lawrence. *The Marble Man: Robert E. Lee and His Image in American Society.* New York: Harper's, 1977.

Cooke, John Esten. *Robert E. Lee.* New York: G. W. Carlton, 1871.

Coolidge, Louis A. *The Life of U. S. Grant.* Boston: Little, Brown, 1922.

Dana, Charles A. *Recollections of the Civil War.* New York: Appleton, 1898.

Dana, Charles A., and H. H. Wilson. *The Life of Ulysses S. Grant.* Springfield, Mass.: Gurdon, Bill & Co., 1868.

Davis, Burke. *Sherman's March.* New York: Random House, 1980.

Davis, Jefferson. *The Rise and Fall of the Confederate Government.* New York: Garret & Massie, 1938.

Davis, Varina Howell. *Jefferson Davis: A Memoir.* 2 vols. New York: Bellford Co., 1890.

Dictionary of American Biography. 20 vols. New York: Scribner's, 1928.

Donald, David Herbert. *Lincoln.* New York: Simon & Schuster, 1995.

Donald, David Herbert, ed. *Divided We Fought: A Pictorial History of the War, 1861–1865.* New York: Simon & Schuster, 1952.

———. *Why the North Won the Civil War.* Baton Rouge: Louisiana State University Press, 1960.

Early, Jubal A. *A Memoir of the Last Year of the War for Independence in the Confederate States of America.* Toronto: LoVill & Gibson, 1866.

Eaton, Clement. *Jefferson Davis.* New York: Free Press, 1977.

Elliott, Charles Winslow. *Winfield Scott: The Soldier and the Man.* New York: Macmillan, 1937.

Evans, Eli N. *Judah P. Benjamin: The Jewish Confederate.* New York: Free Press, 1988.

Foote, Shelby. *The Civil War: A Narrative.* 3 vols. New York: Random House, 1958–1974.

Forsyth, George A. *Thrilling Days in Army Life.* New York: Harper, 1900.

Freeman, Douglas Southall. *Lee's Lieutenants.* 3 vols. New York: Scribner's, 1942–1944.

Freeman, Douglas Southall, and Grady McWhiney, eds. *Lee's Dispatches.* New York: Scribner's, 1957.

Furgurson, Ernest B. *Ashes of Glory.* New York: Knopf, 1996.

Garland, Hamlin. *Ulysses S. Grant: His Life and Character.* New York: Scribner's, 1920.

Gates, Theodore B. *The War of the Rebellion.* New York: P. F. McBreen, 1884.

Gerrish, Theodore. *Army Life: A Private's Reminiscences of the Civil War.* Portland, Maine: Hoyt, Fogg & Donham, 1882.

Gordon, John P. *Reminiscences of the Civil War.* New York: Scribner's, 1904.

Grant, Julia Dent. *Personal Memoirs.* New York: Putnam, 1975.

Grant, Ulysses S. *Personal Memoirs of U. S. Grant.* 2 vols. New York: Webster, 1885–1986.

Guernsey, Alfred, and Henry M. Alden, eds. *Harper's Pictorial History of the Civil War.* New York: Harper's, 1866.

Hastings, William H., ed. *Letters from a Sharpshooter.* Belleville, Wis.: Historic Publications, 1993.

Headley, John W. *Confederate Operations in Canada and New York.* New York: Harper's, 1906.

Hergesheimer, Joseph. *Sheridan: A Military Narrative.* New York: Doubleday, 1931.

Hutton, Paul Andrew. *Phil Sheridan and His Army.* Lincoln: University of Nebraska Press, 1985.

Johnson, Robert Underwood, and Clarence Clough Buel, eds. *Battles and Leaders of the Civil War.* 4 vols. New York: Century, 1887.

Jones, John B. *A Rebel War Clerk's Diary at the Confederate States Capital.* Philadelphia: J. B. Lippincott, 1866.

Kantor, MacKinley. *Turkey in the Straw.* New York: Coward-McCann, 1935.

Ketchem, Richard, ed. *The American Heritage Picture History of the Civil War.* New York: American Heritage, 1960.

Lee, Fitzhugh. *General Lee of the Confederate Army.* New York: Appleton, 1910.

Lee, Captain Robert E. *Recollections and Letters of General Robert E. Lee.* New York: Doubleday, 1924.

Lewis, Lloyd. *Sherman: Fighting Prophet.* New York: Doubleday, 1932.

Lewis, Thomas A. *The Guns of Cedar Creek.* New York: Harper & Row, 1988.

Lincoln, Abraham. *Collected Works of Abraham Lincoln.* Edited by Roy P. Basler, 9 vols. New Brunswick, N.J.: Rutgers University Press, 1955.

Long, A. L. *Memoirs of Robert E. Lee.* New York: J. M. Stoddard, 1886.

Longstreet, James. *From Manassas to Appomattox: Memoirs of the Civil War in America.* Philadelphia: J. B. Lippincott, 1896.

Lossing, Benson. *Pictorial History of the Civil War.* New York: G. W. Childs, 1866.

MacDonald, John. *Great Battles of the Civil War.* New York: Macmillan, 1988.

Maurice, Sir Frederick. *An Aide-de-Camp of Lee: The Papers of Colonel Charles Marshall.* Boston: Little, Brown, 1927.

McFeely, William S. *Grant: A Biography.* New York: Norton, 1981.

McPherson, James M. *Battle Cry of Freedom: The Civil War Era.* New York: Oxford University Press, 1988.

————. *Marching Toward Freedom: The Negro in the Civil War.* New York: Knopf, 1967.

Moore, Frank, ed. *Anecdotes, Poetry and Incidents of the War, North and South.* New York: Putnam, 1866.

Newall, Colonel F. C. *With General Sheridan in Lee's Last Campaign.* Philadelphia: J. B. Lippincott, 1866.

Osborne, Charles C. *Jubal: The Life and Times of General Jubal A. Early, C.S.A., Defender of the Lost Cause.* New York: Algonquin, 1992.

Page, Charles A. *Letters of a War Correspondent.* Boston: Little, Brown, 1899.

Pleasants, Henry, Jr. *The Tragedy of the Crater.* Reprint. Washington, D.C.: National Park Service, 1975.

Pollard, Edward A. *The Early Life, Campaigns and Public Services of Robert E. Lee; With a Record of the Campaigns and Heroic Deeds of His Companions in the Army.* New York: E. B. Treat, 1871.

————. *Lee and His Lieutenants.* New York: E. B. Treat, 1867.

————. *The Lost Cause.* New York: E. B. Treat, 1866.

————. *Southern History of the War.* 4 vols. New York: Charles B. Richardson, 1863–1866.

Porter, Horace. *Campaigning with Grant.* New York: Century, 1897.

Ringwalt, J. R. *Anecdotes of General Grant.* Philadelphia: J. B. Lippincott, 1886.

Rusling, James F. *Men and Things I Saw in Civil War Days.* New York: Eaton & Mains, 1899.

Russell, William Howard. *My Diary North and South.* 2 vols. London: Bradbury & Evans, 1863.

Sandburg, Carl. *Abraham Lincoln: The War Years.* 4 vols. New York: Harcourt Brace, 1939.

Schaff, Morris. *The Battle of the Wilderness.* Boston: Houghton Mifflin, 1910.

Sheridan, Philip. *Personal Memoirs of P. H. Sheridan.* 2 vols. New York: Webster, 1888.

Sherman, William Tecumseh. *The Memoirs of General William T. Sherman.* 2 vols. New York: Appleton, 1893.

Stiles, Robert. *Four Years Under Marse Robert.* New York: Neal Publishing, 1903.

Strong, George T. *The Diary of George Templeton Strong.* Edited by Allan Nevins and Milton H. Thomas. 4 vols. New York: Macmillan, 1962.

Swinton, William. *Campaigns of the Army of the Potomac.* New York: Scribner's, 1882.

Taylor, Walter H. *Four Years with General Lee.* New York: Appleton, 1877.

Thomas, Benjamin P. *Abraham Lincoln: A Biography.* New York: Knopf, 1952.

Thomas, Emory M. *Bold Dragoon: The Life of J. E. B. Stuart.* New York: Harper, 1986.

Trobriand, P. Regis de. *Four Years with the Army of the Potomac.* Boston: Little, Brown, 1889.

Van de Water, Frederick F. *Glory Hunter: A Life of General Custer.* New York: Argosy, 1963.

Warner, Ezra J. *Generals in Blue.* Baton Rouge: Louisiana State University Press, 1964.

———. *Generals in Gray.* Baton Rouge: Louisiana State University Press, 1957.

The War of the Rebellion: A Compilation of the Official Records of the Union and Confederate Armies. Washington, D.C.: n.p., 1880–1901.

Waugh, John C. *The Class of 1846: From West Point to Appomattox.* New York: Warner, 1994.

Whitman, Walt. *Leaves of Grass.* New York: Doubleday, 1926.

Wiley, Bell Irvin. *The Life of Billy Yank: The Common Soldier of the Union.* Baton Rouge: Louisiana State University Press, 1954.

———. *The Life of Johnny Reb: The Common Soldier of the Confederacy.* Baton Rouge: Louisiana State University Press, 1945.

Williams, T. Harry. *Lincoln and His Generals.* New York: Knopf, 1952.

———. *McClellan, Sherman and Grant.* New Brunswick, N.J.: Rutgers University Press, 1962.

Wilson, James H. *The Life of John A. Rawlins.* New York: Appleton, 1916.

Woodward, William E. *Meet General Grant.* New York: Horace Liveright, 1928.

Young, John Russell. *Around the World with General Grant.* 2 vols. New York: Harper's, 1879.

Index